NEW STUDIES IN BIBLICAL THEOLOGY 49

The feasts of repentance

NEW STUDIES IN BIBLICAL THEOLOGY 49

Series editor: D. A. Carson

The feasts of repentance

FROM LUKE–ACTS TO SYSTEMATIC
AND PASTORAL THEOLOGY

Michael J. Ovey

APOLLOS

An imprint of InterVarsity Press
Downers Grove, Illinois

APOLLOS (an imprint of Inter-Varsity Press)
36 Causton Street
London SW1P 4ST, England
ivpbooks.com
ivp@ivpbooks.com

InterVarsity Press, USA
P.O. Box 1400
Downers Grove, IL 60515, USA
ivpress.com
email@ivpress.com

© Estate of Michael J. Ovey, 2019

The estate of Michael J. Ovey has asserted his right under the Copyright, Designs and Patents Act, 1988, to be identified as Author of this work.

All rights reserved. No part of this book may be reproduced in any form without written permission from InterVarsity Press.

InterVarsity Press®, USA, is the book-publishing division of InterVarsity Christian Fellowship/USA® and a member movement of the International Fellowship of Evangelical Students. Website: www.intervarsity.org.

Inter-Varsity Press, England, originated within the Inter-Varsity Fellowship, now the Universities and Colleges Christian Fellowship, a student movement connecting Christian Unions in universities and colleges throughout Great Britain, and a member movement of the International Fellowship of Evangelical Students. That historic association is maintained, and all senior IVP staff and committee members subscribe to the UCCF Basis of Faith. Website: www.uccf.org.uk.

Unless otherwise indicated, Scripture quotations are taken from The ESV Bible (The Holy Bible, English Standard Version) Anglicized, copyright © 2001 by Crossway, a publishing ministry of Good News Publishers. Used by permission. All rights reserved.

Quotations marked NRSV are taken from the New Revised Standard Version of the Bible, copyright © 1989 by the Division of Christian Education of the National Council of the Churches of Christ in the USA. Used by permission. All rights reserved.

Quotations marked VOICE are taken from THE VOICE ™. Copyright © 2012 by Ecclesia Bible Society. Used by permission. All rights reserved.

First published 2019

Set in Monotype Times New Roman
Typeset in Great Britain by CRB Associates, Potterhanworth, Lincolnshire

USA ISBN 978-0-8308-2662-9 (print)
USA ISBN 978-0-8308-5084-6 (digital)
UK ISBN 978-1-78359-896-0 (print)
UK ISBN 978-1-78359-897-7 (digital)

InterVarsity Press is committed to ecological stewardship and to the conservation of natural resources in all our operations. This book was printed using sustainably sourced paper.

British Library Cataloguing-in-Publication Data
A catalogue record for this book is available from the British Library.

Library of Congress Cataloging-in-Publication Data
Names: Ovey, Michael, author.
Title: The feasts of repentance : from Luke-Acts to systematic and pastoral theology / Michael J. Ovey.
Description: Downers Grove : InterVarsity Press, 2019. | Series: New studies in biblical theology ; 49 | Includes bibliographical references and index.
Identifiers: LCCN 2019019941 (print) | LCCN 2019022280 (ebook) | ISBN 9780830826629 (pbk. : alk. paper)
Subjects: LCSH: Repentance--Christianity. | Repentance--Biblical teaching.
Classification: LCC BT800 .O94 2019 (print) | LCC BT800 (ebook) | DDC 234/.5--dc23
LC record available at https://lccn.loc.gov/2019019941
LC ebook record available at https://lccn.loc.gov/2019022280

P	21	20	19	18	17	16	15	14	13	12	11	10	9	8	7	6	5	4	3	2	1
Y	36	35	34	33	32	31	30	29	28	27	26	25	24	23	22	21	20	19			

Contents

Series preface	vii
Preface *Mark D. Thompson*	ix
Abbreviations	xi

1 Repentance: formality, necessity or optional extra? — 1
Introduction — 1
Questions of method: the focus on Luke–Acts — 2
Procedure: from Luke–Acts to systematic and
  pastoral theology — 6
The puzzle: how can the call to repentance
  be universalized? — 7

2 Repentants, unrepentants and feasts — 11
Preliminary: type scenes and feasting — 11
John the Baptist — 14
Feasting in Luke 5:1 – 19:10 — 16
The penitent thief (Luke 23:39–43) — 32
Repentance and forgiveness of sins (Luke 24:46–48) — 33
Conclusion — 33

3 Repentance: for Jew and Gentile — 35
Recap — 35
The appeal to Jews — 38
The appeal to Gentiles — 50
Paul's understanding of his ministry — 57
Objections to a universal call for repentance — 62
Conclusion — 66

4 Repentance: identity and idolatry — 69
Recap — 69
Repentance as recognition — 71
Idolatry as parody — 76
Idolatry as identity — 90

	Idolatry, agnosticism and atheism: objections to using	
	the idea of idolatry	92
	Communicating idolatry	98
	Conclusion	101

5 Repentance: faith and salvation — 103
Recap — 103
The relation of repentance and faith — 104
Faith and repentance? — 105
Barth on repentance — 121
'Faith' without repentance: some pastoral implications — 126
Conclusion — 130

6 Repentance: forgiveness and the people of God — 131
Preliminary — 131
The unrepentant — 133
The repentant — 146
Concluding reflections — 155

Bibliography — 159
Index of authors — 167
Index of Scripture references — 169

Series preface

New Studies in Biblical Theology is a series of monographs that address key issues in the discipline of biblical theology. Contributions to the series focus on one or more of three areas: (1) the nature and status of biblical theology, including its relations with other disciplines (e.g. historical theology, exegesis, systematic theology, historical criticism, narrative theology); (2) the articulation and exposition of the structure of thought of a particular biblical writer or corpus; and (3) the delineation of a biblical theme across all or part of the biblical corpora.

Above all, these monographs are creative attempts to help thinking Christians understand their Bibles better. The series aims simultaneously to instruct and to edify, to interact with the current literature and to point the way ahead. In God's universe, mind and heart should not be divorced: in this series we will try not to separate what God has joined together. While the notes interact with the best of scholarly literature, the text is uncluttered with untransliterated Greek and Hebrew, and tries to avoid too much technical jargon. The volumes are written within the framework of confessional evangelicalism, but there is always an attempt at thoughtful engagement with the sweep of the relevant literature.

By mutual agreement, when the annual lectures of Moore Theological College in Sydney, Australia, have focused on biblical theology, the authorities of Moore College have urged the lecturer to offer his work to NSBT. There has been obligation on neither side, but the collaboration has produced many fine volumes. In 2008 Dr Michael Ovey, Principal of Oak Hill College in London, delivered the lectures, and promptly contacted me, expressing interest in publishing the work under the NSBT banner. He wanted time for revision, however, because he was dissatisfied with their form. Mercifully, he had almost finished their revision before, shockingly, he was taken from us in January 2017. Thankfully, Dr Mark Thompson, Principal of Moore College and longtime friend of Mike Ovey, supervised the final tidying up – and that is why you are able to read the book you are holding in your hand.

Although in some sense this work is a focused biblical-theological study of the theme of repentance in Luke–Acts, grounded in word studies, thoughtful exegesis and sensitivity to the narrative of this pair of biblical books, it is more than that. Dr Ovey moves beyond biblical theology to think through the meaning of repentance in both systematic categories and in pastoral-theological reflection – and we are all the better for it.

D. A. Carson
Trinity Evangelical Divinity School

Preface

Michael J. Ovey delivered an earlier version of the material in this volume as the Annual Moore College Lectures, in Sydney, Australia in August 2008. While they were well received, Mike himself was not happy with them and kept reworking them over the next few years, whenever his busy schedule as the Principal of Oak Hill Theological College in London allowed. He had not quite finished with them at the time of his sudden death on 7 January 2017. In reality all that remained was some minor editorial work, which has now been done in order to allow these important lectures to be available in print.

Mike was a biblical and systematic theologian with a deep pastoral concern. His passion for a theology grounded in and shaped by the Scriptures, and his commitment to providing the best possible training for men and women who will serve the churches in their various ministries, was evident to all who knew him. He was never satisfied with an abstract theological system. Nor was he satisfied with a theology that remained detached from the context in which it is lived out and proclaimed. In this he was not only a biblical and systematic theologian but a public and pastoral theologian as well.

Mike served on the faculty of Oak Hill Theological College for nearly twenty years, the last ten as its principal. He had the enviable gift of exciting his students about the Scriptures, what the Scriptures teach and the God to whom all things are to be referred. He pointed his students to Jesus and the salvation available only through him, but he also modelled the gracious compassion and deep personal interest in the welfare of others that he knew was characteristic of his Saviour. The word most used of him following his death was 'kind'.

The troubled context in which the gospel mission is pursued in the first quarter of the twenty-first century is, Mike became convinced, one in which a critical element of the New Testament proclamation of the gospel, repentance, is far too often ignored, minimalized or dismissed. Yet John the Baptist, Jesus himself and those he commissioned to take his gospel to the nations all spoke of the urgent need to repent. Such repentance consists of a real change, a transforming work of the Spirit of God who does not leave sinners as he found them. That is why it is so threatening to many, of course. But a gospel without repentance as a critical part of its summons (as it clearly is in Mark 1:15; Luke 24:46–47; Acts 17:30–31), Mike realized, quickly distorts our view of God as well as our view of ourselves and one another. It undermines grace and ultimately leads to idolatry. For these reasons, we must not let the fear of legalistic moralism, or of the caricatures of fire-and-brimstone preachers of the past, keep us from speaking unambiguously about the need for all to *repent* and believe the gospel.

Mike called Christians back to the Bible's emphasis on repentance whenever he could: in the college classroom and chapel; in his engagement with the hierarchy of the Church of England, which he saw departing from the authority of Scripture and the gospel of salvation at an alarming pace; and from the platform of the Global Anglican Future Conference in Nairobi in 2013. He knew the issue was serious beyond measure. This is, undoubtedly, why he kept working on this book, determined to ensure he laid out the biblical, theological and pastoral dimensions of repentance with as much care and clarity and persuasiveness as possible.

When Mike died in 2017, global Anglicanism lost one of its foremost theologians. It was, as one friend put it, 'a severe providence'. His wife, Heather, and their children, Charlie, Harry and Anastasia, were surrounded by evangelical men and women from around the world who mourned his loss but gave thanks to God for the gift Mike had been to so many of us. Through the kindness and generosity of the people at Inter-Varsity Press, including senior commissioning editor Philip Duce and copy editor Eldo Barkhuizen, and most especially the enthusiasm and grace of NSBT series editor Don Carson, that gift will continue to bear fruit through this serious engagement with a critical biblical theme.

Mark D. Thompson
Principal, Moore College, Sydney
Friend of Mike Ovey

Abbreviations

AJT	*Asia Journal of Theology*
BTB	*Biblical Theology Bulletin*
CBQ	*Catholic Biblical Quarterly*
CC	*Christian Century*
EBC	*Expositor's Bible Commentary*
Int	*Interpretation*
JETS	*Journal of the Evangelical Theological Society*
JSNTSup	Journal for the Study of the New Testament: Supplement Series
JTSA	*Journal of Theology for Southern Africa*
NovT	*Novum Testamentum*
NRSV	New Revised Standard Version
NTS	*New Testament Studies*
OT	Old Testament
OTM	Oxford Theological Monographs
PRS	*Perspectives in Religious Studies*
SJT	*Scottish Journal of Theology*
TNTC	Tyndale New Testament Commentaries
VE	*Vox evangelica*
WTJ	*Westminster Theological Journal*

Chapter One

Repentance: formality, necessity or optional extra?

'Between the stirrup and the ground
He something sought and something found.'
Mercy.
That's right: Mercy.[1]

Introduction

Pinkie is a character from Graham Greene's novel *Brighton Rock*. He is a teenage gangster, hardened and violent. He knows that his actions are evil and in fact deserve God's condemnation. He still persists in them and comforts himself with the tag of poetry quoted above. He has been taught that God forgives the repentant and assumes he will be able to repent when the time comes. But this prompts some acute questions. How could God ever forgive someone like Pinkie? Will God tolerate such delay in repentance? These questions are further complicated when Pinkie realizes that the poetry is not true. There is no time between the stirrup and the ground to turn to God in repentance: you are too busy fighting death, or your opponent, or are simply too consumed with fear, to think of repentance. For Pinkie repentance proves impossible, and the prospect of forgiveness vanishes. What remains is only bleak despair in the face of death and God's wrath.

But is Pinkie worrying about nothing? Does Pinkie need to repent, or will not God forgive him anyway? Was he told the wrong thing about God and our relationship with him? Behind these questions lies the issue of where repentance fits in Christian faith and life. This issue needs to be faced. For our time in the early twenty-first century in the cultural West is widely described as a time of repentanceless Christianity. The notion of repentanceless Christianity prompts two further questions.

First, is repentance part of the evangelistic message? This affects what we preach in our evangelism. Should a presentation of the gospel

[1] G. Greene 2011: 96.

include a call to repent? In slightly different terms, is repentance really a part of the gospel itself? John Calvin did, of course, talk in just such terms: '[W]ith good reason, the sum of the gospel is held to consist in repentance and forgiveness of sins'.[2] N. T. Wright, however, differs, famously commenting that the gospel is the proclamation that Jesus is Lord.[3] More broadly, the systematic issue at stake is whether a human being needs to repent to be saved. A key practical issue here is how repentance relates to faith. In an evangelistic setting, is it enough to call for 'faith' in Jesus Christ if one does not also preach repentance? What are the long-term pastoral consequences, if any, of neglecting or precluding repentance in a call for faith?

Second, is repentance part of the post-conversion Christian life? Even if one thought that repentance was at least part of becoming a Christian, is there space or need for it thereafter? For some might say that the stress on leading a repentant life is just what gives so much Christian life its joyless, guilt-ridden and dour character. Others, that a repentanceless Christian life is the primrose path to a flabby and finally morally and spiritually compromised Christian life.

So, the subject of repentance touches critical areas: what we say in evangelism and how we expect the Christian life to look and be.

Questions of method: the focus on Luke–Acts

The language of repentance in the New Testament predominates in narrative settings, and in Luke–Acts in particular. Within Luke–Acts repentance occupies a prominent place. In the Gospel of Luke repentance is a consistent thread in the narrative, notably present in the account of John the Baptist's ministry (Luke 3:1–17) and in Jesus' final commission to preach forgiveness and repentance of sins to all nations (Luke 24:47). In Acts repentance is a theme in Peter's speeches to the Jews (e.g. Acts 2:38), is present in Paul's speeches to Gentiles (Acts 14:15; 17:30) and is also significant in his accounts of his ministry (Acts 20:21; 26:18, 20). Of course, given the size of Luke–Acts in the New Testament corpus (over a quarter), and its connections both with Mark and Matthew, as well as Paul's letters, this significant presence within Luke–Acts suggests repentance is theologically significant more generally. However, given the predominance of repentance material in Luke–Acts, attention must focus on this

---

[2] Calvin 1960: 592 (*Inst.* 3.3.1).
[3] Wright 1997: 75, 133.

corpus, and space precludes us here dealing with all the New Testament repentance texts.

Three observations arise connected with this need to focus on Luke–Acts: first, concerning terminology; second, concerning argument by narrative; and third, the focus on people who repent rather than the concept.

Terminology: 'turning' and 'change'

First, concerning terminology. What counts as a reference to 'repentance'? Calvin was not content simply to be confined to the term *metanoia* and its cognates as the textual basis for discussing repentance.[4] His reason was that the concept of repentance was a turning: '[Repentance] is the true turning of our life to God . . .'.[5] Hence, he argued, 'turn', 'return', 'repent', 'do penance', and so on, were used interchangeably. Calvin here in some ways anticipated the argument of S. Porter who suggests that repentance needs to be seen within the semantic domain of changing behaviour.[6]

Yet are Calvin and Porter textually justified in seeing a central concept lying behind several different terms? To anticipate later exegetical work, Paul's speech to Agrippa in Acts 26:17–20 strongly suggests 'change' or 'turning' terms are closely intertwined. For in Acts 26:20 Paul brackets together *metanoein* and *epistrephein* vocabulary as he speaks of God's commission of proclamation. That *metanoein* and *epistrephein* are cognate is further indicated by the way that turning (*epistrephein*) is associated with forgiveness of sins in 26:18, while in Luke 3:3 and 24:47 *metanoia* is associated with forgiveness of sins. Similarly, in Acts 14:15 the call for the Lystrans to repent of idolatry employs *epistrephein*, while the repentance call to Athenian idolaters in Acts 17:30 uses *metanoein*. In Luke itself John the Baptist 'turns' the people towards God (Luke 1:16, using *epistrephein*) and calls Israel to repentance (Luke 3:3, using *metanoia*). These instances suggest at least substantial overlap between 'turning' (*epistrephein*) and 'change of mind' (*metanoia*). Hence usage of both terms is relevant to our study.

Argument by narrative

Second, clearly Luke–Acts is not a straightforward argument. For sure the material is ordered to establish a conclusion in the reader's

---

[4] Calvin 1960: 597–8 (*Inst.* 3.3.5).
[5] Ibid.
[6] Porter 2007: 128.

mind. But this is not a naked argument consisting of categorical propositions arranged in a syllogistic form. Some parts of some New Testament letters may appear more propositional in form. Thus Paul may tell us that if the dead are not raised, then Christ is not raised (1 Cor. 15:16). In one sense, this simply uses the principle that a universal negative proposition (the dead are not raised) must include the particular negative proposition (Christ is not raised), and is valid because Christ is a member of the class of people who have died.

Constructing a more integrated and systematic account of repentance therefore must reckon with the fact that much of the source material is not arranged in straightforward propositional form. Rather, it is cast as narrative, so that there may be a dynamic movement in which our understanding about repentance is cumulatively formed.[7] Moreover, this accumulation will be complex if one assumes, as seems highly likely, that Luke–Acts was to be read more than once. The second- or third-time reader takes an early occurrence of repentance terms in the light of what she or he already knows happens later. Such a narrative form also heightens the possibilities of identification by the reader. J. A. Darr comments that Luke wants to move the reader to a position where he believes the witness of believers in the narrative,[8] and this is surely right in view of Luke 1:1–4.

This all means that a systematic account of repentance must deal responsibly with a position and understanding advocated through narrative, not straightforward logical argument. This emphatically does not, of course, mean that there is no argument in Luke–Acts: rather, the theological argument is carried on in subtler ways and in more dimensions than the argument of a systematic textbook. We do not write systematic textbooks or arguments in the way we do because naked logical argument is somehow superior to narrative argument. Rather, naked logical argument is simpler and more restricted. There is less to confuse the reader, and also, one might say, less to enrich. Sometimes one wants a simple black and white photograph, not because it is in every way better than a colour photograph, but because it may simplify vision, even though it also clearly loses something.

---

[7] Cf. Tannehill (1986, 1: 8), who says, 'The message of Luke-Acts is not a set of theological propositions but the complex reshaping of human life, in its many dimensions, which it can cause.'
[8] Darr 1998: 83.

The focus on who repents and who does not: the question of character

The third observation also concerns the narrative nature of the Luke–Acts discussion of repentance. Luke–Acts does not so much discuss repentance, the theological locus, as people: people who are, and who are not, repentant. This relates to Darr's point that Luke wants to enlist and persuade his reader. He envisages Luke's enlisting the reader as he or she witnesses the interactions between Jesus and other characters: 'In a very real sense, the story functions at two levels: while reading about characters who "witness" the significant events and personages of salvation history, the reader inevitably witnesses in response to them as well.'[9]

Thus there are many episodes which provide examples of positive or negative 'recognition and response'.[10] The characters who respond function as paradigms,[11] for better or worse, orientating readers so that they can know their own position with respect to the plan of God, which R. Tannehill argues is the unifying feature of Luke–Acts.[12]

This means that to discern the values Luke is establishing we must examine the paradigmatic characters he employs. The narrative nature of Luke's work entails examining his characterization.

We can envisage characterization in several ways. Famously E. M. Forster saw a spectrum of characterization between poles of flatness or roundness, depending on the detail and other factors supplied.[13] While not irrelevant, this categorization is not the most helpful for our purposes, which require rather establishing how the narrative establishes values in the reader's mind and the approval or disapproval of particular characters,[14] be they individual or group characters.

D. B. Gowler suggests a more helpful approach.[15] He proposes that characterization in Luke occurs on two sliding scales, one of explicitness, the other of reliability.[16] He writes, 'Reliability is the

---

[9] Ibid.
[10] Ibid. 87.
[11] Ibid. 83.
[12] Tannehill 1986, 1: 2, 'Luke-Acts has a unified plot because there is a unifying purpose of God behind the events which are narrated, and the mission of Jesus and his witnesses represents that purpose being carried out through human action.'
[13] Forster 1927.
[14] Darr 1998: 83.
[15] Gowler 1989; 1991.
[16] Gowler 1989: 55.

measure of the extent to which a speaker can be trusted, whereas explicitness refers to the clarity of the message.'[17]

Reliable speakers in Luke–Acts include the narrator, Jesus (who is established as knowing the secrets of people's hearts; e.g. Luke 6:8) and the voice from heaven. Explicit characterization from these sources carries 'absolute authority'.[18]

Explicit characterization is doubtless important for orientating the reader and can create more sharply contoured characters with less ambiguity about their function in the narrative. On the other hand, indirect presentation, that is, indicators of character that 'show' rather than 'tell' what a character is like,[19] engage the reader differently, enlisting a reader to form judgments.[20] In the nature of a narrative these judgments may harden or modify as the plot progresses. Repetition and contrast are important factors in helping the reader form judgments through implicit or indirect characterization.

These two scales of explicitness and reliability make tension and suspense for readers possible, as they form judgments and identify with characters in the text. Thus two explicit characterizations may exist that are in some ways contradictory. For example, the explicit self-characterization of a person in the narrative may conflict with the characterization provided by Jesus. The Pharisee in Jesus' parable of Luke 18:9–14 exemplifies just this. His self-characterization of what he is not (Luke 18:11–12 in the light of 18:9) implies he is righteous, while Jesus' comment (18:14) shows he is not. Similarly, tension may exist between an explicit self-characterization and the indirect presentation of that character. This kind of tension can force the reader to choose which is correct, and thus whether to share the presentation of Jesus and God's purpose that Luke puts forward.

Procedure: from Luke–Acts to systematic and pastoral theology

Our way forward will be to examine first the biblical material Luke–Acts affords, move to more systematic considerations and then to pastoral theology as we consider repentance in the corporate life of the people of God. Thus the next two chapters will focus on Luke and Acts. In particular we are concerned here with who repents and

[17] Ibid.
[18] Ibid.
[19] Darr 1998: 76.
[20] Gowler 1989: 55.

who does not and the characteristics of both groups. Then in the fourth chapter we shall consider repentance in relation to idolatry, move in the fifth to discussion of repentance in relation to salvation and the *ordo salutis*, and finish in the sixth with considerations about repentance in the corporate life of the people of God.

The puzzle: how can the call to repentance be universalized?

There is, though, a puzzle about repentance. Repentance (turning back) and forgiveness are not simply New Testament concepts but are central to the Old Testament too. Thus Deuteronomy 30:1–10 establishes a framework that envisages sin and curse on Israel (v. 1), Israel's return to God (v. 2) and restoration by God (v. 3).[21]

This framework lies at the heart of key post-exilic prayers of confession and repentance in Daniel 9:3–19, Ezra 9:5–15 and Nehemiah 9:6–37 that plead for mercy and restoration. These prayers give a striking place to covenant thought. Thus in Daniel's prayer, God is invoked as the covenant-keeping God (Dan. 9:4). God is acknowledged as righteous (v. 7), for he has kept his covenant words in bringing judgment on his people for their disobedience (vv. 11–12[22]). Judah and Israel by contrast are liable to shame because they have not kept the words God has given (vv. 7–10).

There is therefore a basic contrast between the covenant faithfulness of God in bringing judgment and curse (just as Deut. 30:1 envisaged) and the covenant faithlessness of Judah and Israel. God, on the one hand, and Israel and Judah, on the other, are characterized, and characterized in relation to each other. God is characterized as faithful to the word he has given to Israel and Judah; Israel and Judah are characterized as faithless within that covenantal relationship whereby they should hear God's voice (Dan. 9:10).

However, God's covenant faithfulness is what lies behind Daniel's plea in verses 15–19. He refers to God's mercy in the exodus, which is an instance of God's remembering his covenant (Exod. 6:2–9; esp. v. 5), he also pleads God's character as merciful (revealed to Moses in Exod. 34:6–7) and concludes with an appeal based on Israel as God's people, who bear his name. The idea of Israel as God's people

---

[21] Millar (1998: 182) notes that a 'basic theological conviction' of the book of Deuteronomy is that human efforts to obey the law 'in practice are bound to fail'. Deut. 30:1–10 therefore deals with reality, not mere conjectural possibility.

[22] Note the stress in v. 12 on God's confirming his word.

is covenantal (e.g. Gen. 17:8; Exod. 19:5), as is the motif of the name of God (Exod. 3:13–15). Thus God's covenant and his given word found the appeal to mercy, and paradoxically God's covenant judgment grounds hope, since, if God keeps his covenant curse, then he will surely be faithful to the covenant promise to restore those who turn to him.

This establishes repentance as having a legal element, for in Daniel 9 it rests on a rule or norm, the rules of the covenant. These rules have been broken. Repentance acknowledges that and returns to the one who has been offended. The one offended may, indeed in the case of Deuteronomy 30:1–3, has promised to, forgive, but a legal element remains, in that a law has been broken. Clearly, this does not preclude a personal dimension, for repentance is also linked to restoring relationship. After all, personal relationships can have rules and obligations attached. For it is a false dichotomy to say a relationship is either personal or legal. Christian marriage, for example, is both: it is personal, resting on mutual love, and carries obligations, such as fidelity.

Here, though, the puzzle about repentance as it appears in the Old Testament emerges starkly. How can one call on a Gentile to repent? For a Gentile is outside the covenant and a stranger to its promises. He has not undertaken covenant obligations as Israel did, and might therefore say he is a stranger to covenant laws. He is not expelled from the Promised Land for his covenant disobedience, and so why should he be restored for repentance under the terms of Deuteronomy 30:1–3? The question here is, 'In what way is repentance a universalizable concept?' Why call on all men and women to repent, as Paul definitely envisages (Acts 17:30)?

Put another way, if Old Testament repentance presupposes some law concerning which one acknowledges breach and pleads for mercy, as Daniel does, what acknowledged legal frame binds the Gentile? There are two aspects, of course, to this. First, objectively, what is the legal framework that binds a Gentile? Second, in what way does a Gentile subjectively acknowledge that frame? More bluntly, what are we asking a Gentile to repent of?

This question whether repentance is universalizable recurs in our examination of Luke–Acts. Clearly, if repentance is not universalizable, then the criticism that gospel proclamation and life in some churches today is repentanceless matters far less.

I am going to propose that repentance is universalizable, and that Luke, for whom repentance is such a major theme, shows this in two distinct stages. In his Gospel he shows that even the apparently faithful must repent. This emerges from his treatment of the apparently faithful character group, the Pharisees, and the apparently unfaithful character group, the tax collectors and sinners. In Acts he shows Gentiles must repent and does this through his description of the proclamation of the gospel to Jews (who must repent for complicity in the Messiah's murder) and then to Gentiles (who must repent for their idolatry).

Chapter Two

Repentants, unrepentants and feasts

Preliminary: type scenes and feasting

This chapter aims to develop the characters of those who do and do not repent in the Gospel of Luke. This does not exhaust Luke's repentance material and it examines the material from a particular perspective, but one that is consistent with Luke's aim of persuading readers as they see a sequence of characters responding to Jesus.

Repentance themes are prominent both in the introduction and conclusion of the Gospel. Thus in Luke 1:16 Gabriel says John the Baptist is one who will turn many of the people of Israel to God, which is language redolent of the covenant repentance terms of the Old Testament. Very near the end of the Gospel the risen Jesus tells his disciples that repentance and forgiveness of sins will be proclaimed in his name to all nations (Luke 24:47). This is significant because, while repentance has been a consistent theme in the teaching and encounters of Jesus throughout the Gospel, this has very largely been within the world of the Jews. Yet now the Gospel concludes that this message of repentance and forgiveness of sins is to continue beyond the horizon of this particular book and that particular nation.

The significance of repentance is not simply a question of prominence and frequency. Significance also arises from the themes with which it appears. Especially striking is the way repentance is bracketed with forgiveness of sins (3:3; 24:47), the joy of heaven and before the angels (15:7, 10) and is the alternative to destruction (13:3, 5).

This means that John the Baptist does not have a fundamentally different, 'legal' ministry and message compared to Jesus. Tannehill rightly says, 'John's call to repentance never ceases to be part of the message of Jesus and his witnesses.'[1] After all, Jesus himself continues the call to repentance (5:32), and his disciples are commissioned to

---
[1] Tannehill 1986, 1: 25.

do this too. Hence material concerning John's call to repent can legitimately help interpret later material, both in the Gospel and in Acts.

We shall focus on material from Luke 5:1 to 19:10, from the call of the first disciples to the encounter with Zacchaeus, shortly after which Jesus goes on to Jerusalem (19:28) and his passion. For Tannehill, 5:32 and 19:10 form an inclusion, giving an introduction and a summary: 'That is, we have similar general statements which serve to interpret the whole ministry which lies between them.'[2]

This introduction and summary establish that Jesus' ministry is to save the lost and call sinners to repentance. Within this section of material there are several type-scenes, notably type-scenes in which Jesus is entertained or feasted,[3] and scenes featuring incidents relating to the Sabbath.[4]

Type-scenes allow both variety and reinforcement. Basically, similar scenes need not be repetitious because details vary in each case, while the setting and use of language permit reinforcement of the values and views Luke wants to impress on the reader.[5] Further variation can arise when these scenes are woven into parables; thus Luke 14 is both a feast or meal (14:1) and also the occasion for Jesus' parable about a meal (14:16–24). This creates tension between the real meal Jesus is attending as a guest of a leader of the Pharisees (14:1) and the parabolic banquet relating to the kingdom of God, which his real-life Pharisee host may be refusing to attend as a guest.

For present purposes the type-scene of the feast or the meal can be seen as two relational triangles.[6] One relational triangle, which we

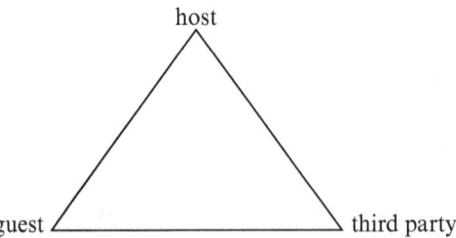

---

[2] Ibid. 106.

[3] Heil (1999: 1) comments that 'the theme of eating and drinking, food and table fellowship appears to be a special Lukan concern'. He notes (2) that 'most of these scenes are unique to Luke-Acts'.

[4] Tannehill 1986, 1: 171.

[5] Cf. ibid. 170.

[6] The idea of relational triangles has been strongly and helpfully developed by S. Karpman in his analysis of the Victim Triangle, consisting of three roles: victim, persecutor and rescuer.

may call the triangle of hospitality, deals with the relations of the feast or meal itself, and has three roles which interact with each other: host, guest and third party.

In this relational triangle, the third party may be another guest, or someone outside the meal altogether.

However, the feast/meal type-scenes in Luke 5 – 19 frequently have elements of conflict in them, usually with three characters, that feature Jesus.[7] This creates a second relational triangle, a triangle of conflict. Typically, the conflict arises from some criticism voiced and there are again three roles: critic, Jesus and other.

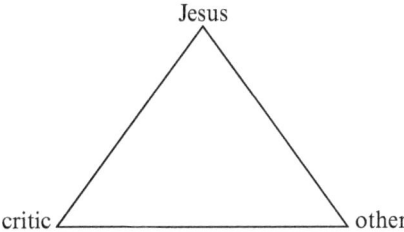

In this relational triangle the critic may be the host or third party from the first triangle, although Jesus is typically the guest in the triangle of hospitality. The other may be the object, or victim, of the critic, although the other may in fact side with the critic against Jesus.

The interplay between the triangles of hospitality and conflict permits considerable variation, since the critic may occupy different positions in the triangle of hospitality (host or third party), while the stability of the triangle of hospitality allows ready reinforcement and accumulation of meaning. But the two triangles in some ways conflict with each other, and this conflict can generate interest and concern in the reader. For, aside from other eschatological associations, hospitality can easily speak of fellowship, peace and enjoyment. Such seem to be, for instance, the associations in the father's mind in Luke 15:11–32 and the parable of the lost son. But fellowship, peace and enjoyment sit uneasily with the kinds of conflict described in these type-scenes. A feast is not the fitting occasion for such conflict.[8] Thus the conflicts at the meal scenes have an added poignancy in the already prominent theme of conflict in Luke. For example, the meal of Luke

---

[7] Malina and Neyrey (1991: 97) comment, 'At every turn, Luke's story of Jesus and his disciples narrates scenes of conflict' and include the meals with Simon (7:36–50) and Zacchaeus (19:1–10) as examples.

[8] Equally, the conflict in the Sabbath type-scenes is perhaps unfitting for the Sabbath.

11:37–52 culminates in deep hostility to Jesus (11:53–54), while the parable of the prodigal son lacks any explicit peaceful resolution on the part of the elder brother (15:32).

John the Baptist

Gabriel's announcement to Zechariah (1:16) signals John's task as one who will call to repentance. The significance of this turning is developed in Zechariah's song in 1:77, as John is described as one who will give God's people knowledge of salvation by the forgiveness of sins. This links John's call to repentance with salvation, and suggests that the content of salvation at least includes the forgiveness of sins. The connection between repentance and forgiveness of sins is therefore no surprise in 3:3, when John's ministry is actually in progress. Moreover, the statement that this fulfilled the prophecy of Isaiah 40:3–5 underlines the importance of this call, for Luke has stated that his programme includes showing fulfilment of prophecy (1:1–4).

All this establishes John as a reliable speaker for the purposes of Gowler's proposal that reliable speakers are important in establishing character.[9] John's own characterization of the repentant is both significant and interesting. The reader is told (3:7) only that there are 'crowds' (*ochloi*) who come, leaving their religious affiliations and geographical origins vague.[10] John's reaction (3:7–9) to the repentant crowds is striking. They are a brood of vipers (3:7), who are attempting to flee the wrath to come, who must bear the fruits of repentance (v. 8) and who are warned against presumption on the grounds of descent. The seriousness of fruits of repentance is stressed by the reference to the axe that cuts down trees that do not bear fruit (v. 9). Again this is a judgment image.

In terms of character, this implies that the repentant are bad. John is a reliable, divinely ordained speaker in Luke; and by depicting the repentant as a brood of vipers, he establishes the thought that the repentant are not simply modest humble people who are aware of their faults: they are bad. They are fleeing coming wrath, but the warning about fruits of repentance suggests misgiving about the sincerity of their repentance. They are also clearly ethnic Jews, given the rebuke about ethnic presumption (3:8), which also hints at a tendency to inappropriate pride.

---

[9] Gowler 1989: 55.
[10] Unlike Matt. 3:7, which specifically mentions some Pharisees and Sadducees attending; and Mark 1:5, which includes the point that Jerusalemites have come.

John suggests the value of being repentant, since the baptism of repentance is something that stands against the wrath to come and seems a way out of it. Strictly, repentance is seen as fruit-bearing. The content of fruit-bearing is teased out in what follows. Three categories of people ask what they should do, and contextually this is asking what the fruits of repentance look like for them.

First, the crowds are instructed in 3:11 to share if they have two coats. Strictly, Jesus does not assume that all do, and arguably the possession of more than one coat does not necessarily suggest prior bad conduct.

The second category is different, though. In 3:12 the focus moves to tax collectors. This subgroup of the crowd now emerges into a sharper, but unflattering, focus. The construction of verse 12 suggests that the tax collectors' presence is unexpected: 'even tax collectors' (NRSV) came to John, aptly translating *ēlthon de kai telōnai*. The fruits of repentance for tax collectors also illuminate what they are like. They are told to collect no more than their due (3:13), which suggests they have been collecting more than their due, and, since they are to be taken as descendants of Abraham given the block address of 3:8 to the crowd as descendants of Abraham, this implies not merely that they collude with the occupying power, but that they batten on fellow-Jews. Moreover, as the Gospel progresses, such greed will be seen as an increasingly serious sin, for greed and the actions it breeds are deeply criticized by Luke. Wealth is in fact depicted as an idol competing with God for the faithful service and worship of men and women (16:13),[11] and the fatal nature of the ill-use of wealth emerges in the parable of the rich man and Lazarus (16:19–31).

Tax collectors will emerge as a highly significant group of the repentant, so it is worth clarifying where these initial hints lead. The presence of tax collectors suggests that, contrary to expectation, even tax collectors may repent. This may provoke hope or outrage: hope that if even tax collectors repent, so can the reader;[12] outrage, because of the sense that tax collectors are deeply sinful. For the reader even now has the thought that they may have much of which to repent, namely wealth dishonestly acquired.

The third group which asks John about the fruit of repentance is the soldiery (3:14). The fruit here takes again a financial turn, with

---

[11] Bock (1996, 2: 1336) comments on Luke 16:13, 'Mammon is here personified and treated as if it could be an idolatrous threat to God.'

[12] Nave (2002: 154) comments that the inclusion of soldiers and tax collectors shows repentance is available to all.

the stipulation not to extort and to be satisfied with wages. This again creates the negative suggestion that soldiers have extorted and been discontented with their wages. Soldiers do reappear from time to time, and sometimes in a favourable light (the centurion of Luke 7, the centurion at the cross in 23:47 and Cornelius in Acts 10). Equally, the participation by soldiers in the mockery of Jesus in Luke 23:11, 36 is unfavourable,[13] but they are not strongly developed as a character group in relation to repentance.

Feasting in Luke 5:1 – 19:10

The first feast: Luke 5:27–32 and the feast with Levi

Luke 5:32 provides the programmatic statement that Jesus has come to call sinners to repentance. This connects Jesus' own ministry both with John the Baptist's and also his disciples', who will be called to proclaim repentance and forgiveness of sins. The context of this saying, though, repays close attention. It emerges after Levi has responded to Jesus' call (5:28) and given a banquet for Jesus at his house (5:29) and forms a comment on that incident.

The call of Levi itself has to be seen within the framework of chapter 5 and the three major incidents that have happened earlier in the chapter: the call of Peter, the healing of the man with leprosy and the healing of the paralytic. In 5:1–12 Jesus has called Simon to follow him, after the miraculous catch of fish in verse 6. Two things stand out about Peter's call: his self-definition (v. 8) and Jesus' response to that (vv. 10–11). Thus, first, Peter, after the catch of fish, defines himself as a sinful man and envisages this means Jesus must distance himself from Peter (5:8), 'for a sinful man cannot associate with one who wields divine power', comments Tannehill.[14] Jesus does not disagree with Peter's self-description, and the fact that it is a self-description against interest, a confession of guilt, tends to carry conviction. Peter characterizes himself as sinful. This, though, secondly, colours Jesus' subsequent call of Peter: Jesus will not just be close to sinful Peter; he will include Peter and have Peter as his follower (v. 11), who will serve him as a fisher of people (v. 10). Jesus' response to Peter is not to exclude himself from sinners, but this inclusion is not because Jesus has denied that Peter is sinful.

---

[13] Conceivably, these two incidents cover both Jewish and Roman soldiers.
[14] Tannehill 1986, 1: 204.

The healing of the leper connects with the idea of exclusion, which Peter at any rate anticipated in 5:8. For leprosy is par excellence a condition which excludes, and intriguingly the vocabulary is not simply 'healing' but related to cleansing (vv. 12–14). If one is clean, one need no longer be excluded.

Third, the healing of the paralytic (5:17–26) connects the ideas of healing and forgiveness of sins. This in turn is closely linked with the paired ideas of 5:31–32, healing and repentance. For repentance by now has been tied to forgiveness of sins through the ministry of John the Baptist.

The call of Levi, then, and the feast that follows, can be seen as tightly integrated into the themes of Luke 5:1–32 as a whole. Luke 5:29–30 represents a triangle of hospitality and conflict. Thus the roles are distributed as follows: Levi is host and other, the Pharisees are third party and critic, while Jesus is guest.

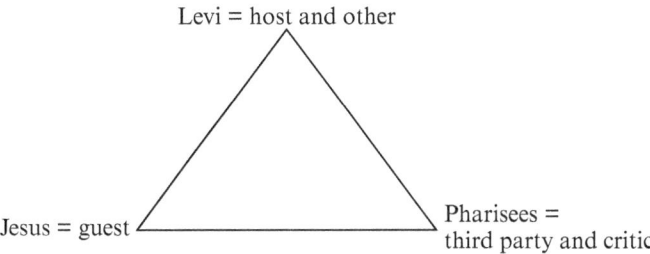

The Pharisees' criticism is voiced to Jesus' disciples, but aimed ultimately at Jesus, for the banquet Levi gives is for Jesus. The thought ultimately is that Jesus should not eat with tax collectors and sinners (v. 30). The criticism is double-edged. First, there is the unmistakably negative pairing of tax collectors and sinners at Levi's feast. For the reader, the undertone of 3:12–13 will lend support to a negative view of the tax collectors, and this will be reinforced by the pairing with sinners, who in the Psalms are associated with rapacity at the expense of the poor and righteous.[15] Second, there is the assumption that Jesus should be separate from such people and he has broken this norm. Such separation, though, is an exclusion theme, specifically the proper exclusion of sinners, and relates to the exclusion theme assumed by Peter earlier in the chapter.

The valuation given to the Pharisees here is ambivalent. On the one hand, there is an apparent concern for holiness and this has continuity

---

[15] Roth 1997: 118.

with John's criticism of the 'brood of vipers' (3:7). Moreover, the antipathy is to a tax collector in particular, and one might therefore wonder if such antipathy did not have some foundation. On the other hand, the Pharisees seem to be excluding the repentant, and this stands at odds with John's ministry. This impression of possibly obstructing the work of God is increased by the context of the healing of the paralytic, where the Pharisees seem at least initially to deny that Jesus has authority to forgive sins.[16]

This sense of ambiguity is heightened by Jesus' own statement in 5:31–32. Are the Pharisees really 'healthy' and 'righteous'?[17] If they are, then Jesus implies some distance between himself and them, for they lie outside the scope of his mission. This represents an odd reversal: there is distance between the 'righteous' and Jesus, but not between Jesus and repentant sinners, while the Pharisees envisage distance between Jesus and, apparently, even repentant sinners, while not seeing distance between themselves and Jesus. The oddness of this reversal is heightened by the way that 'righteous' hitherto in this gospel has been given a positive value.[18] The question this poses for the readers is whether they should identify as 'righteous' or not. To do so would distance them from Jesus, whom Luke has already established as God's promised king.

The repentant in this feast are represented by Levi. He is identified with Peter in that, like Peter, he leaves all to follow Jesus (5:11, 28). He is like the man with leprosy in that there is no longer exclusion (or uncleanness), for Jesus is with him. He is like the paralytic in that his sins seem to have been forgiven.[19] There is, though, an intensification of Levi's moral state compared to that of Peter and the paralytic. Peter's confession defined him as a sinner but the reader has no further data to support this. The reader must infer that the paralytic is sinful from the way Jesus sees it necessary to pronounce forgiveness, and this presupposes sin. But the circumstances of Levi's call are that he is seated at the tax booth, and is therefore called in the very act of committing sins in pursuit of his greed. This underlines the scope of Jesus' call: that it touches the sinful tax collector who is caught red-handed. The reader is also, though, hastened almost breathlessly

---

[16] Obstructing the work of God becomes progressively more strongly identified with the unrepentant.
[17] Some, e.g. Morris (1974: 120), take the reference to being righteous as 'ironical'.
[18] As Heil (1999: 27) notes, citing 1:6, 17 and 2:25.
[19] Heil (ibid. 22) writes that in the light of John's baptism of repentance for forgiveness and the healing/forgiveness of the paralytic 'the audience deduces that Jesus has forgiven the sins of the repentant Levi'.

through Levi's change of heart, for his response is immediate, total and translates apparently immediately into a feast.

As a repentant, Levi bears fruit, as John insisted, for he has left all, and the possibility of his, as a tax collector, taking more than is appointed, has gone. But, perhaps most strikingly, the feast Levi the repentant tax collector gives suggests joy and celebration. Moreover, a grandeur hangs about the celebration. The feast is large (*dochēn megalēn*), and the attendance extensive (*ochlos polys telōnōn*). In view of other material, we properly associate repentance with mourning for sin (e.g. Dan. 9:3), but here joyful celebration is also present. On reflection this may be less surprising, for repentance has already been associated decisively by Luke with the forgiveness of sins, and that is surely joyful. The obvious challenge for the reader is whether his or her own attitudes to repentance mirror Levi's.[20]

Finally, mention must be made of the disciples. The initial question from the Pharisees and their scribes is addressed to them,[21] and poses the question about their table fellowship with Levi and his party of tax collectors and sinners. It may be Jesus who answers, but the disciples' participation in the feast is necessarily implied. This raises the question of acceptance of the repentant by other followers of Jesus, a theme that gathers momentum throughout the Gospel and Acts.

The second feast: Luke 7:36–50 and the feast with Simon

In the second feast Simon the Pharisee invites Jesus to eat with him (7:36). By this stage, though, Luke's narrative has acquired significant momentum. Luke 6 has further developed the characterization of the Pharisees.

In the first scene featuring Sabbath-breach (6:1–5) the Pharisees have appeared as those challenging Jesus for the sake of the Sabbath (6:2).[22] This is quite compatible with their being righteous people concerned for the law. But in the second Sabbath-breach scene the narrator (6:7) reveals the Pharisees' motives, which is to find grounds for accusation rather than a simple regard for God's law. This opens the door to the thought that the Pharisees' devotion to the law may not be simply what it seems. This unfavourable impression is heightened in Luke 6:11 as they are filled with fury at Jesus' healing. Since

---

[20] Cf. ibid. 27.
[21] As the plural verbs *esthiete* (you eat) and *pinete* (you drink) show.
[22] This first Sabbath controversy also features eating while with Jesus (Heil 1999: 32).

healing has been linked with forgiveness and salvation (5:12–16 and 17–26 respectively), this angry reaction raises the question whether the Pharisees will obstruct Jesus' ministry or not.[23]

Luke also paves the way for further unfavourable characterization of the Pharisees in 6:39–42 as Jesus teaches about a judgmentalism that ignores its own faults while attacking the faults of others (v. 41). The reader has certainly seen the Pharisees critical of the faults of others by this point. Such people are described as hypocrites, and Jesus later attributes exactly this to the Pharisees (12:1).

However, the strongest explicit depiction of the Pharisees before Simon's feast comes in 7:29–30. Here the Pharisees stand in contrast to the tax collectors and sinners. The latter, in accepting John's baptism, a baptism of repentance for the forgiveness of sins, acknowledge God's justice. As we have seen, the question outstanding at the end of 5:32 was whether the Pharisees were among the sinners who should be called to repentance. The implication of 7:30 is that the Pharisees and lawyers should be counted among the 'sick' who need healing and the sinners who need repentance and forgiveness. For in refusing John's baptism of repentance, they have rejected God's purpose. This is chilling since the reader is told this by the authoritative voice of the narrator. It creates further tension because hitherto the defence of God's honour has been associated with the Pharisees, and this now seems questionable.

Further ambiguity is introduced by the way Jesus recites the charge (7:34) that he has come eating and drinking and is a friend of tax collectors and sinners. Yet this is almost immediately followed by Jesus' eating and drinking with a Pharisee (7:36). The implicit question is whether Jesus is on this occasion eating and drinking with a sinner.

The roles in the triangles of conflict and hospitality have changed from the previous feast. Again the host is named (7:43), while the third party remains nameless. The Pharisee Simon is now the host and critic, Jesus remains guest, while the woman is third party and other. The triangle of relations is as shown in the figure opposite.

The theme of the dialogue between Simon and Jesus is forgiveness and love. Forgiveness, though, has already been associated with repentance, and there is a curious parallel between Levi's feasting response to Jesus and the woman's. Simon has been a poor host,

---

[23] Arguably this may also tie the feast type-scenes to the Sabbath-healing type-scenes. Several feast scenes feature the forgiveness and acceptance of the repentant, which the Pharisees frequently oppose, while Sabbath healings are connected with salvation and forgiveness, and again the Pharisees are found opposing this.

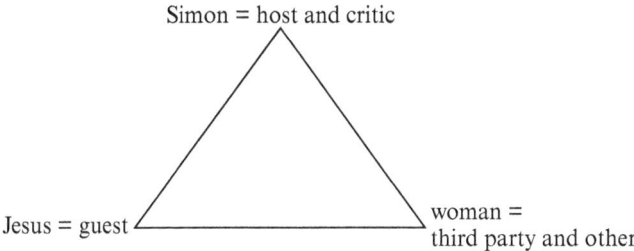

providing no water, no kiss and no anointing (7:44-46). Tannehill rightly observes that 'In her own strange way the woman supplied all of these things.'[24] She is, oddly, 'hosting' Jesus at the feast. The sinner does what the Pharisee should have done.

The hosting provided by the woman is worth appreciating, for her hosting shows intensity, intimacy and costliness, but also, emphatically, humility. Where Simon provided no water for Jesus' feet (v. 44), the woman herself, not a servant, has provided water, and from her own tears rather than a pitcher. She has, moreover, dried the feet of Jesus with her hair, i.e. from her head, 'an honoured part of her own body'.[25] This underlines her humility before Jesus. This humility is reinforced by the detail that her kiss, which supplements Simon's omission of any kiss, is not on the cheek of Jesus, but on his feet, and is performed repeatedly (v. 45). Finally (v. 46), she does not anoint Jesus' head, but his feet, and not with olive oil, but with ointment from an alabaster jar, something more costly.[26] There is, of course, no doubt about her sinfulness. The authoritative voice of the narrator has introduced her as this (v. 37) and Jesus, whose credibility as one who knows hearts has been underlined in this episode, is explicit (7:47).

The attitude of the repentant, then, is one of love and humility, born out of a recognition of the magnitude of forgiveness. This prompts readers to wonder whether their own response matches hers. Such self-examination is also prompted by the example of Simon. He has conformed to the pattern of 5:30 in his attitude of exclusion towards the woman, which rests on a sense of superiority. Yet the parable that Jesus tells (7:41) is explicit that both are debtors. This implies that Simon too is a debtor or sinner in need of forgiveness.

---

[24] Tannehill 1986, 1: 117.
[25] Heil 1999: 46.
[26] Heil (ibid. 47) speaks of the anointing indicating 'both the humility of her repentance and her exuberant appreciation of the worth of Jesus'.

The event itself implies that Simon has not realized he corresponds to a debtor in the parable. In this way the ambiguity of 5:32 over whether Jesus' mission really includes Pharisees starts to clarify: it seems they need forgiveness too. Further, their lack of love towards Jesus (and sense of superiority towards others) seems associated with a lack of awareness of their own sin.

In terms of the woman's reaction, love is certainly what is foregrounded. But stress has been rightly laid on her tears, and the implication that there is sadness here, traditionally a grief at personal sin. J. Nolland rightly sees that this is consistent with her gratitude: 'The sorrow of regret is suffused with the warmth of grateful affection.'[27] There is a complexity to this repentant woman's state, loving the forgiver and grieving at what necessitated forgiveness.

The third feast: Luke 11:37–54 and the feast with Pharisees and lawyers

By the time the reader reaches the third feast, Luke has underlined the importance of repentance by Jesus' warnings about repentance in 10:13–15 and 11:29–32. In the first passage, Chorazin, Bethsaida and Capernaum are warned that their lack of repentance compares unfavourably to the proud and tyrannical Gentile cities of Tyre and Sidon. Capernaum in particular is warned of its overthrow, not its exaltation. In a similar vein, the responsiveness of Nineveh (11:30) to the message of Jonah contrasts with 'this generation'. Both passages, however, turn on a reversal: that those one would not expect to repent do so, and those who might be expected to respond to God's purposes do not do so.

Two other contextual factors require comment. As the reader approaches another feast with the law-focused Pharisees, he or she does so with the summary of the law in mind (10:25–29) and with expansion of the law of love of neighbour in terms of showing mercy (10:29–37). Besides this, Jesus has rather unnervingly raised a serious question of self-examination in 11:35: that one should consider whether 'the light in you be darkness'.

The third feast varies the relationships again. This time an unnamed Pharisee is host and critic, Jesus again is guest, but the third party or other is a lawyer, who sides with the Pharisees against Jesus. Thus the triangle of hospitality and conflict looks as shown in the following figure.

---

[27] Nolland 1989: 354.

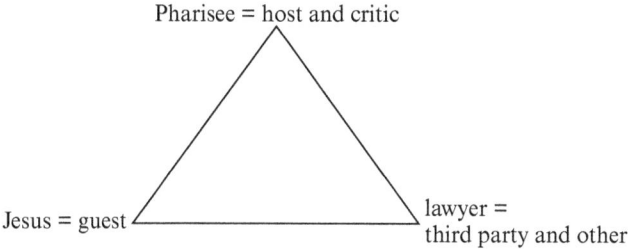

Jesus is here challenged about not washing before eating (11:38).[28] His response becomes a full attack on the Pharisees' moral character and their concerns with cleanness.[29] The reader has been prepared for this in two ways. Jesus' authority as one who knows the secrets of people's hearts has emerged at several points. But also the Pharisees' character as a group devoted to honouring God has become increasingly problematic. Now Jesus completes the task of unmasking the Pharisees' true nature.

The feast has a number of paired ideas:

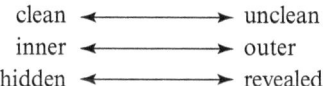

These themes interweave to explain the Pharisees' true nature and the perplexing way they behave. For the Pharisees do present a riddle. Their implicit claim is to be those who honour God and keep his law. This implicit claim emerges from their questioning of Jesus over his alleged infringement of the divine prerogative to forgive sin, and their defence of the Sabbath. Such a posture of questioning is not merely a questioning of another (in this case Jesus), but presents the questioners as those seeking to honour God. Yet this implicit claim stands starkly at odds in the reader's mind with their attitude to Jesus, who is the one who fulfils God's promises.

Thus to the world of men the Pharisees' outer appearance is shown or revealed as clean. But, of course, outward cleanness hides inner uncleanness, but what is inner will be revealed (as Jesus goes on to

---

[28] Heil (1999: 84) sees an ironic play on words: Jesus (v. 38) 'did not wash' (*ou . . . ebaptisthē*), while the Pharisees and lawyers (7:30) have 'rejected being baptized' (*mē baptisthentes*).

[29] Jesus' response has an added authority since it is a response of 'the lord' (v. 39). Cf. Heil 1999: 84.

explain in 12:1–3). The contradiction between the Pharisees' self-presentation as loyal friends of God and their hostility to Jesus is thus resolved by the explanation that the Pharisees' inner and outer natures are themselves in contradiction. So, outer cleansing of utensils contrasts with inner rapacity and wickedness (v. 39). Outward obedience to the law contrasts with a reality in which they disobey the summary of the law (for they neglect justice and the love of God, 11:42, which relate to the laws of love to God and neighbour). The Pharisees do have a 'love', for they love seats of honour among men (11:43).[30] This reverses the Pharisaic appearance of honouring God rather than men. Another reversal appears in the way the group that is ostensibly concerned with cleanliness and purity and fears being made unclean is in fact a group that makes others unclean, an unmarked grave (11:44). However, Jesus repeatedly frames these diagnoses of the Pharisees in terms of 'woe', something that implies future judgment for these things, and the need to repent of them. Since judgment awaits this inner uncleanness, it is clear that inner uncleanness cannot be hidden indefinitely, as 12:1–3 makes clear. Moreover, since judgment is in view, there is again a strong, if implied, call to repent. For John's baptism was linked to fleeing the wrath to come (3:7).

A lawyer attempts to defend the Pharisees, only to be met with ripostes that outline how the lawyers in fact burden people, are identified with persecutors of God's agents and hinder entry to knowledge. Unsurprisingly, the meal ends in heightened hostility (11:53) and Jesus goes on (12:1–3) to warn the crowd about the Pharisees and specifically their hypocrisy. Hypocrisy hinges on a difference between inner and outer, in which inner uncleanness remains hidden. Jesus' point is that it will not remain hidden but will be exposed. Hypocrisy, though, becomes the key designation of the Pharisees, a 'master status' for them in the Gospel.[31] By now the group is identified by the narrator as rejecting repentance (7:30), as seeing itself as righteous, and as needing to repent, while pretending it does not.

---

[30] Again there is a wordplay between *tēn agapēn tou theou* (v. 42; 'the love of God') and *agapate tēn prōtokathedrian* (love the best seat). Cf. Heil 1999: 86.

[31] Malina and Neyrey (1991: 101) comment, 'The *master status* engulfs all other roles and labels. Hence Judas was "the traitor"; the Pharisees were "hypocrites"'; emphasis original.

The fourth feast: the leader of the Pharisees and the man with dropsy (Luke 14:1–24)

The next incident involving feasting blends two different type-scenes: the type-scene of a dispute at a meal and the type-scene of a Sabbath healing (Luke14:1–6). Further complexity is added by Jesus' advice about where to sit at banquets (14:7–11) and by the parable of the great banquet (14:15–24).

The healing itself takes place after the emphatic statements of 13:1–5 that speak of the necessity to repent. The instruction to repent stands against the alternative of 'perishing'. The term for this is drawn from *apollymi* and this is the terminology that will appear prominently in chapter 15 with the lost sheep, the lost coin and the lost son. The instruction to repent also harks back to the message of John the Baptist where repentance is in the light of the coming wrath, and, critically, Jesus' instruction is quite general. Naturally, this puts the refusal of the Pharisees to repent in an even more unfavourable light.

Further characterization of the Pharisees comes in 14:1–24. The opposition to Jesus' ministry is emphasized, as the lawyers and Pharisees watch Jesus closely (14:1) to see if he will heal. For Heil, Jesus' questions of verses 3 and 5 are designed to appeal to the Pharisees and lawyers 'to share his compassion for the urgent healing of the man with dropsy'.[32] Jesus' earlier comments from 11:43 that the Pharisees love prominence and honour are now vindicated as the narrator describes the guests seeking places of honour (v. 7). Lastly, the theme of rejection of the purpose of God is revisited in the parable of the great banquet, for it seems precisely the mention of the kingdom of God (14:15) that prompts a description of those who refuse the invitation to a great banquet. The great banquet itself continues the theme of reversal that Jesus has introduced in 14:11 and which the reader is starting to pick up as the apparently spiritually unpromising group of sinners and tax collectors are responding with feasting and love, while the Pharisees increasingly exclude themselves: something still more strongly developed in the next feast.

The fifth feast: for the lost son of Luke 15

The next relevant feast is again contained within a parable, one of three told by Jesus in response to the criticism of the Pharisees and scribes of Jesus' practice of eating with sinners (15:2). The parables

---

[32] Heil 1999: 100.

of the lost sheep and lost coin both feature a search for what is 'lost', using cognates of *apollymi*, which after Luke 13:1–5 carries highly ominous associations. Both also conclude with the joy of heaven and before the angels over a repentant sinner (vv. 7, 10). 'Joy' in fact is a major theme that links all three parables.[33]

Two relevant features emerge. First, the joy of the successful shepherd and householder corresponds to divine joy over the repentant.[34] This helps explain the priority that Jesus adopts in his mission (Luke 5:32), and the idea that he has come to call the sinners rather than the righteous to repentance. This joy of heaven complements the notion of festal joy by the repentant themselves that the example of Levi suggests. Both the repentant and the one who brings them to repentance rejoice.

The joy of heaven adds something, though: if this is the attitude of heaven to the repentant, then should not people on earth imitate it? D. Harrington comments, 'God wants us to rejoice over the repentance of sinners.'[35] In fact, given the parables, one might put this more strongly: God commands joy. For the shepherd and the householder speak in imperatives to their friends and neighbours (*syncharētei*; 15:6, 9). Yet this joy in heaven, and its invitation or command, contrast horribly with the scribes and Pharisees. Unrepentant themselves, they have also proved obstructive and antagonistic towards those who seek repentance.[36] This reinforces and expands the notion that the unrepentant reject the purpose of God (7:30): not only do they do so for themselves; they also oppose, it seems, repentance for others.

Second, the repentant are sought and found.[37] This qualifies any idea that repentance is a salvific work by the repentant, who simply 'find' God. J. Donahue sums this up well: 'Repentance is not climbing a ladder of sorrow and regret toward God, but the joy of being discovered by a searching God.'[38]

The parable of the lost son at first glance appears slightly different. It is longer and more complex, having three central characters rather

---

[33] So too Heil (ibid. 125), commenting on the prevalence of *chairō* (rejoice) and its cognates in the three parables (15:5–7, 9–10, 28, 32).

[34] Joy in heaven (v. 7) and before the angels of God (v. 10) are best taken as periphrastic references to God's joy.

[35] Harrington 2007: 39.

[36] Cf. the comment of Morris (1974: 240) on the parable of the lost son: 'those who reject repentant sinners are out of line with the Father's will'.

[37] Morris (ibid. 238) cites C. G. Montefiore, who saw here a distinctive and revolutionary note: 'God actively seeks out sinners and brings them home.'

[38] Donahue 2001: 30.

than simply one or two. It is also clearly very closely tied with the setting described in 15:2, where there is murmuring against Jesus on two counts: that he receives sinners, and that he eats with them. Terminologically, one might add, *diegongyzon* in 15:2 recalls the 'murmurs' in the wilderness.

Both these elements of criticism, receiving and eating, are picked up in the parable. Thus the father does indeed receive his son, with both compassion (*esplanchnisthē*; 15:20) and joy. Joy is exhorted in 15:23 (*euphranthōmen*) and a necessity in 15:32 (*euphranthēnai de kai charēnai edei*). This emphasis on joy links this parable with the two preceding it, and the repeated exhortation and note of obligation intensifies the challenge to the Pharisees and scribes to join in rejoicing over the repentant. As for eating, the father also sets a feast for his lost son, which the elder son refuses to join. The feast itself features the fatted calf, implying 'a meal of sumptuous and abundant nourishment',[39] thereby emphasizing both the satisfaction of the younger son's craving but also the intensity of the father's joy at his son's restoration.

Relationally this creates a triangle of roles like this:

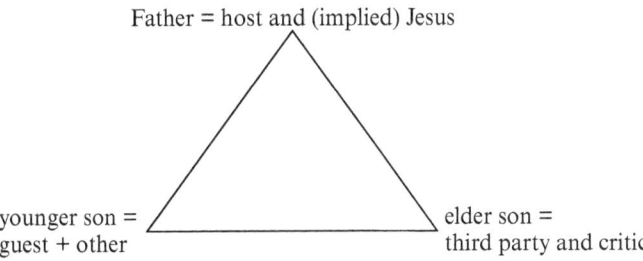

Father = host and (implied) Jesus

younger son = guest + other

elder son = third party and critic

The father seems identified with Jesus since the issue of 15:2 is Jesus' reception of and eating with sinners, which is the elder son's objection to the father.

The elder son's refusal is destabilizing for the hearer or reader. The elder son claims (15:29) he has never disobeyed his father, but this immediately follows his father's summons or entreaty to come in and join the feast (15:28). G. Forbes remarks of the elder son, 'The audience cannot miss the irony here. He has just shamed his father by refusing to enter the celebration!'[40]

---

[39] Heil 1999: 123.
[40] Forbes 1999: 222.

The elder son is therefore manifestly disobedient and dishonouring to his father. This poses the question 'What is the real difference between the elder and younger sons?' The elder son does not refuse joy, for he speaks of rejoicing with his friends (*meta tōn philōn mou euphranthō*), but nevertheless will not rejoice at his brother's restoration. This distances him from his father, for within the frame of the parable they rejoice at different things; and given the parables of the lost sheep and lost coin, the implication is that the elder son does not rejoice in the same things as heaven. This in turn, since the Pharisees and scribes are being challenged about the extent they conform to the elder son, raises the question about how much the Pharisees and scribes really share the values of heaven. Their actions too imply disobedience. This distancing is reinforced as the parable closes with the feast taking place and the elder brother excluding himself from it, refusing the invitation or call to a banquet. Such a refusal, of course, carries uncomfortable associations after the parable of the great banquet in 14:16–24.

However, this parable develops previous images of exclusion, which revolved around the Pharisees barring association between Jesus and the group of tax collectors and sinners. Previously, tax collectors and sinners were the ones being excluded, so to speak. Here, faced with the inclusion and welcome of the lost son, who stands for tax collectors and sinners, the one who wants to exclude others finally excludes himself. In the context of repentance, the elder son's refusal of his brother's repentance implies his own lack of repentance: thus he has doubly no share in the feast of repentance, begrudging repentance to others and shunning it for himself.

The parable, however, underlines the necessity of repentance in line with 13:3, 5. For the father repeats his description of the younger son's plight: lost and dead, with the language of lostness (*apolōlōs*) not merely echoing Luke 15:6, 9 but also the ominous 'lost' terms of Luke 13:3, 5. Lost and dead is dramatic and grave language. In this way Jesus does not adopt a libertine attitude to sin. The younger son's words of 15:21 reflect the seriousness of what he has done, and the repeated lost and dead terms underline the consequences of that sin.

The sixth feast (Luke 19:1–10): the feast with Zacchaeus

The final feast that falls for consideration is influenced by three major incidents. First, Luke 16 provides extended material characterizing the Pharisees' attitude to wealth. Following the parable of the dishonest manager (16:1–9), Jesus warns of the perils of seeking wealth:

it can amount to trying to serve two masters (16:13). This warning strongly resembles a warning not to commit idolatry and break the first commandment.[41] The language of loving a master recalls the summary of the law (10:27) and the duty to love God. This command already has a sharp pertinence after Jesus' charge that the Pharisees neglect the love of God (11:42), and the edge is sharper still as the reliable voice of the narrator observes the reaction of the Pharisees to Jesus (ridicule) and connects it with their love of money (16:14).

Thus the Pharisees are now seen as possessing just the characteristic implied for tax collectors in 3:13: greed. This negative assessment is reinforced both by Jesus' response, which is to describe the Pharisees as those who justify themselves, and by the parable of the rich man and Lazarus.

Second, the theme of those who trust in themselves for righteousness is picked up in Luke 18:9–14, where a parabolic tax collector and Pharisee stand as contrasting types. In Luke 18:14 Jesus characterizes both: one humbles himself; the other exalts himself. Thus the Pharisee typifies self-exaltation, which comprises precisely what the reader has now come to associate with the group character: a contempt for others who are sinners, combined with a self-congratulation connected with law-keeping and acts of piety (Luke 18:11–12). The reader, however, has been forewarned to treat such self-estimation with suspicion.[42] By contrast the tax collector is one who humbles himself. His prayer has two elements. He defines himself, admitting his identity as a sinner.[43] There is a conspicuous lack of self-congratulation. The second element relates to who God is, for it asserts and relies on God's character rather than his own.

Of course, this parable not only links God's exaltation of the humble with justification, but his response to the plea for mercy is met with justification. In fact, righteousness language at this stage clusters around the Pharisees and their self-image. Jesus speaks of them (16:15) as those who justify themselves in the sight of others and the narrator characterizes them as those who trust in themselves that they are righteous. Since this self-image as righteous is connected with contempt for other Jews (both Pharisee and tax collector are worshipping in the temple; Levi in ch. 5 is apparently a Jew), this righteous status cannot be simply an ethnic self-righteousness of

---

[41] Cf. Bock 1996, 2: 1336.
[42] Note Jesus' criticisms of 11:42–44 and 13:7–9, and his statement of 16:15, that God abominates what humans may prize.
[43] As Peter had done earlier in 5:8.

covenant membership contrasting itself with those outside the covenant. It is a contempt directed at other Jews, as the kinship in the parable of the lost son in chapter 15 also makes clear. It is, though, a delusive self-image, for Jesus has already characterized the Pharisees as those who disobey God's law (11:42) and who are inwardly unclean (11:39).

The third incident that contextualizes the feast of Zacchaeus is that of the rich ruler of 18:18–25. By now the reader knows that wealth is a snare for tax collector and Pharisee alike. Initially the ruler is introduced as one seeking eternal life (v. 18) and who sees himself as a law-keeper (v. 21). Jesus' command of verse 22, with its challenge to sell all and follow Jesus, exposes the ruler's love of wealth. He is sorrowful (v. 23) and it is unclear whether he responds or not. Yet there are some who have already responded by 'leaving and following', namely Peter and Levi in chapter 5.

This brings us to Zacchaeus in Luke 19:1–10. He is (v. 1) a 'chief tax collector' (*architelōnēs*) and 'wealthy' (*plousios*). This characterization creates certain tensions. The description of Zacchaeus leaves the reader with an ambiguity, given previous characterizations surrounding wealth and tax collectors.[44] The reader has been emphatically warned about greed, and has recently seen apparent failure in the rich ruler, and here is another rich man about to meet Jesus. A chief tax collector, however, might plausibly be expected to have all the typical faults of his group in abundance, yet the tax collector of the parable went home justified: will this one?

There are motifs of exclusion in this incident. Not only can Zacchaeus not initially see Jesus (v. 3), creating the impression of a man shut out,[45] but later the crowd grumbles at Jesus' accepting Zacchaeus's hospitality.[46] There are, then, three characters: Zacchaeus, Jesus and the crowd, which creates a triangle of relationships as shown in the figure opposite.

This triangle of hospitality and conflict is fundamentally similar to that featuring Levi in chapter 5. The tax collector is host and Jesus is criticized for accepting hospitality from such, because the

---

[44] Cf. Heil 1999: 151.
[45] Cf. Tannehill's (1986, 1: 123) remarks: 'Zacchaeus' isolation from the community is clear in v. 7 and is a major issue in the scene as a whole. The crowd as physical barrier and Zacchaeus' strange position up in a tree can serve as spatial symbols of his isolation from his community.'
[46] There is a possible irony in the way Zacchaeus's name means 'clean' or 'innocent' in Hebrew.

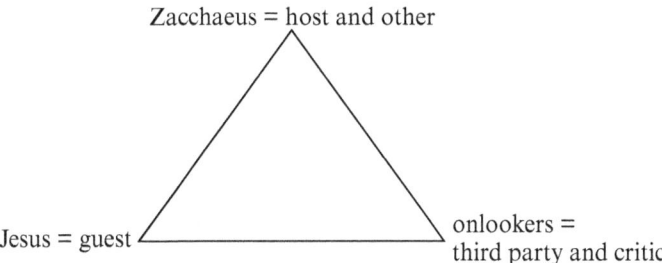

presupposition is that people like that should be excluded. Yet several features require comment.

To begin with, the grumbling critics at this feast are not Pharisees but the onlookers (v. 7). This gives point to Jesus' earlier warning (12:1–3) to beware of the leaven of the Pharisees. The group character, 'the Pharisees', have no monopoly on the 'Pharisaical' attitude.

Second, Zacchaeus's response bears similarity to Levi's in 5:27–32, for Zacchaeus responds promptly (19:6), corresponding to Levi's immediate departure from the tax booth, and bears fruits of repentance. Levi likewise symbolized rejection of his former ways in leaving the tax booth, and Zacchaeus promises restitution to those he has wronged, and offers to give half his wealth to the poor. The rich giving to the poor has been introduced by Jesus in 18:22, but here Zacchaeus makes his offer of half his estate spontaneously. It should be added that the restitution offer strongly implies Zacchaeus has been avaricious, and Jesus' statement of verse 9 implies forgiveness for Zacchaeus rather than the notion that he has nothing for which to be forgiven.

Third, Zacchaeus is depicted as a son of Abraham (v. 9). This reminds us that the contrasting characters of Pharisee and tax collector / sinner are characters within the framework of Judaism.

Fourth, Zacchaeus exemplifies Jesus' mission: he came to seek out and save the lost (v. 10). The motif of seeking recalls the parables of the lost sheep and lost coin, while the terminology of 'lost' (*apolōlos*) recalls both the three parables of chapter 15, but also the language of 13:1–5. Tannehill writes, 'This final statement turns the story of Zacchaeus into a key example of Jesus's mission as a whole, which is concerned with restoring the outcast of Israel to their rightful place as participants in the salvation promised in Scripture.'[47]

---

[47] Tannehill 1986, 1: 125.

He adds that this reference to the Son of Man's seeking makes the reader reconsider the incident. It is less a case of the lost Zacchaeus seeking Jesus, although the incident is initially introduced in this perspective (19:3), as of Jesus' seeking him, which is the authoritative perspective Jesus sets out (19:10). The significance of Jesus' mission is underlined within the incident itself by Jesus' use of the language of necessity (*dei*; 19:5) about his entertainment by Zacchaeus.[48] This too casts an unfavourable light on the crowd's resistance to Jesus' welcome of and table fellowship with Zacchaeus. Are they like the Pharisees in resisting God's purpose?

Fifth, Zacchaeus's reaction to Jesus is one of joy (v. 6), and a feast is in view (v. 7), if not actually stated. Thus the ministry between 5:32 and 19:10 is enclosed by the festal and rejoicing reactions of repentant tax collectors, who bear the fruits of repentance. The response of joy on the part of the repentant, which was implicit in the feast of Levi, is now explicit. Heil aptly comments that Zacchaeus provides a 'stunning model of true repentance'.[49] As one contemplates Zacchaeus, the rich chief tax collector, one naturally asks if any more conspicuous sinner could be found. This brings us to the penitent thief.

The penitent thief (Luke 23:39–43)

The incident of the penitent thief provides another contrast between the repentant and unrepentant. The two men crucified beside Jesus stand against each other. The contrast does not lie in their moral worth, for both are designated criminals (*kakourgoi*) by the narrator (vv. 32, 39). Both are also suffering exclusion, for, as Tannehill writes, with some understatement, 'Execution as a criminal is an extreme form of exclusion from society,'[50] and crucifixion with its connotations of curse intensifies this. The most obvious contrast between the two is in their treatment of Jesus. At this moment of undoubted personal agony at the hands of the authorities, one criminal nevertheless identifies himself with those crucifying both him and Jesus. For he derides Jesus in the same terms (v. 39) as the leaders (v. 36), inviting Jesus to save himself.[51]

---

[48] Heil 1999: 152–153.
[49] Ibid. 163.
[50] Tannehill 1986, 1: 126.
[51] Such identification is significant given Luke's later account of the believers' prayers in Acts 4:25–28, which interpret the murder of Jesus as a fulfilment of the conspiracy and concerted action of the nations and rulers against God's anointed.

In contrast, the other thief both confesses his own (and his companion's) wrongdoing but asserts Jesus' innocence and kingship. He asks for Jesus to remember him in his kingdom (v. 42), to which Jesus responds with a promise of paradise (v. 43). There are parallels with the prayer of the tax collector in Jesus' parable of 18:9–14. Like the tax collector, the penitent thief has defined himself as a sinner, and asked, in effect for mercy, not moral desert. The difference is that the plea for mercy is directed through his confession of Jesus as king. But, like the parable, the plea for mercy by a self-identified sinner is met by an indication of mercy.

Repentance and forgiveness of sins (Luke 24:46–48)

The concluding words of the risen Jesus both recall the start of Luke's Gospel and provide perspective on some of the events relating to Jesus' crucifixion. The speech of the angel Gabriel introduced John the Baptist as one who would turn many in Israel to God, and John's ministry of calling to repentance has been continued and amplified by Jesus; now the proclamation of repentance is to be taken to all nations. Luke also introduced the idea of fulfilment in 1:1–4. Fulfilment is to the fore here since Jesus now relates both his resurrection and the proclamation of repentance and forgiveness to the fulfilment of the Scriptures (v. 46). The fact that one, the resurrection, has been fulfilled lends credibility to the other: the proclamation to all nations.

However, these final words also connect with the repentant criminal of Luke 23:39–43. Jesus promised the criminal a place in paradise, and his resurrection implies fulfilment of this promise, which is associated with the forgiveness of sins. Repentance and forgiveness of sins are in Luke 24 connected with the name, or authority and identity, of Jesus. To that extent repentance and forgiveness come to have a Christological element. This expands on the repentant prayer of the criminal in Luke 23, who confessed both his own guilt and the innocence and kingship of Jesus. His faith and repentance are Christological.

Conclusion

Over the whole Gospel, Luke develops the character of both the repentant and the unrepentant. The repentant appear predominantly as the group comprising tax collectors and sinners. It is assumed that the sins of tax collectors and sinners are real, wicked and dangerous, since repentance is necessary to avoid divine judgment. The repentant are associated with self-humbling, a grief at sin and an admission of guilt, but also with joy and feasting and trust in Jesus. Strikingly, while repentance is necessary for all, it also seems open to all, for the issue of who repents comes to a head in the examples of Zacchaeus the rich chief tax collector and the criminal on the cross. Lastly, repentance bears fruit, in terms of restitution and deep love.

The unrepentant are largely represented by the character group comprising the Pharisees. As the Gospel progresses they are increasingly placed on a level with tax collectors: like them, tending to idolize wealth, and not full law-keepers, for they do not love God, nor their neighbours, but do love prestige and position. They are proud, self-reliant and hypocritical. Their plight is acute because this is scarcely their self-image, yet the authoritative words of Jesus and the narrator tell the reader this is the reality. As the narrative develops, the Pharisees are, in the reader's eyes, cast down and, although they are unaware, humbled, as their true character is revealed. This undoubtedly destabilizes the reader, for one must ask whether one does not harbour the same pride in oneself and contempt for others.

In all this, repentance becomes something that locates us relationally with respect to Jesus and God and others. With respect to God, it locates the repentant as those rejoicing in his mercy, mourning over sin and who are objects of his rejoicing as we repent. Repentant people love God and bear fruit. Repentant people are humble before God and Jesus, knowing that because of sin all they bring is an empty and undeserving hand.

With respect to others, the repentant can have no pride towards others, for repentance means acknowledging one's own sin. Nor, by implication, should they adulate others, for others, too, can only be trophies of grace.

Lack of repentance, on the other hand, is associated both with rejecting God's purpose for oneself, so excluding oneself from his grace, but also with the obstruction of grace to those who are repentant. Thus in the feast of repentance the unrepentant are consistently portrayed as those who, as well as excluding themselves, unjustifiably attempt to exclude the people who are the objects of Jesus' mission. Lack of repentance features dislocated relation both with God and with others.

Chapter Three

Repentance: for Jew and Gentile

Recap

In the last chapter we saw how Luke accumulates a picture of repentance in his Gospel. We examined the way Luke articulates his theology of repentance by characterization of two groups in particular: the tax collectors, who largely represent the repentant, and the Pharisees, who largely represent the unrepentant. Of course, Luke is too skilful a writer and too astute a theologian to envisage all tax collectors as repentant, or all Pharisees as unrepentant. Apart from anything else, Acts features an archetypal Pharisee, Paul, who comes to repentance and faith, just as the Gospel in the figures of Zacchaeus and the criminal on the cross feature what one might call the stereotypical dregs of society coming to repentance and faith. What strikes the reader, though, is whether he or she identifies himself or herself with the repentant or the unrepentant.

Who should repent?

The range of figures who repent in the Gospel open up the wonderful possibilities of repentance for the reader. If someone as compromised and embedded in sinful structures as Zacchaeus can repent, then the net of repentance is very widely spread indeed. The possibilities of repentance are opened up in another way, though, by Luke's Gospel, as the class of 'sinner' is gradually extended to cover even the apparently law-keeping Pharisees. The implication is that if even the Pharisees must be classed as sinners, then surely all must be. The Gospel envisages an apparently universal scope to the call to repentance at two points: Luke 13:1–5 (with its stress on the need to avoid judgment) and Luke 24:47 (where repentance is linked to forgiveness of sins). The failure of even such dedicated law observers as the Pharisees justifies this universal emphasis.

What are the repentant like?

By the end of the Gospel the reader has a number of characteristics in mind for the repentant. They are sinners; they love God and Jesus, for they are acutely aware of how much has been forgiven them. They have defined themselves as sinful and bound for God's wrath and rely not on themselves but on his mercy. They are objects of divine joy, the ones to whom Jesus was sent, and their repentance is associated with a festal joy on their part. They also mourn at sin, and are to show the fruits of repentance in their repudiation of the typical acts and attitudes of their previous life, something shown sharply in the rich tax collector Zacchaeus's giving restitution to those he defrauded and succouring the poor. They are humble and are called on in their turn to show mercy to others as they themselves have received mercy.

What are the unrepentant like?

The group that stands so much in contrast to these characteristics of the repentant, the unrepentant, nevertheless have one critical characteristic in common with the repentant: they are sinners too. Luke is at great pains to draw this out with respect to the character group the Pharisees, who are finally shown to have remarkably similar characteristics in important ways to the tax collectors they so despise: they too love money and are grasping. However, close attention shows that the Gospel resists a simple demonizing of the Pharisees, in which, so to speak, the reader is led to substitute a new villain for the old villains of the tax collectors. For the love of money is not restricted to the Pharisees. And the thirst for prominence, worryingly, can be present even among the disciples themselves. For the disciples can ask for high places in heaven when Jesus' reign is realized (Luke 9:46–47, and compare also Luke 22:24–27 and the dispute as to who is the greatest). As such it is a risky business for readers to congratulate themselves on not being a Pharisee: 'Lord, I thank you that I am not like other men and not like this Pharisee here', to paraphrase the parable of Luke 18.

Where the unrepentant fundamentally differ from the repentant is critically in the area of self-justification and pride. This leads to some striking attitudes. Concerning themselves, they imagine they are already righteous, and so have no need for repentance. At root, then, the unrepentant are deceived about themselves.

The point that the unrepentant are deceived about themselves is so important that it justifies a digression. Let us take New Testament scholarship first. Considerable efforts have been made, understandably, to investigate the understandings of Second Temple Judaism, and equally understandably this has led scholars not only to scrutinize the texts of this Judaism in order to understand it, but to accept at some level that Judaism's self-description.[1] It is, though, obvious that if Jesus had followed this method he would not have said what he did in Luke 11:39–52. He comments devastatingly that the Pharisees do not do justice and do not love God (11:42) but actually make people unclean (11:44). This was scarcely what they would say about themselves. Rather, they imagine they are precisely concerned with proper cleanness – it was, after all, with ostensible Pharisaic concerns for cleanness that the controversy of Luke 11 started (see v. 38). Jesus warns in Luke 16 about the dangers of loving wealth, as if it is an idol, and the narrator immediately associates this with the Pharisees' love of money in 16:14. Jesus' critical point in Luke 12:1–3 is that the Pharisees are hypocrites. This necessarily implies that their self-testimony and public discourse are not the reality of their hearts. That reality will indeed be revealed. In fact, the reality of their hearts is much darker, as the cross, one would have thought, amply demonstrates. In the debates about Second Temple Judaism one needs to hear more strongly, perhaps, that the Judaism one may read on the page, even supposing one could talk of a single Judaism, is not the same as the belief in the heart of a first-century Jew. And Jesus deals with and diagnoses the latter, not Judaism the abstraction.

This leads to a pastoral point: quite simply, people are self-deceived about how good they are. Inevitably this affects gospel proclamation as much in our day as it did in Luke's. The proclamation that Jesus is Lord, clearly right in itself, is to a particular kind of person, not merely to one who has a lord of whom they were previously ignorant, but to one who has offended that lord already, before the proclamation has even been made. We are reminded, too, of the evil of having an unrepentant person trying to proclaim the gospel. There might very well be problems for their calling for others to repent of hidden sin when they themselves are in denial about their own sinfulness. One possibility is that an unrepentant minister, therefore, will simply preach a gospel void of repentance, and be content with the admittedly awe-inspiring information that Jesus is lord, but not supplement it with the very call Jesus deems necessary, of repentance and

---

[1] It is, naturally, by no means clear that one can speak of a single Second Temple Judaism. See Carson, O'Brien and Seifrid 2004.

forgiveness of sins. And if such people do preach repentance to others, they may well bring the gospel into disrepute because, while they may deceive themselves about their sin, their need for repentance may become all too apparent to those who have to listen to their pomposities. Luke does not intend his readers to be unrepentant proclaimers of repentance to others. We must now return to the main point.

Given the self-understanding of the unrepentant that they do not need repentance, they are shown as loving God little, if at all, and this frigidity towards God is compounded by seeking the approval of humans rather than him and 'loving' the things of this world, notably wealth.[2]

This self-understanding also affects attitudes to others. It involves the begrudging of God's mercy and forgiveness to repentant sinners, and implies that those who hold this attitude do not forgive others. Instead, the attitude to the sinner is one of contempt, which underpins consistent attempts to exclude. Failing the attempt to exclude others, the unrepentant exclude themselves, and are objects of wrath.

There are, then, major differences between repentant and unrepentant in their understanding of themselves, God and others. But the difference is emphatically not that the repentant have a merit that the unrepentant do not have: both are sinners.

However, so far in Luke's account the question of repentant as against unrepentant has been played out within the confines of the covenant people. We turn now to consider Acts, and will follow the basic structure that the book provides: that the message Jesus committed to his disciples in Luke 24 is taken first to the Jews, the covenant people, and then to the Gentiles.

The appeal to Jews

The proclamation of Jesus' message of repentance and forgiveness of sins to Jews is most extensively described in Acts 1 – 7. Clearly, proclamation to Jews continues throughout the book, for the missionary strategy of Paul and others is characteristically to go to diaspora synagogues, and Acts 28 concludes with Paul's encounter with Jews in Rome. Nevertheless, the focus on proclamation to Jewish audiences is intense in chapters 1–7, while a major theme in what follows is that the gospel of salvation is going to the Gentiles (Acts 13:47; 28:28).

---

[2] Heil (1999: 86) draws out that this is the Pharisees' 'love'.

Acts 1 – 7, which focuses on this proclamation to the Jews, again features two groups: one responsive and repentant; the other unresponsive and unrepentant. Here, though, the two groups that embody these attitudes are, on the one hand, the crowds, who are repentant and responsive, at least in the sense that some respond to the apostles' preaching, while on the other hand the temple authorities are predominantly unrepentant and unresponsive.

This recasting of who is and who is not repentant is intriguing. The crowds in Luke 19:1–10 have behaved in ways that have previously characterized the Pharisees, for they show excluding attitudes to the repentant and there is an implied sense of superiority. Yet in Acts 1 – 7, as we shall see, the people are capable of repentance. Moreover, Saul the Pharisee, part of the group so negatively portrayed in the Gospel of Luke, is converted. In this way Luke does not allow us easy categorizations of who is beyond repentance.

Yet there is also continuity in Luke's recasting. One of the features of the Gospel of Luke was the motif of reversal, and how the mighty or proud are cast down (1:52). The portrayal of the unrepentant Pharisees should be related to this especially in the light of the parable of the tax collector and the Pharisee (18:9–14), where Jesus says precisely that those who exalt themselves will be humbled, while the humble will be lifted up. In Acts 1 – 7 there are 'mighty' figures who are being challenged, and, one might say, humbled by the progress of the gospel proclamation. But the mighty are not at this stage the Pharisees but another sector of the Establishment (to use a slightly anachronistic term), the temple authorities, notably the Sadducees. One must here admire Luke's artistic portrayal. A central feature of the witness of the apostles in Acts is to the resurrection of Jesus,[3] and what more appropriate group of naysayers to Jesus' resurrection could one focus on than a group systemically committed to the denial of any resurrection?[4]

Acts 2:37–42: Peter's sermon at Pentecost

The first call to repentance in Acts comes at 2:38, as Peter speaks at Pentecost. By the time Peter begins his address Acts 1:7–8 has prepared the reader for the apostles to fulfil the promise from Luke 24:47: that Jesus' message will be preached from Jerusalem to the ends

---

[3] E.g. Acts 1:22 has witness to the resurrection as a criterion for apostleship, while proclamation of and witness to the resurrection is evident in 2:32; 3:15; 4:10; and 5:31–32.

[4] See Luke 20:27.

of the earth. Peter also targets his speech: in Acts 2:14 he addresses himself to 'Men of Judea and all who dwell in Jerusalem', phrasing anticipated by 2:5 but which also recalls the order in which Jesus envisages the proclamation would go forth, and makes it clear that the context for the call to repentance that will follow is still the covenant people. This in-house aspect is reinforced by the subsequent reference to the audience as 'men of Israel' (2:22), a covenant name, and the employment of the terms 'brothers' to one another by the apostles (2:29) and the audience (2:37).[5]

Turning to the speech's content, H. F. Beyer stresses the way Peter's speech recalls Old Testament and intertestamental traditions of prophetic calls to Israel on account of God's mighty works.[6] Certainly, the theme of God's mighty works cannot be overlooked, since the audience itself refers to them (2:11),[7] and Peter speaks of the signs and wonders done by Jesus (2:22), before going on to describe the resurrection of Jesus as God's work (2:24, 32), a resurrection put into the context of prophetic fulfilment.

But Peter's speech is not only about testifying to the resurrection and consequent lordship of Christ. Jesus' resurrection by God implies accusation as well as fulfilment. This is evident in the narration of the Pentecost sermon. Structurally, Acts 2:14–40 comes in three parts. First (vv. 14–36) Peter explains the tongues the audience has heard and describes Jesus' death and resurrection. In doing so, however, he ends by joining Jesus' lordship with the point that Jesus was murdered by 'you' (v. 36). This prompts the second section, strictly an interruption to Peter's talk, as the audience asks what it should do (v. 37). This leads to the third section (vv. 38–40), in which Peter answers by calling for repentance and baptism, so that their sins may be forgiven (v. 38), and continues with a declaration of God's promise and an exhortation to the audience to save itself.

Three observations should be made about this structure. To begin with, the first section comes to a crescendo with the accusation that the Jews and the dwellers in Jerusalem have murdered God's Messiah. Verse 36 itself climaxes not in Jesus' lordship but in accusation: 'God has made him both Lord and Christ, this Jesus whom you crucified' (*kai kyrion auton kai Christon epoiēsen ho theos, touton ton Iēsoun hon hymeis estaurōsate*). The sentence ends with the deed of the people, not the appointment of Jesus. C. M. Green speaks rightly of

---

[5] Cf. Tannehill 1994, 2: 27: the speech is mainly concerned to 'address all Israel'.
[6] Bayer 1998: 263.
[7] In some confusion, since they hear them proclaimed in their own languages.

Peter's 'careful and accusatory use of "you"' in this passage.[8] The emphatic use of 'you' also markedly contrasts with God, thereby emphasizing 'the conflict between the actions of the audience and God'.[9]

The second observation is the dramatic weight of the crowd's response in verse 37: they are cut to the heart. There is a realization of who Jesus really is, and consequently the true nature of their own actions. They have lifted their hands against the Lord's anointed. Tannehill sees this as a kind of recognition, an *anagnōrisis*: 'The Pentecost speech is part of a recognition scene, where, in the manner of tragedy, persons who have acted blindly against their own best interests suddenly recognize their error.'[10]

There is, though, a double recognition here. There is the recognition of who Jesus really is, but this recognition and the revaluation of him that it brings, carries a corollary: a recognition that their own actions are not what they thought, but have a very different and more sinister quality. The two recognitions are reflexes of each other.

Third, the crowd's response of verse 37 gives a higher profile to Peter's response in verse 38. By interrupting Peter's speech in verse 37 the significance of the accusation is underlined. So far, Luke's account is that the audience has listened in silence. Now they react and their reaction is to the accusation they have murdered the Messiah, not it seems to the mere proposition that Jesus is Lord. However, since the accusation has acquired weight by the audience's interruption, corresponding weight is thrown on Peter's response in verse 38, which is to enjoin repentance for the forgiveness of sins. Rhetorically, the significant point in the speech is what Peter finally asks the audience to do. Accepting the resurrection is a step on the way to this, but is not the final destination: the command to repent is. The audience is not invited merely to accept the proposition that Jesus is Lord: it is told to repent.[11]

Of course, given what has happened in Jerusalem this is perfectly intelligible. The audience has a very specific sin from which to repent: the collective murder of Jesus. Repentance here has a very clear focus:

---

[8] C. M. Green 2005: 51.
[9] Tannehill 1994, 2: 35.
[10] Ibid. The motif of recognition, derived from Aristotle's *Poetics*, will be further developed in a later chapter.
[11] For Tannehill (1994, 2: 35–36) the scene is comparable to a tragic 'recognition' scene, where a character is brought to a real understanding of his or her actions, and is designed to issue in repentance out of that recognition.

it is with respect above all to the murder of Jesus, and it leads to the forgiveness of sins.[12]

Two points should be made before moving to Peter's second speech. First, the scope of repentance and forgiveness is by implication huge: one may repent and be forgiven even of the murder of the Messiah. We rightly stress the wonder of salvation encompassing Gentile as well as Jew, the ends of the earth as well as Jerusalem. One may equally wonder that repentance and forgiveness are offered to this audience so soon after the murder of Jesus the Christ. This surpasses perhaps the impact of repentance and forgiveness in Luke's Gospel. There the reader has seen the, by implication, avaricious and collaborating Levi caught *in flagrante delicto* at the tax booth and he is still called by Jesus; and the criminal beside Jesus on the cross, self-confessedly enduring a just punishment is promised he will be with Jesus in paradise. But here in Acts there is forgiveness for the murder even of the Messiah.

Second, the structure of Acts 2:14–40 makes one somewhat uneasy with a statement that proclaiming the gospel means proclaiming 'Jesus is Lord' and that alone. Such a statement seems to stop Peter's speech at verse 36a, but Luke has not done so: he builds to accusation, a sense of guilt and a call to repentance. Considered as rhetoric, the call to repentance is what Peter is aiming for. This is the response he seeks to his message. That Jesus is Lord is not a mere fact to be grasped. This call relationally locates Peter's audience with respect to the proposition that Jesus is Lord.

This relational location of Peter's audience is vital. Clearly, virtually any theory of communication considers who a recipient is in relation to what is communicated. Thus a proclamation in a Roman garrison town on the Rhine that, say, Vespasian is now emperor, can strike different people in very different ways. An ordinary Roman citizen may hear it with a sense that this is now the person in whose name he will be taxed and to whom he owes allegiance. A visiting German from the far side of the Rhine will not feel he owes allegiance to Vespasian but may be mindful that his own king must now deal with Vespasian and that jests in the tavern about Vespasian's parentage may now be injudicious. The garrison commander, however, may hear the news as the stroke of doom, having backed Vespasian's rival for the purple. The relational locations of citizen, German and

---

[12] I. H. Marshall (1980: 80) notes that Peter speaks of baptism as well as repentance, but rightly indicates that the two are to be taken together.

commander make all the difference to the nature of the news. It is precisely relational location that Peter brings out by his accusation of verse 36b, and it is from this that appropriate response springs in verses 37–42.

A further illustration by way of contrast may help. In J. R. R. Tolkien's *The Lord of the Rings* the rightful claimant to the ancient throne of Gondor, Aragorn, is finally manifested to those who are his rightful subjects. The proclamation of Aragorn's kingship is a proclamation of something long prophesied, but now unlooked for and beyond hope, but it does not call for repentance. It does call for acceptance in that whoever now does not accept Aragorn is from this time onwards committing treason against his or her rightful lord. Such a person is not, though, committing treason before the announcement of the news. This, though, does not capture the progress of Peter's address, for ultimately he emerges, in Bayer's words, 'as a prophetic preacher of repentance in Jerusalem'.[13] Repentance certainly includes acceptance of Jesus' lordship, but, as the comparison with Aragorn's rise to the kingship shows, acceptance does not necessitate repentance. The omission of repentance (even in the name of simply saying the gospel is 'Jesus is Lord') in the Pentecost address would be fatal. It would sweep the great sin that the people have committed under the carpet.

Acts 3:17–26: Peter's sermon in Solomon's Portico

Peter's next speech, in Solomon's Portico after the healing of the lame man at the Beautiful Gate (Acts 3:17–26) takes a similar form to the Pentecost address. It carries covenantal notes, for Peter calls the audience 'men of Israel' (v. 12) and goes on to speak in terms that presuppose the covenant (the God of Abraham, Isaac and Jacob; v. 13).

Again Peter lays an accusation against the audience: he sets out what the audience has done in verses 13–15. The compact list of verbs in the second-person plural, with little ornamentation or expansion, adds force and vividness to what has been done, culminating in the statement they have murdered the Author of life (v. 15). Poignancy is added to the accusation of murder by the contrast between the one whom they asked to be released, a murderer who takes life (v. 14), and

---

[13] Bayer 1998: 262. Cf. Witherington (1998: 141), 'Peter's speech is not just an attempt to defend the experience of his fellow-disciples, but a call to Jewish repentance, especially of course to those Jews most directly responsible for Jesus' death.'

the person they killed, who is the Author of life (v. 15), and by implication a giver of it.

In this way the hearers are revealed as profoundly at odds with God. They ask for a murderer to be released in preference to Jesus, while God raises and releases Jesus from death. They are takers of Jesus' life, while God is the restorer of Jesus' life. They emerge, so to speak, as pro-death, for they are on the side of 'life-taking'. This is doubly the case, for it is shown both in preferring a murderer and also in being murderers themselves, while God's Servant is Author of life and God is a life-giver. Life and death represent fundamental oppositions in human experience. Hence the murder of Jesus comes to speak of a people who are deeply estranged from God and what he prizes, and who are opposed to him, as death is opposed to life.

Thus the audience again has a specific sin of which to repent, and again, as in 2:36, is challenged to a twofold recognition, a re-evaluation of Jesus in the light of who he truly is, and, as a corollary, a re-evaluation too of their own actions in colluding in his murder. If anything, however, Luke relates the sin that is the presenting issue more emphatically to an underlying distance from God, so that the people are revealed as fundamentally at odds with him. B. Witherington perceptively comments, 'It is not just a matter of turning from sin (repentance-*metanoia*), but of turning to God.'[14] His implication is that the people are turned from God.

Several other features emerge from Peter's call for repentance (vv. 19–26). First, terminologically, *metanoein* and *epistrephein* terms are bracketed together in Peter's call (v. 19). This is important, since Peter uses 'turning' vocabulary again at the end of the speech. The verbal ties between verses 19 and 26 create conceptual connections too.

Second, the importance of repentance is evident in the way forgiveness of sins in some ways depends on it (v. 19). This is how forgiveness of sins is appropriated, it seems. This naturally raises the question of the relationship between repentance and faith, to which we shall return in a later chapter.

Third, the work of Jesus is put in covenant terms, fulfilling the promise given through Moses to raise up a prophet (vv. 22–23) and the promise of Genesis 12:3 to Abraham to bless the families of the earth (vv. 25–26). Clearly, this underlines the themes of fulfilment and the unity of God's plan for salvation that are so important to Luke's

---

[14] Witherington 1998: 184.

account. However, verse 26 explains that this blessing is associated with God's turning (*en tōi apostrephein*) one from one's evil ways. This turning language, given the earlier connection between repentance and turning in verse 19, cannot easily be separated from repentance. This means the covenant blessings promised through Abraham to all people come through repentance. Moreover, given that earlier link, the blessing of the nations through Abraham relates to the forgiveness of sins,[15] for this is where repentance leads.

However, God's role in turning is to the fore here. Turning and repentance are not acts in which we are uniquely active. Rather, God's action is emphasized here. This process of repentant turning is linked with the forgiveness of sins and the blessing promised through the Abrahamic covenant. Although the speech is addressed to Israelites, this reference to the final blessing of the Abrahamic covenant takes one to the blessing of the nations by the forgiveness of sins. Peter's theology of divine turning and repentance for the forgiveness of sins has universalizing implications.

Acts 5:29–32: Peter's speech to the councils

Peter's next speech dealing with repentance differs from the two earlier speeches, which clearly resemble each other. To begin with, Peter's speech is addressed to the high priest, council and *gerousia* (senate) of Israel (5:21), rather than a relatively indiscriminate group of Israelites. A slight differentiation has already occurred between people and rulers in Peter's earlier speech in Acts 3:17, and there is a sense in which the speeches of Acts 4 and 5 are to this second, distinct, group, or subgroup, of Israelites involved in the murder of Jesus.

The speech of Acts 5:29–32 is set, however, against a bleaker backdrop of hostility and rejection than either the Pentecost speech or the speech in Solomon's Portico. It is closely related to the speech in Acts 4:8–12 and the prayer of 4:24–30, which follows. To begin with, 4:1–2 strikes a slightly ominous note, as the Sadducees are specified as being part of the group that takes offence at the words of the apostles, and the grounds of the offence is the proclamation of 'the resurrection of the dead in Jesus' (*en tō Iēsou tēn anastasin tēn ek nekrōn*).[16] This slightly cumbersome phrasing clearly refers to Jesus' own resurrection, but the phrasing 'the resurrection of the dead in

---

[15] Cf. Rom. 4:7–9, with its thought that forgiveness is blessing (v. 7) and that this blessing is not just for the circumcised (v. 9).

[16] Taking the clear majority reading of 4:2.

Jesus' takes one to something more general: that in or by Jesus there is resurrection from the dead, and not just for Jesus individually. Jesus seems to be the focal point for general resurrection.

This opens up two considerations. First, this is utterly consistent with the emphases seen so far in Acts: that the apostles witness to the resurrection of Jesus. Second, proclaiming the resurrection of Jesus will be highly offensive to the Sadducees in particular given their repudiation of any kind of resurrection. The Sadducees and the groups they are connected with seem necessarily set on a collision course with the apostolic proclamation in which resurrection is so central. The Sadducees are brought to the reader's attention again in 5:17 as part of the audience to Peter's speech.

Peter's speech in Acts 5 is also given context by other factors. In some ways it is a continuation of the speech from Acts 4:8–12, and the introductory words of the high priest in 5:28 envisage continuity between the two incidents. The speech of 4:8–12 contains key themes that have been encountered previously: an assertion of resurrection, an accusation (both v. 10) and a reference to the possibility of salvation (v. 12), although it is now explicit that Jesus alone saves. There is no explicit call to repentance.

The reaction is intriguing. A sign has been done, just as signs preceded the two earlier speeches. There is no denial that a sign has taken place (4:16), but there is no positive reaction to it. This contrasts with the reaction of the people in 3:10. The reader, given the way Luke has constructed the narrative, feels an appropriateness to the people's reaction. There is, though, an irrationality to recognizing a sign has occurred and then refusing to allow it to be spoken of, as the rulers do. It speaks of a certain obstructiveness.

This is compounded by the instructions given in 4:18 not to speak in the name of Jesus. 'Name' has been a feature throughout the incident of the lame man. He is healed in the name of Jesus (3:6), Peter explains his healing in terms of the name of Jesus (3:16) and the rulers ask in what name or authority the healing has been done (4:7). Peter concludes his speech by saying salvation is possible only in this name (4:12). Thus as the rulers forbid speaking in the name of Jesus, they oppose themselves to the purpose of God, which the reader of the Gospel and Acts knows is precisely to have the name proclaimed to the ends of the earth. Moreover, in attempting to obstruct the apostles' proclamation, the rulers are cutting off the offer of salvation and forgiveness to others. This puts them at odds with the covenant purposes of God outlined in 3:25–26, which is to bless all the families of the earth by turning them from their wicked ways. They emerge, in effect, as anti-covenant people.

The sense of deep antagonism to God from the rulers is reinforced by the prayers of the believers in 4:24–30. This prayer construes the opposition to Jesus as a fulfilment of Psalm 2, in which the rulers of Israel are part of a coalition with the Gentiles against the Lord's anointed (4:27–28). The rulers, precisely the people one might think would and should behave as the covenant people of God, show themselves deeply identified with Gentiles in rebellion against God.[17]

The speech of Acts 5:29–32 continues these themes. Again the rulers are faced with a sign (the release from prison) that perplexes them (5:24) but does not bring them to repentance. By now the refusal to reckon with the resurrection and with the sign, combined with the inability to produce alternative explanations, increases the reader's perception that this group is profoundly irrational. They go on to recognize that they are being accused of murder (5:28), which Peter immediately underlines (5:30). There is, though, no recognition in the dramatic sense, an *anagnōrisis* in which they revalue Jesus and their own actions in putting him to death. The reader of 5:28 who has been brought to share Luke's narrative world reacts to the rulers' complaint with a sense that the rulers are indeed being accused of murder and justly so. The reader may also experience discomfort. The rulers, like the people addressed in the previous speeches, clearly need repentance and the forgiveness of sins. The possibility of repentance and forgiveness of sins is set out by Peter in 5:31 for Israel, despite their rejection of the Messiah. Yet this possibility seems distant for the rulers at this point, given their unrepentance in the face of Jesus' murder. Strikingly, Peter has issued imperatives to repent (*metanoēsate*; Acts 2:38; 3:19), but issues no imperative here. The gift of repentance and forgiveness of sins through Jesus is available to Israel generally, but is not realized in these lives; not yet at any rate.

Indeed, the gift aspect of repentance is again prominent. The exaltation of Christ by God is said to be with the purpose of giving repentance to Israel. The activity of God is stressed here as the one from whom the gift of repentance ultimately comes.[18] Peter has

---

[17] Cf. the cry before Pilate from 'the Jews' recorded in John 19:15 that they had 'no king but Caesar'.

[18] Strictly there is an ambiguity as to whether God exalts Jesus so that he (God) might give repentance and forgiveness, or whether God appoints Jesus so that he (Jesus) might give repentance. Either way, divine action is stressed, as is, by implication, the necessity of Jesus for salvation.

previously phrased his account of repentance in ways that take it away from being a purely spontaneous human-generated decision, but one that has to be seen in the light of the action of God who 'turns' hearts (3:26). Calvin writes:

> Repentance is indeed a voluntary conversion, but what is the source of this willingness except that God changes our heart, making a heart of flesh out of a heart of stone, one that is pliable out of one that is stiff and hard, and, finally, one that is upright out of one that is crooked? And this happens when Christ regenerates us by His Spirit.[19]

The only thing to add about the characterization of the high priest and those with him, the Sadducees, is that they are filled with jealousy (*eplēsthēsan zēlou*; 5:17). This jealousy is in response to the progress Luke describes in 5:12–16, in which the apostles are highly regarded (v. 13), believers are increasing in number (v. 14), signs are being performed (vv. 12, 15–16) and crowds are gathering (v. 16). The jealousy, then, appears to be in reaction to the prestige and attention the apostles have acquired. The attentive reader of the Gospel will recall that one of the marks of the unrepentant Pharisees was the lust for prominence, and jealousy at this 'success' of the apostles connects the Sadducees with this trait.

Acts 8:20–24: Peter's warning to Simon Magus

The next occurrence of repentance language comes in the incident surrounding Simon Magus. The setting is in some ways a transitional one, Samaria (8:5). Clearly, the reader recalls Jesus' words of Acts 1:8 in which the progress of the proclamation starts in Jerusalem and proceeds as it were through Judaea and Samaria to the ends of the earth.

Simon's spiritual status is, of course, debated. In 8:13 he is described as amazed at the signs Philip is doing. After the example of the rulers in Acts 4 – 5 one might well feel that accepting intellectually a sign has taken place is not necessarily a sign of conversion, but 8:13 also states that Simon has been baptized and has believed. This has suggested to some an authentic belief. Witherington's diagnosis is that Simon's sin is greed.[20] Certainly, money is involved, but as what Simon

---

[19] Calvin 1552: 149.
[20] Witherington 1998: 286.

offers rather than what he explicitly wants (8:18). It is quite plausible that Simon envisages being able to distribute the gift of the Spirit for reward later, but 8:10–11 emphasizes rather the prestige that Simon had among the Samaritans as someone great before Philip came. Certainly, prestige and financial gain are consistent with each other and Simon might well have made money out of his prestige.

However, both issues, money and prestige, connect with traits associated with the unrepentant character group, the Pharisees, in Luke's Gospel. There is also, though, a connection with material in Acts, for Ananias and Sapphira, who are apparently believers, sin with regard to the proceeds of sale of their land (Acts 5:1–11). The example of Ananias and Sapphira certainly relates to money, and that of Simon plausibly relates to prestige and possibly money. This shows the problem of these archetypal sins persisting within the community of believers or apparent believers.

Simon is called on to repent by Peter (8:22), but this in itself is a note of hope for Simon: that forgiveness is possible. Calvin writes:

> In urging him to repent and pray, he is leaving the hope of forgiveness open to him. For the only man who will be moved by any feeling of repentance is the one who is confident that God will deal favourably with him. On the other hand, hopelessness will always rush men headlong into presumption.[21]

In this way Calvin opens up the thought that repentance depends not merely on a sense of wrongdoing or sin, but on a conviction that God will be merciful. It also underlines, on the view that Simon was a believer, that repentance continues in the Christian life, just as sin continues to be a reality in Christian life in this world. However, we should not miss the implication that post-conversion sin is forgivable.

Review

In looking at the issues of repentance in the major speeches made to Jewish or closely related audiences, several things emerge clearly. First, there is the consistent charge that people and rulers have murdered the Messiah and, indeed, this is merely a continuation of a history of rejecting God's messengers. This sin is depicted in terms that underline the depth of estrangement between the covenant people and the

---

[21] Calvin 1965: 240. Cf. Ambrose, *Concerning Repentance* 2.4.23, 'And yet he did not exclude him from the hope of forgiveness, for he called him to repentance' (Schaff and Wace 1979, 10: 348).

covenant God, in which there is an antithesis of values. Second, while this certainly is a sin, forgiveness and repentance are possible even for this catastrophic sin. Third, there are the traits of the unrepentant. The unrepentant are no longer strongly identified with the Pharisees but with the rulers, who not only do not repent themselves but obstruct the purpose of God and the repentance and forgiveness of others by their attempts to silence the witness of the apostles.[22] The unrepentant are, though, people who should know the truth of what they hear, have the means to know it, and may even have some intellectual grasp of it, yet refuse it.

The appeal to Gentiles

The proclamation of the gospel in Samaria begins a major transition to the world of the Gentiles. In what follows in Acts there are again two character groups that demand attention: repentant Gentiles and the unrepentant synagogues in the towns that Paul and others visit. As with the unrepentant rulers in Acts 1 – 7, a key trait for the unrepentant is their envy as repentant Gentiles come to faith.[23]

Acts 11:15–18: Peter's account of God among the Gentiles

Luke carefully prepares the way for the reader to understand the conversion of the Gentiles. Thus in 9:10–16 Ananias has a vision that introduces not just Saul, but Saul's mission to the Gentiles (v. 15), explained in terms of Jesus' name. This phrasing both plays with Saul's original mission to imprison those who call on Jesus' name (v. 14) and recalls the significance of the name of Jesus in chapters 4 – 5. In chapters 10 – 11 Peter's vision is told twice and brackets the events of 10:34–48 in which Gentiles hear Peter's message and receive the gift of the Spirit (v. 44). The vision raises two themes already present in Luke's Gospel. First, the vision is about cleanness and uncleanness, in the first instance about foods, but applied by Peter to his encounter with the Gentile Cornelius and his household: unclean people rather than simply unclean food.[24] Second, the vision contains the possibility of human resistance to divine action. Peter initially refuses to eat and is commanded not to call unclean what God has

---

[22] Although compare the description of the Pharisees in Luke 7:30.
[23] Note esp. Acts 13:45, *hoi Ioudaioi . . . eplēsthēsan zēlou* (the Jews . . . filled with jealousy). Cf. 5:17 and the reaction of the high priest and Sadducees.
[24] Tannehill 1994, 2: 135.

called clean, reprising the theme of both the Gospel and Acts of human resistance to God's will.²⁵

Peter is challenged at Jerusalem in terms that again recall the gospel: he has eaten and associated with those with whom a good Jew should not (11:3), actions that recall Jesus' table fellowship.²⁶ Yet on the basis of the vision Peter can recognize the events of 10:44–46 as God's giving the same gift, the Spirit, whom he gave to Jews when they believed (11:17). Peter then asks whether he can hinder God. The implication is that of course he cannot. He has also spoken earlier of the impossibility of withholding baptism from those who have received the Holy Spirit even as he and the circumcised believers had (10:47), which underlines the motif of not resisting what God has been doing.²⁷

However, by this time the reader of the Gospel and the earlier chapters of Acts knows that some precisely do try to hinder the progress of proclamation. And it is therefore with some relief that one reads in 11:18 that the Jewish believers were not merely silenced but praised God, for this is not merely recognition of the progress of the gospel, but also reveals something about the authenticity of the Jewish believers. They associate themselves with, and submit to, the purposes of God, and do not exclude those whom he has included.

This becomes still clearer in their description of God's action: they understand the Gentiles as having been given repentance by God. To a reader of Luke's Gospel this immediately identifies the Jewish believers with the values of heaven, for heaven rejoices at the repentant, as Luke 15:7, 10 indicates. It naturally also distances them from the authorities and their response to the proclamation of the name of Jesus.

However, the phrasing of the believers indicates other things too. One cannot miss the emphatic placement of the phrase relating to the Gentiles, *Ara kai tois ethnesin ho theos tēn metanoian eis zoēn edoken* (even to the Gentiles God has given the repentance that leads to life). God's part in turning people from their wickedness has already been connected earlier with keeping the promise of blessing under the Abrahamic covenant to all the families of the earth (Acts 3:26). Here

---

²⁵ Cf. ibid. 132, 'The command gains its force by presenting a sharp warning of the potential conflict between divine and human action.'

²⁶ Heil (1999: 258), noting the criticism in Luke 19:7 and 15:2.

²⁷ The astonishment of the circumcised believers at the Gentiles speaking in tongues and praising God (10:45–46) resembles the scene at Pentecost.

that covenant promise is being fulfilled. For repentance is God's gift, not restricted to Jews, and not a human achievement in which one may boast. Repentance, too, is something that leads to life.

Repentance, further, is used in 11:18 to describe what happened in 10:42–48, in which people hear the promise of forgiveness to those who believe in Jesus' name and receive the Spirit. Repentance in that sense relates to faith and baptism in the Spirit,[28] and these are three closely related concepts. In fact, this section shows just how closely faith and repentance must be kept together. For the same Peter who can phrase his call which leads to the forgiveness of sins as a call to believe (10:43) is the one who in earlier speeches has spoken of repentance as the instrument leading to forgiveness (2:38; 3:19; 5:31).

Acts 14:5–18: Paul's call to repent at Lystra

Before Paul comes with Barnabas to Lystra, there have been several incidents in which the gospel has been opposed. Herod has had James murdered (12:2), while Paul and Barnabas themselves have faced persecution instigated by the Jews (13:50; 14:2). However, it is not a simple case of pagan Gentiles always responding to the gospel: as 14:4 shows, just as in Jerusalem among the Jews, so among the nations, some respond and some do not, but rather side with unbelieving or unrepentant Jews.

In Lystra Paul and Barnabas are faced not with a mixed audience of Jews and God-fearers (as in 13:16) or God-fearers (10:34 – note the description of Cornelius as a God-fearer in 10:2). Both Jews and God-fearers were at least monotheistic but the situation in Lystra is one of pagan polytheism, so that the healing of 14:10 is construed in polytheistic terms. For the Lystrans this sign does not immediately point to God. Paul and Barnabas react with horror (14:14) and explain that they are bringing the gospel (*euangelizomenoi*). This gospel is then explained as a call to turn from 'these worthless things' to the living God. The reference to these worthless things recalls Old Testament polemic against idols, so that the content of repentance in the Lystran situation is a turning from idolatry.[29]

Witherington comments that not only does this resemble the speech at Athens in 17:22–31; it also resembles Paul's writings in

---

[28] Cf. Calvin (1965: 326), who suggests that since repentance is unto life, repentance is clearly not to be separated from faith.

[29] Marshall (1980: 238) says, '[in Lystra] It was necessary to begin a stage further back with the proclamation of the one true God.'

REPENTANCE: FOR JEW AND GENTILE

1 Thessalonians 1:9–10 and Romans 1:18–32.[30] The corrupting effect of idolatry is certainly signalled in Romans 1:18–23, where it is associated with corruption of mind (Rom. 1:21) and of appetite (Rom. 1:24). The wrongness of idolatry is signalled in the present passage, both by the intensity of Paul and Barnabas's reaction to the would-be sacrificers, by the indications that the living God has exercised forbearance in the past (Acts 14:16), and by the implication that idolatry has left them estranged from their Creator (for why would they need to turn to him if they were not estranged? See Acts 14:15). This last point bears emphasis: it speaks of a situation where not just are some things wrong in the Lystrans' lives, but there is a fundamental disorientation and dislocation of life. After all, for a creature to be estranged from the one who created it and all things is to be dislocated indeed.

Acts 17:22–31: Paul's call to repent at Athens

Before Paul addresses the Athenians at the Areopagus the conversion or turning of the Gentiles to God has come under discussion in the Council of Jerusalem in Acts 15. The believers have received with joy the news Paul and Barnabas bring of Gentile conversion (15:3), thereby identifying themselves again with the joy of heaven at repentant sinners, and distancing themselves from the envy of the rulers and some of the diaspora Jews. As regards the outcome of the council, in some respects the rules of 15:29 can be seen as a call to bear fruits of repentance.

In Athens itself the context of Paul's speech is idolatry. This is what has inflamed him (*parōxyneto to pneuma autou en autōi*; 17:16). Of all the things that might have offended Paul in the life of Athens, it is this that is highlighted.

In the Areopagus speech itself it is the religious life of Athens that is scrutinized and criticized.[31] Paul begins with a reference to religiosity in his carefully ambiguous description of the Athenians as 'very religious' (*deisidaimonesterous*), which could be good or bad. In contemporary terms one might say it could be either the positive-sounding 'very spiritual' or the negative 'very superstitious'. In a sense the speech is an unfolding of the way Paul resolves the ambiguity. However, the speech is ultimately a piece of rhetoric designed to propel its audience to action, and the actions commended emerge in

---

[30] Witherington 1998: 425–426. Marshall likewise observes (1980: 290) the resemblance to 1 Thess. 1:9.

[31] Hansen (1998: 309) stresses the contact with OT polemic against idolatry.

verses 29–30: that 'we' must not think of God in certain ways, and that God commands all people everywhere to repent. As with other pieces of epideictic rhetoric, the rest of the speech has to be construed with these commended actions in mind.

In moving to this rhetorical goal Paul picks out the theme of ignorance.[32] It is an astute move, because a confession of ignorance implicitly acknowledges that action may have to be taken when ignorance is replaced by knowledge. More pointedly here, the ignorance concerns a person, and ignorance is something this person will no longer overlook. This emerges in 17:30–31, where the command of God to repent is explained in terms of the coming judgment of the world. One cannot safely enter that judgment in ignorance, because the times of ignorance, which God would overlook, have finished. This 'overlooking' of the times of ignorance implies the ignorance was ethically wrong and that repentance is with respect to this culpable ignorance and with a view to judgment. This aspect of wrongness implies that Paul is not merely providing cognitive correction, or better information, to an audience that is unenlightened through no fault of its own.[33] Ignorance, after all, has already been acknowledged by Peter with respect to the Jerusalem crowd, but this does not remove the wickedness of their actions or their consequent need to repent (Acts 3:17). Rather, 'ignorance', albeit on different topics, is now seen to link both Jew (the Jerusalem crowd) and pagan Gentile (the Athenian Areopagus).

Thus the speech implies that ignorant idolatry is itself the ground of judgment. This is highlighted by the other action laid down for the Athenians in the exhortation of verse 29, that 'we should not think' (*ouk opheilomen nomizein*) of God in the ways the Athenians have. The call not to think of God in these terms arises from Paul's radical undermining of Athenian religious life.

Paul starts with the altar to the unknown God (Acts 17:23). On reflection, there is a slight tension in this thought: on the one hand, the Athenians concede ignorance of this god; on the other hand, they seem to know enough about him, they imagine, to worship in the traditional way, using an altar. The presupposition is that one deals

---

[32] Witherington 1998: 524.

[33] This stands against the argument of Talbert (1998: 144), which envisages some conversions in Acts as moral, involving 'issues of sin and forgiveness' (citing Acts 2:38; 3:19; 5:30–31; 10:43; 13:38; 26:17–18), and others as cognitive, involving 'a shift of basic paradigms about the world' (citing Acts 13:4–12; 14:8–18; 17:22–31). It will be argued later that conversion, as in repentance for Jew and Gentile alike, involves both elements.

with a god with this kind of cultus or approach. But do they know enough to make this judgment? Paul speaks of the living God as one who does not dwell in temples made by hands (17:24), nor does he need food and service (17:25). The shrine and temple-based worship of pagan Athens implied just that: location and dependence. This Creator and sovereign of all is not rightly approached or worshipped in this way because such worship in fact treats him as what he is not. There may be an inkling of God in the human heart but no adequate response.[34]

Thus it is that the Gentile Athenians, like the Gentile Lystrans, can be profoundly religious, yet guilty of the sin of idolatry. It is precisely in their religious life, in their purported acts of due reverence, that the sin for which they are called to repent lies. Again this can be seen as a challenge to recognition, similar to, although clearly different in detail from, the challenges issued to the crowds in Jerusalem in chapters 2–3. In Jerusalem the purported acts of reverence in the killing of the allegedly blasphemous Jesus are revealed to be acts of rebellion against the Lord's anointed, as Jesus' true identity is disclosed. In Athens the purported acts of reverence to the unknown god are revealed to be things that belittle and misrepresent him, as the true nature of God is revealed.[35]

Three other things, though, emerge in relation to the call to repent at Athens. First, idolatry is presented as a pervasive Athenian problem. It is just the pervasiveness that enrages Paul in 17:16 and the prevalence of religious practice that he refers to in 17:22. Idolatry is no trivial, incidental, part of Athenian life. It appears fundamental.

Second, the call to repentance in 17:30 is clearly universal, with the double emphasis of all people in all places. This arises from the idea of universal judgment,[36] expressed in verse 31 as a judgment of 'the world' (*tēn oikoumenēn*) and is connected with the thought of 1 Thessalonians 1:9–10, that the Thessalonians are delivered from coming judgment. Repentance, of course, presupposes an admission of wrongdoing. Thus universal repentance in the face of universal judgment presupposes that no human being can rely on his or her own righteousness. This is not a new theme in Luke–Acts given the criticism of the self-reliance of the unrepentant Pharisees; but here,

---

[34] Cf. Witherington 1998: 523.
[35] The incident at Lystra in Acts 14:11–13 also features some misconceived acts of reverence.
[36] Stott 1990: 288.

of course, it is extended to Gentiles. Thus, while the offer of salvation is universal, so is the problem with which salvation must deal.

This universality is grounded clearly in relationships applicable to all humans, not just those born within the Abrahamic covenant. The universal relationships in question are those of Creator and created. Commenting on how Paul universalizes the gospel proclamation, Tannehill states:

> The necessary resources are found through reflection on the relation of the Creator to the creation. This is a relation that transcends every ethnic and racial difference. It is a relation rooted in creaturely existence as such, embracing, therefore, Jews and Gentiles equally.[37]

Third, Paul relates his claims and commands to the resurrection. In this respect there is a fuller account than in the speech at Lystra. There is also, naturally, continuity with Peter's speeches in Jerusalem. There the resurrection was used to show the people and rulers that their rejection and murder of Jesus was wrong and required repentance. Here the resurrection is connected to universal judgment and thus to the imperative to repent. Yet whether the audience is Jewish or pagan polytheist, resurrection is related to repentance. Intriguingly, resurrection is also a stopping point here in Athens as it was in Jerusalem. Some of the Areopagite audience behave like Sadducees, mocking the resurrection (Acts 17:32). To the reader of Luke–Acts, who has been brought to see the centrality and certainty of Jesus' resurrection, this mockery smacks of foolishness and obduracy.

Review

At the close of the speech to the Areopagus a picture emerges of the Gentiles to whom Paul speaks as profoundly religious at one level, yet nevertheless guilty of sin in their idolatry. An intriguing picture therefore emerges in Acts, that whether in Jerusalem or Athens, repentant and unrepentant alike are 'religious' in one sense, but all alike are under the obligation to repent.

It is fitting here to focus on the problem of religiosity. Two points are especially noteworthy. First, Luke consistently highlights the dubious religiosity to be found in the pagan Graeco-Roman world in which Paul ministers. Second, this religiosity is not dissimilar to the

---

[37] Tannehill 1994, 2: 211.

false religiosity to be found in Jerusalem. We must develop these briefly.

Thus, in relation to the dubious religiosity of the pagan world, Acts has consistent references to demonic or sorcerous activity: Bar Jesus (13:6); the spirit-possessed slave girl (16:16–18); the sons of Sceva (19:14–16); and the burning of the Ephesian magic books (19:19–20). The power of pagan idolatry is underlined both in the incident at Lystra (14:11–18), where polytheism is the lens through which the Lystrans construe the miraculous healing (their world view), and by the riot in Ephesus initiated by Demetrius (19:23–41).[38] The power of the Artemis cult is evident through the length and unity of the chant 'Great is Artemis of the Ephesians!' (19:34). Luke presents pagan religiosity as a major obstacle against which Paul must (rightly) struggle.

False religiosity is also something common to both Jerusalem and the pagan Gentile world. There is a grim parallelism between the fears of the Jerusalem authorities about Stephen (see the accusation of 6:14, which includes the destruction of the temple) and the fears of Demetrius and the silversmiths (Artemis's temple will be discredited; 19:27). This is further compounded by the parallel between the riot in Ephesus instigated by Demetrius and the riot in Jerusalem initiated by the Asian Jews. Tannehill comments that the description is similar, and so is the reason: '[M]embers of an established religion are protesting the effect that Paul's mission is having on their religion and its temple'.[39] To this extent, Jew and Gentile have a common problem: false religion.

The unrepentant in this section of Acts, which details mission to the pagan world, emerge with two characteristics especially. First, there is envy, manifested in those Jews who attempt to obstruct Paul and his various companions; and second, there is rejection of the resurrection, manifest in the reaction of some of the Areopagites. Both these traits are found in the Jerusalem section of Acts as well.

Paul's understanding of his ministry

As well as providing examples of the way Peter and Paul conducted their apostolic ministries, Acts also provides us with material showing

---

[38] Note that Demetrius attributes to Paul the argument that man-made gods are not gods at all (20:26). Paul has evidently critiqued Ephesian idolatry.
[39] Tannehill 1994, 2: 242.

how Paul understood his ministry. We turn now to two examples of this.

Acts 20:17–24: Paul's ministry in Ephesus

The point is frequently made that Paul's speech to the Ephesian elders at Miletus matters greatly given both his closeness to the Ephesian believers (having ministered there for two years or so; 19:10) and his anticipation he would not see the elders again (20:25). Under these circumstances he summarizes the shape of his own ministry with a view to commending it to them also.

In this summary Paul speaks about the character and manner of his ministry: humble, persevering, God-serving and diligent (20:19–20). He also speaks of the content (v. 21): 'I testified to both Jews and Greeks about repentance toward God and faith toward our Lord Jesus Christ' (NRSV).

Paul, then, has one message, which applies to both Jews and Greeks alike.[40] Despite the uniqueness of Israel's historical experience as the covenant people, there is nevertheless one message for both Jew and Gentile. This is no surprise given the movement within Acts from Jerusalem out into the pagan Gentile population.

That message includes both repentance and faith. For Calvin these two elements summarize Paul's teaching.[41] Witherington supports this, countering accusations that this account is not Pauline by pointing both to Romans 2:4 and also, importantly, to 1 Thessalonians 1:9–10, where the Thessalonians are described as turning to God and waiting for Jesus.[42]

For Calvin the two elements, repentance and faith, are not synonymous, nor one part of the other. Yet they are not simply two unrelated things:

> Indeed, I admit they cannot be separated, because God does not illuminate anybody with the Spirit of faith, without regenerating him to new life at the same time. Yet they need to be distinguished as Paul does in this verse.[43]

---

[40] The fact that Paul does not differentiate between Jew and Gentile here tells against the view of Talbert (1998: 144), which differentiates conversions into moral or cognitive categories.
[41] Calvin 1966: 175.
[42] Witherington 1998: 617.
[43] Calvin 1966: 176.

Calvin goes on to state what the distinction is in his view:

> For repentance is a turning round to God, when we compose ourselves in the whole of our lives to His obedience. On the other hand, faith is the receiving of the grace which is presented to us in Christ.[44]

For Calvin this means that it is not possible to preach repentance in a distinctively Christian way without preaching Christ and the possibility of reconciliation that he offers. Such faithless preaching of repentance is indistinguishable, he feels, from secular philosophy.[45] However, while envisaging that repentance cannot be taught properly without faith, he does not discuss the question whether faith can be taught without repentance. Logic suggests it cannot. Material elsewhere in Calvin supports this; for if repentance is here related to obeying God, faith is related to a knowledge of his will,[46] which is closely linked to obedience. We shall return to this relation of faith and repentance in a later chapter.

Acts 26:12–23: Paul's commission from Christ

Paul also describes his mission in his speech to Agrippa in Acts 26. Here, though, this is in the context of Paul's own commissioning by the risen Jesus, and his statements about how he has fulfilled it.

Acts 26:16–18 reads:

> But get up and stand on your feet; for I have appeared to you for this purpose, to appoint you to serve and testify to the things in which you have seen me and to those in which I will appear to you. I will rescue you from your people and from the Gentiles – to whom I am sending you to open their eyes so that they may turn from darkness to light and from the power of Satan to God, so that they may receive forgiveness of sins and a place among those who are sanctified by faith in me. (NRSV)

Paul continues in verse 19 that he was not disobedient to this vision. What follows therefore in verses 20–23 serves to explain what the commands in the vision entailed.

---

[44] Ibid.
[45] Ibid.
[46] Calvin 1960: 549 (*Inst.* 3.2.6).

Paul in verse 21 mentions speaking to both Jews and Greeks, and the content of what he says is that they should repent and turn to God and do deeds consistent with repentance. This reinforces the idea that Paul had one message for Jew and Gentile alike, albeit differently presented in different settings. Stenschke writes:

> Paul has one and the same message of all people: repentance in its most general sense is needed; the Jewish sin of rejecting Jesus is not particularly in mind. All people are away from God and need to turn to him.[47]

Terminologically, as I have indicated before, repentance as *metanoein* and turning as *epistrephein* are very closely related. Paul also is prepared to summarize a message that elsewhere he sees in terms of repentance and faith (20:21) as one of repentance and turning to God. This supports the view that faith and repentance are closely interwoven. What may be striking from a contemporary viewpoint is that repentance and turning are used by Paul as the overarching category to cover the whole. Unsurprisingly, given the disputes of the Reformation and the importance of the letters to the Romans and Galatians in those disputes, much emphasis in theology is laid upon faith, and this is rightly and understandably reflected in evangelism, where there are calls to faith. But Paul here emphasizes the call to repentance (and this is evident in Peter's commands to repent earlier in the Jerusalem speeches in Acts). In terms of earlier material the stress on deeds that fit with repentance recalls the ministry of John the Baptist, who called for the fruits of repentance.

However, 26:18 is especially important because it gives us a glimpse of the theological value attached to repentance. It deals with two pairs of ideas. The pairs are darkness–light on the one hand, and power of Satan–God on the other. Those pairs each contain contrasting ideas rather than similar ones. Repentance is a turning from the first member of each pair to the second member of each pair. The pairs no doubt interpret each other, so that power of Satan is glossed to some extent by darkness, and light by God:

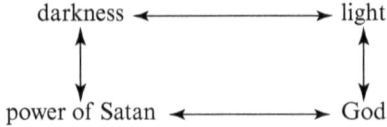

---

[47] Stenschke 1998: 142.

This means that Paul is envisaging repentance as a turning from darkness and the power of Satan to light and God. Elsewhere light is associated with salvation in Luke–Acts (e.g. Luke 1:78–79),[48] and this associates the God to whom one turns in repentance with salvation, and darkness with being unsaved. The status of unsaved is even gloomier when darkness is associated with the power of Satan, so that repentance is a turning from being under alien dominion. Calvin, recalling the language of John 8:34, speaks of being 'slaves to sin'.[49] This is applied to both Gentiles and Jews alike.[50]

This presentation of the plight from which people must be turned in repentance does not easily reduce to either a purely cognitive turn (where the problem fundamentally is lack of information), nor simply an ethical or moral dimension.[51] It doubtless has elements of both.

What is perhaps initially surprising is the way this seems to apply even to the covenant people, the Jews. For the natural question is how one could say they, the covenant people, were under satanic dominion. But at this stage it is worth recalling how strongly Peter paints the opposition and estrangement between the Jewish people and their rulers on the one hand and God on the other. As we have seen in 3:14–15, the people and rulers are associated with rejection and death, in contrast to God, who gives life; while in 4:25–27 they are interpreted as standing in a rebellious confederacy against God and his anointed in fulfilment of Psalm 2. Moreover, in Luke the unrepentant Pharisees are lovers of money rather than God and seek praise and prominence from men. One may well say, then, that they behave fundamentally like pagans. The prevalence of idolatry and sorcery among Gentiles equally clearly speaks of a world under satanic dominion.[52] The common nature of this plight is underlined as one sees Luke describing the problem of false human religion both in Jerusalem and in the pagan world. J. Green perceptively writes, '[I]n subtle but important ways, Luke underscores the idolatry of even the Jewish people'.[53]

---

[48] Witherington (1998: 745) says, '[T]hroughout Luke-Acts the movement from darkness to light is used as a metaphor for salvation in dependence on the Isaianic ideas . . .' (citing Isa. 42:6–7; Luke 1:77–79; 2:30–32; Acts 13:47).

[49] Calvin 1966: 277.

[50] Jesus has, of course, pointed to satanic slavery for his Jewish interlocutors in John 8:34.

[51] Contra Talbert 1998: 144.

[52] In this connection note that Paul does link idolatry with demonolatry: 1 Cor. 10:19–20.

[53] J. Green 2002: 7.

THE FEASTS OF REPENTANCE

Thus, whether Jew or Gentile, it is from no neutral position that one repents and turns to God. Paul refers to a plight that is indeed desperate. Outside salvation one is under the power of Satan; while in turning to God there is salvation, forgiveness of sins and freedom from the dominion of Satan. Understood this way, the motifs of feast and joy that are so clearly linked with repentance in the Gospel of Luke become well-judged and appropriate responses to the wonder of God's saving deeds. We should also note in passing that this set of motifs is paralleled in the Pauline corpus by the description of salvation in Colossians 1:13–14, while in John the passion is represented, among other things, as a conflict with the ruler of this world.[54]

Acts 28:26–28: Paul's understanding of God's purposes

The final reflection on repentance and turning again features the matter of who refuses and who accepts. In Acts 28:25–28 Paul comments on the failure to believe on the part of at least some of his Jewish audience in Rome. By quoting Isaiah 6:9–10, Paul locates the refusal to believe within the framework of prophetic fulfilment and thus within God's plan. There is at least a hint that this is in fact God's dispensation and that he has not given the gift of repentance. The idea of refusal by at least some Jews, though, is present throughout Acts, as is the optimistic view that salvation will go to the Gentiles, at least some of whom will listen. Again this has been amply demonstrated within the narrative at least since Acts 8 and the conversions in Samaria.

Objections to a universal call for repentance

The objection outlined

However, it may be objected that Luke–Acts does not in fact support a strictly universal call for repentance. This objection may be outlined in the following way. To begin with, Luke designates some characters in a positive moral way. Thus Zechariah and Elizabeth (Luke 1:6), Simeon (Luke 2:25), Joseph of Arimathea (Luke 23:50) and Cornelius (Acts 10:2, 22) are all described in positive moral terms in the authoritative voice of the narrator.[55] In particular, these characters are called *dikaios*, among other things.

---

[54] See e.g. John 12:31; 13:27; 16:11.
[55] Acts 10:22 is only a partial exception to this, since the positive evaluation there coincides in substance with the narrator's description in 10:2.

62

However, the *dikaios* terminology occurs at two highly significant points. First, Jesus defines his mission as calling sinners, not the *dikaioi* (Luke 5:32). Second, Jesus speaks (Luke 15:7) of the joy of heaven at the repentance of the sinner as against the ninety-nine righteous people (*dikaioi*) who 'have no need of repentance' (*ou chreian echousin metanoias*).

This furnishes data from which an objection to a universal call to repentance might be constructed. For, it might be said, Luke envisages an actual existing class of people who are 'righteous' (*dikaioi*). A human person who is *dikaios* is not a mere hypothetical. This class of people is not called by Jesus (Luke 5:32), for they are not sinners. Instead, because they are not sinners, they have no need for repentance (Luke 15:7). Such people are not deprived of eschatological life, since they are righteous, not sinners, and the call of Acts 17:30 to all people everywhere is a generalization, rather than a strict universal command. The Pharisees fit within this pattern not as righteous, but simply as people who wrongly think they are,[56] and are therefore subject to the command to repent, since in reality they are sinners.

The objection considered

Much of the force of this objection depends on the weight to be attached to the description of someone as *dikaios*. Certainly, there is a line of commentators on Luke 1:6, where Zechariah and Elizabeth are described in *dikaios* terms, that decline to take this as denoting literal sinlessness. Morris's comment is representative: 'This means, of course, that they served God faithfully, not that they were sinless.'[57] The question, of course, is whether this is simply special pleading.

There are a number of factors that tell against seeing *dikaios* simply as sinless or faultless. Zechariah is not without fault in his response to Gabriel's announcement (Luke 1:20 says he did not believe the angel). This weighs against seeing Zechariah as *dikaios* in the sense of sinless. Moreover, the *dikaioi* in the birth narrative respond with joy at the coming of salvation, and this joy seems to have a personal application. This is clearest in Zechariah's song (Luke 1:68–79), which repays attention. It is authoritative (for he is filled with the Holy Spirit; Luke 1:67) and it rejoices at God's salvation (vv. 68–69). Yet Zechariah envisages himself as a beneficiary of this salvation ('a horn of salvation for us'; Luke 1:69), and goes on to bracket salvation very

---

[56] Note the preamble to the parable of the tax collector and the Pharisee in Luke 18:9.
[57] Morris 1974: 68; see also e.g. Calvin 1972a: 6–7; Bock 1996, 1: 77; Liefeld 1984: 982.

closely with the forgiveness of sins (Luke 1:77). This suggests he regards himself as included among those receiving salvation in the forgiveness of sins. This implies he does not regard himself as sinless, and at this point in the narrative speaks with authority.

In a similar but less clear vein Simeon's song (Luke 2:28–32) speaks of the coming of salvation, something relevant both for Gentiles and Israel. It is difficult to see Simeon as anything other than a member of Israel, the covenant people, and in this sense a salvation that bears on Israel is salvation for him too. Nor will it do to confine Israel's salvation simply to liberation from Rome, since Zechariah's song has already linked salvation to forgiveness of sins.[58]

Moreover, it becomes clear in Acts from the example of Cornelius that one can be *dikaios* and a beneficiary of forgiveness of sins. Tannehill aptly comments that Cornelius, despite being a Gentile, is presented as truly pious.[59] Whatever else *dikaios* is capable of meaning within Luke–Acts, its application to the Gentile Cornelius means that *dikaios* is not confined to faithful, law-keeping Israelites, for Cornelius has not been circumcised and is counted as a Gentile,[60] despite the favourable depictions of him. However, the message that Peter goes on to teach Cornelius includes the element that forgiveness of sins comes through belief in his name (Acts 10:43). This would, of course, be irrelevant to Cornelius if *dikaios* meant sinless. But the surrounding narrative does not permit the reader to think Cornelius is a sinless believer in Jesus, for Peter's account of the conversion of Cornelius and his household is construed by believers in Jerusalem as being the grant of repentance that leads to life (Acts 11:18). Cornelius and his household, in being given the Spirit, are seen as being given the gift of repentance, and repentance involves a turning from sin. Cornelius was not therefore without sin.

This naturally poses the question of what meaning then is to be attached to 'righteous'? For Tannehill a key consideration is the emphasis in the text in case of both Simeon and Joseph of Arimathea that they were awaiting or expecting some kind of fulfilment of God's saving promises.[61] Tannehill comments on the birth narrative:

---

[58] Note that later Jesus' visit to Zacchaeus is the coming of salvation, in which the lost are saved; Luke 19:9–10.

[59] Tannehill (1994, 2: 133) says, 'Cornelius is clearly an uncircumcised Gentile (cf 11:3), yet his piety parallels that of a devout Jew.' Cornelius prays, gives alms, is a God-fearer and of good repute, as well as being *dikaios* (righteous); Acts 10:2, 22.

[60] As Marshall (1980: 183) observes.

[61] The 'consolation' (*paraklēsis*) of Israel in Simeon's case; the kingdom of God in Joseph's case.

The central characters are described as devoted to the law and to the hope of Israel's redemption . . . Thus the birth story is not only steeped in the Old Testament but also takes a very positive attitude toward the Torah obedience and hope of pious Jews. The story is shaped to attract our sympathy to devoted men and women who have waited long for the fulfilment of Israel's hopes and who are now told that the time of fulfilment has come.[62]

Joseph naturally fits easily into these sympathetic presentations from the birth narrative,[63] as do, one might add, the travellers on the road to Emmaus who, by implication, likewise are among those who await the promised Messiah.

This association with faithful waiting for the fulfilment of Old Testament promise can be supplemented in the case of Zechariah and Elizabeth (Luke 1:6) with an adherence to God's law, but which need not, as the later example of Cornelius shows, mean that complete and perfect obedience to the law is in view.[64] This provides a positive content to *dikaios*, without eliminating the need for repentance among those so described.

Such a view fits with the broader theology of Luke–Acts, and its view of Jewish legal observance. Luke stresses the uniqueness of the salvation that Jesus offers (e.g. Acts 4:12), as well as the universal nature of the offer of salvation (Luke 24:47).[65] This implies an incompleteness in what the Old Testament law could by itself offer. This point becomes explicit in Paul's address in Pisidian Antioch, where he speaks of believers in Jesus being forgiven for sins and justified in all the things of which they could not be justified in the law of Moses (Acts 13:38–39).[66] For Marshall, the point here is that 'justification is not possible at all through the law' rather than that Jesus simply provides justification for more things than the law.[67] Notably, Paul makes his appeal here to a synagogue audience quite general. The proclamation is 'to you' (v. 38), not simply those who

---

[62] Tannehill 1986, 1: 19.
[63] Cf. Liefeld (1984: 1046), who says, Joseph 'joins others in Luke whose piety and expectation of the Messiah validates their testimony (e.g. Simeon and Anna, 2:25–38)'. For Calvin (1972c: 217), 'this waiting for the kingdom of God was the root and source of his [Joseph's] righteousness'.
[64] For Cornelius is not circumcised, and can still be contemplated as 'unclean'.
[65] 'Universal' in that all kinds and conditions of human beings may be saved; not universal in the sense that all necessarily will be.
[66] The justification terms are drawn from *dikaioō*.
[67] Marshall 1980: 228; Calvin 1965: 384; Stott 1990: 225.

are not *dikaios*. In fact, at no stage do the apostles in Acts seem to envisage that their proclamation of repentance and forgiveness in the name of Jesus is unnecessary for some members of their audiences because those members are already perfect. Rather, the testimony is to Jews and Greeks alike of the need for repentance and faith (Acts 20:21).

This takes us to alternative explanations of Luke 5:32 and 15:7. In the former case it makes good sense to follow Morris in seeing the reference to righteous as 'ironical'.[68] Certainly, this would challenge a reader who gradually finds his or her view of who is righteous constantly challenged as the true nature of the apparently religious is unmasked.[69] In the latter case perhaps the most plausible reading is that of Bock, who sees Jesus' use of the word as rhetorical.[70] This is rendered all the more attractive by comparison with the parable of the lost son, where the older brother does have something of which to repent (he too has defied his father), even though in the earlier stages of the parable this does not appear to be the case. The force of the observation of 15:7 is, then, Jesus' love for the 'lost', those who are in current spiritual danger,[71] and his joy at their rescue. This, of course, tallies with what appears in the encounter with Zacchaeus.

For these reasons, then, the objection fails.

Conclusion

The repentance theme in Acts has developed in two directions. First, repentance is now clearly demanded of the Gentiles. From the initial speeches in Jerusalem that called the Jewish people to repentance, although implying a wider scope, Paul's speech in Athens marks a quite general call, not even confined to the immediate situation of the Areopagus, but on all people everywhere.

This relates to the second way repentance has developed. From repentance initially being proclaimed on the basis of the sin of

[68] Morris 1974: 120.
[69] Liefeld (1984: 884) also canvasses the idea that 'righteous' here is simply used relatively. Naturally, this is possible but arguably provides a less satisfying or thought-provoking reading than the alternative (he also deals with the possibility that Jesus speaks with sarcasm).
[70] Bock 1996, 2: 1302.
[71] As Morris (1974: 238) observes. He says they have already been found, which carries the implication that all may at some point have needed finding. Calvin (1972b) envisages that the repentance in view in 15:7 is that of a person's first or saving turning to Christ, and this implies that those already in the sheepfold have 'no need' to repent in this sense, for they have already done it.

murdering Jesus, repentance for Gentiles has now been asked for on the basis of idolatry. Given all the evils in pagan society to which Paul's letters bear witness, it is striking that this is the basis on which pagan Gentile conduct is judged and found wanting. Behind this stands an understanding of who humans are outside Christ: under the dominion of Satan and in darkness. Stenschke rightly suggests Luke has an anthropology against which salvation is proclaimed, in which all people are alienated from God and face his judgment.[72] In this way there is an equality between Jew and Gentile, just as in the Gospel of Luke there was an equality between tax collector and Pharisee.

Repentance is proclaimed among Jew and Gentile on the basis of the resurrection. The resurrection vindicated Jesus as God's Messiah, and so condemns the Jewish people and rulers, setting out their presenting sin of murdering the Messiah for which they must repent. The resurrection is also indicated in the call on Gentiles to repent, for it is connected with a universal judgment. This, of course, is consistent with the idea that the resurrection vindicates Jesus as God's promised Messiah, but the appeal to fulfilment of Old Testament promise is understandably not to the fore in the crucial speeches in Lystra and Athens, where Paul is not addressing God-fearers who may well be familiar with the Old Testament promises.

The characteristics of the repentant are not as strongly delineated in Acts as in the Gospel of Luke. As in the Gospel, there is an expectation that the repentant will bear fruit ethically. The repentant also seem to be people of faith, since repentance towards God is related to faith in Jesus, not a substitute for it. What further marks believers out is a joy at the news of others repenting and believing. Thus the Jerusalem believers rejoice at the news of Gentile repentance and turning to God. Such an attitude is just what Jesus enjoins in the parables of Luke 15.

However, this marks them out from the unrepentant, who are associated with envy, whether it is the envy of the rulers at the apostolic success in Jerusalem, or the envy of the diaspora synagogues at the conversion of Gentiles. The unrepentant, obliquely in Jerusalem through the guise of the Saducee party, and more overtly with the rejecters in Athens, are also associated with rejection of the resurrection and the apostolic witness. Since Luke is at such pains to help the reader see the certainty of the resurrection and the reliability of

---

[72] Stenschke 1998: 142.

the witness, the reaction to those who refuse this witness is that they are irrational and blind to the obvious works of God. These themes of unrepentance are anticipated in Luke's Gospel, of course, for the grudging envious attitude to others who respond to Jesus is seen in the Pharisees, while the parable of the rich man and Lazarus warns exactly that people may not listen even if one should rise from the dead (Luke 16:31).

Repentance is associated with God's gift, rather than simply as a work humans provide. It is moreover a means by which God fulfils prophecy and keeps his covenant promises, for the promise to bless all the families of the earth is kept as God turns people from their wickedness.

However, the resting point that Acts provides when it comes to the place of idolatry in the discussion of repentance is neatly caught by one of the Anglican *Homilies*:

> Repentance, as it is said before, is a true returning unto God; whereby men, forsaking utterly their idolatry and wickedness, do with a lively faith embrace, love, and worship the true living God only, and give themselves to all manner of good works, which by God's word they know to be acceptable unto him.[73]

---

[73] From Homily 32, 'Of Repentance and True Reconciliation unto God' (Bray 2015: 499).

Chapter Four

Repentance: identity and idolatry

[H]e hath ever but slenderly known himself.[1]

Recap

We begin this chapter with a question: 'Is repentance moralism?' There is a fear that teaching repentance, especially evangelistically, comes across as an exercise in moralizing criticism, followed by implicit demands for self-improvement. Such demands can undercut the offer of free grace and the principle of salvation by grace alone. John Calvin noted just this possibility of repentance becoming moralism when he stressed how Paul joined repentance with faith in Acts 20:21.[2] Without this connection, Christian calls for repentance differed little, Calvin felt, from secular philosophy's exhortations about how to live well.

This is perhaps compounded by our desire to inject realism into any call to repentance by making matters as specific as possible, and talk of particular sins. A little knowledge of an audience can naturally add a great sense of relevance. At one point in the 1980s, for instance, there was a spate of cases in England in which solicitors had embezzled their clients' funds. Any sermon addressed to English solicitors could quite plausibly and realistically have spoken of the temptations of greed.

It is important that this point is not misunderstood: we are not decrying the need to apply the calls of Scripture as specifically as possible, nor the advantages in understanding that the spiritual struggles and temptations of a middle-aged English solicitor are often very different in detail from those of a teenager. At their best, such specific applications drive home the reality of sin in our own lives rather than leaving us feeling that sin is a problem for others than us, whoever those others may be. There is also, though, a risk of creating

---

[1] William Shakespeare, King Lear, Act 1, scene 1.
[2] Calvin 1966: 176.

an impression of being obsessed with minutiae and detail, and thus of being, in that great pejorative term, 'legalistic'. We may well feel that such a charge is profoundly unfair, but the very detail may convey a sense that Christian faith is not really dealing with the great, fundamental matters of life. John Stott writes, 'Many people are rejecting our gospel today not because they perceive it to be false, but because they perceive it to be trivial.'[3]

At this point we must recall the progress of Paul's call to repentance in Acts. Acts details the progress of the gospel's proclamation from Jerusalem and the setting of ethnic Judaism to Rome and a Graeco-Roman world that was not even monotheistic. This represents in one sense the universalization of the gospel, for God is bringing his good news of salvation to the ends of the earth. But the universalization of the gospel message also inevitably brings a universalization of repentance.

The call to repentance to Gentiles in Acts is not predicated on participation in the murder of Jesus. It is, no doubt, theologically true that all races do participate in the murder of God's anointed, who is the Author of life, through the representative nature of those actually there. The accounts of Jesus' crucifixion stress the breadth of both class and also race of those despising and mocking Jesus. Nevertheless, the call to Gentiles to repent is not put on these grounds. The issue of participation in Jesus' murder certainly is central to the calls for repentance in the Jerusalem and Jewish setting of Acts 2 – 7, and is closely related to the status of Jews as covenant people. They have rejected the one whom the covenant God appointed and sent. But by definition an appeal in which the Abrahamic covenant plays a part will seem irrelevant in a Gentile setting: they are not covenant people.

Paul, in his two major speeches to the pagan Gentiles does not, of course, refer overtly to covenant fulfilment by God and breach of the Abrahamic covenant by the Gentiles. Nor does he, in the summaries Luke provides, point to the very detailed sins of everyday life that were no doubt all around him in a pagan Gentile setting. Thus the marketplace in Athens (Acts 17:17) would surely have afforded numerous examples of slave-trading, immorality and financial greed, things we know from elsewhere he regards as sins that invite the judgment of God. Instead, he starts with idolatry, as he did at Lystra, but not this time because of circumstances forcing him to do so: this is what he discerns in Athens (Acts 17:16) and is the focal point of

---

[3] Stott (1990: 290), commenting on Paul's speech at the Areopagus.

his call to repentance. Moreover, Luke stresses the power and prevalence of pagan religious systems in Paul's missionary encounters. We know, further, from his description in 1 Thessalonians 1:9–10 that this understanding of turning to God is not simply specific to Athens, and from Romans 1:18–32 that he sees the idolatry principle as fundamental to humanity's spiritual plight and how humans understand the world.[4] And John Stott observes after his comment on the perceived triviality of Christianity, 'People are looking for an integrated worldview, which makes sense of all their experience.'[5]

In this chapter we shall be discussing the way Paul's calls for repentance over idolatry in fact include a call for turning from, and a repentance of, what we would now call the world views held by those who do not believe. It is not, of course, startlingly new to propose that repentance must be seen ultimately in terms of idolatry.[6]

Repentance as recognition

Before we look at the theological significance of idolatry as the sin ultimately of which we repent, we must recall some more general ways in which the terms of repentance are used. Repentance is associated with 'confession': thus Daniel's great prayer of repentance and sorrow in the face of Israel's sin is a making of confession. In one way this confession is a recital of what Israel has done, and in this recital various actions are detailed. These actions are detailed against a moral or ethical frame: evil has been done and laws have been broken.

However, actions can establish character. Both in reading and in everyday life we frequently describe who people are on the basis of what they have done. This is particularly the case when the actions are repeated and apparently habitual. The recurrent themes in Daniel 9:3–19 of rebellion, disobeying and not listening establish a character for the people: their repeated acts of covenant breach establish them as faithless. In this way confession of sinful *actions* can be a confession of *character*, not merely of what we have done, but of who we are.

---

[4] Note too Demetrius the silversmith complains of Paul's attack on idols as no gods at all (Acts 19:26). It seems that Paul's message in Ephesus, as well as Athens, Thessalonica and Lystra, dealt with the idolatry question.
[5] Stott 1990: 290.
[6] As already noted, the Anglican *Books of Homilies* do envisage repentance as a forsaking of idolatry: 'Repentance, as it is said before, is a true returning unto God; whereby men, forsaking utterly their idolatry and wickedness, do with a lively faith embrace, love, and worship the true living God only . . .' (Homily 32; Bray 2016: 499).

Notably such a confession of character or identity is set against an ethical or legal understanding.

Confessional repentance, though, does not merely establish who we are in our ethical or legal character, but who we are in relation. For confession acknowledges, as in Daniel 9, that one has offended another, and that the relationship between us and another stands in a particular way or status because of who we are, and what we have done. The identity that is disclosed in confession is not a self-characterization that is purely solipsistic and deals only with the I. It is a self-characterization of who I am in relation ethically or legally to another.

This is certainly true of Daniel's confession and others like it. Daniel's confession does not merely disclose that Israel and Judah are wicked, but it goes further in specifying with regard to whom they have been wicked, and in what relational context. In the case of Daniel and Israel, of course, that relational context is given by the covenant. This relational location also features, naturally, in the confession or repentance that one human being may show to another. Thus the parable of the lost son of Luke 15:11–32 contains a double confession by the lost son: one planned (v. 17); the other carried out (vv. 18–19). These confessions involve acknowledging who the son is or has become in his relationships (sinning against heaven, i.e. God, and before you).

We may also say, though, that confessional repentance acknowledges not merely who one is in relationship ethically or legally; it deals with a common identity for the one who confesses: an identity for the confessor that both sides of the relationship share. In the parable of the lost son we are told that the son 'came to his senses' (*eis heauton de elthōn*; v. 17), which may well imply that up to that point he had not seen or acknowledged himself as one who had sinned against heaven and before his father. In the parable the son comes to accept the relationship his father offers (that they are father and son; the feast is predicated on this; Luke 15:24). This stands in contrast to his earlier refusal to accept common identity. For his demand for his share of the inheritance is in an important sense a denial of the relationship between himself and his father. After all, he is acting as though his father is dead and the property is consequently fallen for division.

This common identity, however, is one that the repentant does not establish, but recognizes. Repentance is a recognition of one's true identity. The scenes of repentance, for example of the Jerusalem crowd stricken to the heart at Peter's address in Acts 2, are recognitions of what one truly is, despite what one might have thought. 'Recognition' (*anagnōrisis*) scenes have since Aristotle been acknowledged for their dramatic power. Aristotle summarizes them thus:

> Recognition is, as its name indicates, a change from ignorance to knowledge, tending either to affection or to enmity; it determines in the direction of good or ill fortune the fates of the people involved. The best sort of recognition is that accompanied by *peripeteia* [reversal of fortune], like that in the *Oedipus*.[7]

Aristotle's statement lends itself to two points. He saw Sophocles' *Oedipus the King* as a near-perfect expression of tragic form, and the *anagnōrisis* in the *Oedipus* is Oedipus' discovery of his own identity: that in reality he is the son of Laius, whom he has killed, and Jocasta, whom he has married. Repentance is not least a self-recognition, a dealing with one's own identity. Further, repentance as *anagnōrisis* does indeed feature a change of fortune (*peripeteia*), for it is the way to forgiveness of sins and removal from darkness into light.

The common identity the repentant confessor acknowledges is the identity the other party believes the repentant has: in repentance one may accept someone else's valuation of who one is. Thus Daniel acknowledges the justice of God's treating Israel and Judah as faithless covenant-breakers (e.g. Dan. 9:14). We should pause here to reflect how odd and indeed offensive this sounds in a modernist or postmodernist setting. To accept that another's view of one is the true one shatters the claims of autonomy common to both outlooks.[8]

With these general notions in mind of repentant confession as an acknowledgment of identity in relation to another, we must consider the specific self-recognition that the data of Acts seem to enjoin. We are to repent of our acts of idolatry, and to this extent are to repent of being idolaters. To this identity of idolaters we now turn.

Recognition of idolatry

The point is often made that idolatry is an inaccessible concept in the modern world, or in the cultural West, at any rate, because physical

---

[7] Aristotle 1972: 1452a.
[8] Oyserman (2004: 13), in reviewing current social research on self-concepts, comments on North American and West European cultures that 'they socialise members to believe in individual rights and personal freedoms, the centrality of personal pleasure and autonomy, and the personal, private, and unique self'.

objects are not normally objects of worship. Indeed, some may continue that one of the marks of the modern cultural West is its secularity and lack of any 'sacred canopy', as well as its tendency, at least superficially, to endorse forms of atheism.[9] These latter points weigh heavily because they affect how it is that we may preach and teach repentance. How can one repent of something one simply either does not recognize or thinks too trivial to count?

However, a frequent and well-made response is that this fails to grasp the subtlety of the Bible's thought about idolatry. It is not simply related to the worship of a physical object as if that object were divine itself or the dwelling-place of the deity. Thus Ephesians 5:5 counts covetousness as idolatry. Moreover, Paul well understands that a physical object used in worship is in one sense nothing (1 Cor. 8:4). In Acts 17:29 Paul does refer to the physical objects of devotion, but analyses this in terms of a deeper cause. His point is that such objects are representations arising from the human mind and artistic instinct. This insight is well developed by the influential apologist of the early church, Tertullian, who does not see a physical object as essential to idolatry: 'Yet idolatry used to be practised, not under that name, but in that function; for even at this day it can be practised outside a temple, and without an idol.'[10]

Instead, idolatry arises when something is treated 'in place of God, against God'.[11] Tertullian sees this predominantly in terms of the replacement of the Creator by something within creation. Stott summarizes things slightly differently:

> In brief, all idolatry tries to minimise the gulf between Creator and his creatures, in order to bring him under our control. It actually reverses the respective positions of God and us, so that, instead of humbly acknowledging that God has created and rules us, we presume to imagine that we can create and rule God.[12]

Thus for Stott the key feature is the reversal of relationship between the human creature and the divine creator of that creature. This can no doubt take place in a number of ways. An idol is the means by

---

[9] There is considerable literature devoted to establishing a secularization thesis for the modern West, but this has also been significantly questioned.

[10] Tertullian, *On Idolatry* 3: 'Nam et hodie extra templum et sine idolo agi potest' (Roberts and Donaldson 1980, 3: 62).

[11] '[P]ro deo aduersus deum', *On Idolatry* 4 (Roberts and Donaldson 1980, 3: 63).

[12] Stott 1990: 287.

which this reversal takes place. Tertullian's principle of 'in place of God, against God' also refers to the distortion of the creation relationship, since a creature treats another as his or her Creator. The two accounts are not, of course, incompatible, for in elevating something within creation to be an object of worship a human acts sovereignly, even if tacitly and without full reflection, as if he or she were God, and not a creature. The critical point in Tertullian's account is that the object set in place of God is set there by humans, even if, in Tertullian's thought, it may have been put there at the prompting of demons.

In this way we can see idolatry as a perversion or distortion of the relation that exists between creature and Creator. That distortion may arise in two ways. First, by an attempt to rule God and act as creator towards him, which is very clearly present when humans shape God as a golden calf, according to human art and imagination (Acts 17:29), although such shaping may be aniconic and ideological rather than a physical shaping. It is an awesome, or rather, awful, thing to say 'I like to look at God as . . .' and then fill in the blank as one desires. The second way that the relation is distorted is by treating something within the created order, a creature, as if it were a creator, or the Creator, and so substitute this for the one true God.

At root the idea of idolatry in passages like Isaiah 44 or Jeremiah 10 revolves around the idea of worshipping what is not God, either because it is a created object within creation or because it is not truly God who is worshipped. In this idea of worshipping what is not God, two further presuppositions are involved: that there is a true God, and that there are things that are not truly God. We may add in passing that some forms of atheism and projection theories of religion, such as L. Feuerbach's, can in some ways be understood as a further distortion of this idea, insisting that it is not just some things that are not God, but that nothing is God.

The true God is a living and uncreated God who is creator of all (e.g. Jer. 10:12). As Creator he stands in a relationship to his creatures, and the appropriate response for a creature is worship and honour (e.g. Rom. 1:21; Rev. 4:11). But as Romans 1:21–22 also makes clear, wrong response is possible, so that he is not honoured rightly, *as God*. Precisely because God is who he is, the true and living God, standing in a particular kind of relationship to us, there is the possibility of wronging him by denying that relationship. In denying that relationship and committing idolatry there is also a denial of God's identity towards us of Creator. But equally, because of who God is, the true and living God, whose will cannot ultimately be frustrated, there is the possibility of salvation. Recognition of who God truly is can bring both horror at sin and yet also hope. That sounds paradoxical but it is one of the features of Calvin's thought on repentance, of course, as well as being present in confessional passages like Daniel 9. Both the hope and the horror arise from a recognition of who God truly is.

The other presupposition, that there are things that are not truly God, is, as it were, the polar opposite. Instead of being the uncreated creator of all, the idol is in reality the created non-creator of anything. Thus in Jeremiah 10, after stating that God is the true God (v. 10), Jeremiah goes on to speak of the gods of the nations, 'who did not make the heavens and the earth' (v. 11), before going on to assert that it is the Lord, Yahweh, who made the heavens and the earth (v. 12).

Thus to acknowledge oneself as an idolater in this way is to acknowledge there is the true God, and that there are things that are not. Those things that are not God, but are treated as if they are, are lies.

Recognition of one's own identity

However, recognition of idolatry is not simply a recognition of these bare truths: that there is a true God and there are false gods. At some level, it involves the recognition of one's personal standing or one's location with respect to these truths, that the true God has been wronged by not being responded to rightly, and the response that should have been offered to him has been offered elsewhere. Yet, as I have said, this is not simply an action, or even a set of actions, but rather our actions reveal our characters as idolaters. We turn now to the significance of that identity.

Idolatry as parody

One understanding of idolatry and what it does to us is that idolatry is parody. In idolatry various aspects of authentic life and existence are parodied, so that ultimately in sin and idolatry not merely do we parody God but we also become parodies of what humans should be. Idolatry affects and changes us. G. Beale summarizes this dynamic aptly: '[W]e resemble what we revere'.[13]

---

[13] Beale (2008: 22), where he notes this is the 'primary theme' of his book. See also on this theme Meadors 2006.

Idolatry as the parody of real relationship
I–Thou and I–It relations

The first area we need to explore is the area of relationship. It may be helpful here to recall the framework for relationship proposed by Martin Buber. To use the terms Buber made famous,[14] human relations can be classified into two major categories: I–Thou and I–It relationships. I–Thou relations are interpersonal, in which one personal subject relates to another personal subject, and does so recognizing that personal dimension to the other. In such relations, writes Buber, 'The *Thou* meets me.'[15] One may add that this meeting is reciprocal. Each meets the other, because the Thou who meets me is in turn from his or her perspective an I who is met by a Thou, namely me.

In contrast, I–It relations occur when an I relates to the other as an object, identified, knowable and masterable. We must note that the difference between I–It relations and I–Thou relations is not a simple difference between bad and good ways of relating. For the I–It relation can be powerful and appropriate, so that the discovery of the properties of, say, penicillin in the natural world is rightly an I–It relationship. However, that does not mean that such I–It relationships are value free and without moral constraint. For the It that I investigate and scrutinize may be an object in the world, but may not belong to me. In fact, of course, the reservation of the fruit of the tree of knowledge and the need to grant the right to eat meat indicates precisely that while humans have a proper dominion in creation, this is not an absolute right of disposal.[16]

The significance of Buber's distinction, of course, is that some ways of treating the other may be wrong. If I treat someone as an It, to be known and mastered, then I seem to deny that person human personhood. I am not treating him or her as he or she truly is. We rightly see this as a fundamentally wrong and also inadequate way of relating to others. And this point is not, of course, confined simply to dealings between human persons, but must also include relations between God and humans. H. Thielicke perceptively comments in this regard that 'Anyone who deals with truth – as we theologians certainly

---

[14] Buber 1958.
[15] Ibid. 11.
[16] An important point for considering the argument made in ecological theology that the dominion language of Gen. 1:26–30 inevitably degenerates into the unqualified mastery of domination.

do – succumbs all too easily to the psychology of the possessor.'[17] This applies both to claims of truth (where the language of mastering, say, John's Gospel, can readily speak of exhausting what it has to say) and to God himself.

Naturally, this invites the objection that Buber's classification ceases to be so useful in a postmodernist era. The argument would run that to treat another I meet in the world as an object that is masterable and knowable is to make just the kind of mistake we would associate with extreme modernism. It speaks of a commitment not simply to rationality but to rationalism, in which I master the world by my reason, and possess it. After all, a strong component in the postmodern mood is exactly a suspicion and rejection of claims about 'what the world is really like', and to be able to access an objective reality. Hence, so the argument might run, the danger that Buber observed does not arise in postmodernism.

It is certainly true that Buber's thought predates the postmodern turn in its stronger forms. Even so, there are strands in Buber's thought that do still, perhaps, illuminate this question. Buber was, of course, trying to ensure that we encounter what is other than ourselves in the world rightly. Thus he has a place for I–It relationships. His concern is that these do not obscure the Thou from me when I meet another. Moreover, in *The Eclipse of God* Buber spoke of the way that the ego, the individual 'I' in modern life might become so swollen as to obscure others, including God. The 'I', he feared, was coming to stand more and more in the foreground.[18] As it does so, it comes to exclude or eclipse others, most notably God.[19]

It is at this point of the 'swollen ego' that postmodern attitudes seem so vulnerable. For an attitude that asserts one cannot say 'the world is really like that', and that one cannot access other things in it, readily becomes an attitude in which one accepts oneself but nothing else. Everything else seems not even allowed to be an It, except in so far as I perceive and value it. And if I assert that the other

---

[17] Thielicke 1966: 16–17.
[18] Buber 1953: 126.
[19] For Buber, this relates to a distorted swelling of the I–It relation (1953: 129). Similarly, one might relate the solipsistic tendencies of postmodernism not simply to a reaction against modernism (the opposition to rationalism clearly is a reaction), but to a development of one aspect of modernism, namely its sense of the imperial ego. In some respects one may see postmodernism not as anti-modernism but as ultra-modernism. Wells (2005: 133) rightly quotes F. Nietzsche's remarks in *Beyond Good and Evil* concerning the 'noble type of man', who is a 'creator of values': this represents a very considerable self-aggrandisement.

is inaccessible to me, then I seem to be saying that a Thou cannot meet me: all there is is my own 'I', and the other cannot disclose him or herself to me; at any rate not as he or she really is.[20] I may perceive others, but not meet them as they are.[21] They are what I perceive them to be. This is scarcely the I–Thou relation of which Buber wrote. Rather, it seems to be an I–only non-relation.

In this way, whether one thinks of modernist tendencies to see all as I–It relations, or the postmodern turn to I–only non-relations, what is at stake is the existence of interpersonal I–Thou relations in which the other person may meet and encounter one and disclose himself or herself.[22]

God and I–Thou relations
Within Buber's classification, relationship with God is certainly I–Thou rather than I–It, for we do not exhaustively master God when we meet and know him. It is certainly not a postmodern I–only non-relation, for we meet someone who is what he is independently of us and our perceptions. For Buber, the only way in which one can talk of a relationship with God is in I–Thou terms: 'But it is only the I–Thou relation in which we can meet God at all . . .'.[23] The reason for this is not far to seek. If we meet God as an It, we meet him fundamentally as what he is not, and that is not an encounter with who he truly is.

However, while we should describe our relation with God as I–Thou, it is a unique I–Thou relationship. Barth adopts similar terms to Buber and states God 'speaks as an I and addresses by a Thou'.[24] But unlike our relations with others, we meet a Thou who is our Lord, not simply another person to whom I relate on a basis of fundamental equality at the level of being.[25] The reason why we encounter God as a Thou who is Lord is, of course, because he is our Creator. We exist by his will and plan (Rev. 4:11), and for his

---

[20] There is a gulf between what a person or thing is in itself and what it is in someone's perceptions. This gulf between the object-in-itself and the object-as-perceived is deeply inscribed in Western European thought after Immanuel Kant.
[21] Barth laid great stress on existence in encounter. For Barth (1960: 250) a basic criterion for being in encounter is that 'one man looks the other in the eye', so that one sees and is seen.
[22] Barth also lists (ibid. 252–256) mutual speech and hearing as requirements for being in encounter, which he develops in terms of self-disclosure and being addressed by the other.
[23] Buber 1953: 128.
[24] Barth 1975: 307.
[25] Barth (ibid. 306) comments, 'God reveals Himself as the Lord.'

glory. Barth is apt therefore in drawing out two aspects to this address to us by God: not only is he our lord, with the connotations of sovereignty that brings, but he addresses us in his freedom, without being constrained by us.[26]

Correlative but asymmetrical relations
However, the consequences of this need to be teased out. Since we exist only by God's will and plan, our relationship with God is inevitable. It is a relationship one cannot escape. To exist at all for a human being is to exist as a creature: it is the only way one can be human. Yet to exist as a creature presupposes there has been an act of creation, and that there is a Creator. The relation of creature and Creator is correlative, just as one might say that there is a correlative relationship in trinitarian theology between Father and Son.

We may, though, do well to stay with this trinitarian analogy for a moment. When expounding orthodox Nicene trinitarian theology in contrast to the denial of the Son's deity by Arianism, Athanasius sees the Father's fatherhood as co-relatively related to the Son's sonship.[27] To change the latter is to change the former, and the fatherhood of the First Person is, to Athanasius, the primary way in which he is.[28] This leads Athanasius to a profound insight about the significance of the Arian attack on the Son's true deity. Ostensibly Arianism was upholding the unique dignity of the Father in denying that the Son was truly divine. But if one says that 'Once the son was not,' one thereby insists on his status as a creature, for the Son becomes someone with a beginning. But this means, in turn, that fatherhood is something that happens to the Father, who is not truly and eternally father. The Father's identity is also changed. In a relationship of correlativity, an attack on one partner in the relation, or a redefinition of who that partner is, is inevitably an attack on, or a redefinition of, the other.

We must apply this pattern of thought to the correlative relation of human creature and divine Creator. If a human creature denies his Creator, then the correlative nature of the creation–Creator relationship means that the creature is not merely saying something about God, but about himself or herself. Our accounts of who God is

---

[26] Ibid. 307.
[27] As in *Four Discourses Against the Arians* 1.17–19 (Schaff and Wace 1991, 4: 316–317).
[28] E.g. ibid. 326. Lyman (1993: 134) and Widdicombe (1994: 159–160) comment on this.

inevitably affect who we think we are. This is, naturally, deeply rooted in Calvin's thinking, who tells us that the knowledge of God and the knowledge of ourselves are 'joined by many bonds'.[29]

This certainly relates to the idea, fashionable in recent years, to see personal relationship as constitutive.[30] Nevertheless, suspicions have been voiced about this. Thus H. A. Harris queries this fashionable stress on becoming persons through relations.[31] She points out this implies that, without relations, personhood is not established.[32] This results in what she calls 'relational determinism'. Rather, she contends, we should admit persons are prior to relations.[33] No doubt part of the fear here is that the motto that one becomes a person through relations gives too much power to those with whom one is in relationship. Thus, if one is treated as a slave, and that is the relationship, does one not become a slave, in the sense that this is indeed who and what one is? Conferring identity lies with those with whom one is in relationship and the possibilities of abuse are great.

Yet in the present case of Creator and creature it cannot be said that persons are prior to relations.[34] The only way I can exist at all is as a human creature, in a relation of creation with my Creator. Other relationships may be important, and fruitful, or debilitating, but they are not essential in this way. Creation means there is one relationship that is indeed determining. At this most fundamental level humans are not self-determining or self-creating.[35] Moreover, this is not at all a self-determining relationship, or even one in which we work synergistically with another to determine ourselves.

We need now to address how this discussion of relationship affects an understanding of idolatry. Idolatry involves worshipping what is not God, either because it is a created object within creation or because it is not truly God who is worshipped, but rather an understanding that humans themselves create. In this way idolatry features the Creator–creature relationship and distorts it. As such it parodies an I–Thou relationship between humans and God. The original relationship is real enough, and inevitable. It does have, though, particular

---

[29] Calvin 1960: 35 (*Inst.* 1.1.1).
[30] Particularly under the influence of theologians such as John Zizioulas (1985).
[31] H. A. Harris 1998: 214.
[32] Ibid. 217.
[33] Ibid. 227.
[34] Nor is this Harris's contention.
[35] For an early, and highly articulate, defence of the individual human ego as self-creating, see Stirner (1907), who in some ways anticipates both the solipsistic tendencies of F. Nietzsche and twentieth-century French and German existentialism.

contours, which cannot be altered. While the relationship is co-relative and mutual in that way, it is not a reversible or symmetrical relationship. Relationships such as brother and brother are reversible, for, if A and B are brothers, being a brother is equally applicable to both. In the Creator–created relationship, for a human to apply to himself or herself the role of Creator, or to God the role of created is a distortion and parody of the real relationship.

No doubt sometimes the parody can be frighteningly close to the real thing. After all, this is just what one might say of the presentation of the Pharisees in Luke's Gospel, that they are parodies of real relationship, and that the reality of the reversal of the true shape of relationship is revealed in Peter's description that the people have murdered the Author of life. In such parodies of relationship it is right to echo Buber's phrase: there has been no real meeting with God, and in being alienated from the Creator the creature is alienated from his or her own true identity.

Idolatry as lie

This understanding of idolatry as parody of true relationship also connects with another central biblical understanding of idolatry: idols are presented as lies (e.g. Isa. 44:21).[36] The lie consists either in lying about God (e.g. that he is not faithful to his word, the great lie about him in Gen. 3) or in lying about something created (e.g. that it, rather than God, created things).

The idea of lie, however, features prominently in the Bible's explanation of the human predicament. The archetypal sin of Genesis 3 involves the serpent inducing a 'false faith' in God by lies.[37] The lies themselves may be comparatively delicate and oblique. Thus one might see Genesis 3:4 as posing a suggestive question, 'Will you surely die?' But even so the sense is to induce disbelief in God's truthfulness, by implying that the curse of Genesis 2:17 will not come to pass. There is, moreover, the suggestion that the reason behind the command of Genesis 2:17 is envy rather than goodness and generosity. The serpent therefore has lied by suggesting to, and inducing, Eve to disbelieve two things about God that the narrative of Genesis 1 – 2 has been at pains to emphasize. First, that God's word is truthful, for he speaks and it is so. Second, that God treats his

---

[36] Cf. Keyes (1992: 37), who stresses that idols are lies in the way they counterfeit aspects of God; typically either his immanence or his transcendence.
[37] Beale (2008: 133) sees Gen. 3 as idolatry since Adam comes to trust himself and, possibly, Satan, rather than God.

creation benevolently, for he makes it good and blesses it. Eve now disbelieves exactly these things.

Yet this is not a simple absence of faith. Eve does have beliefs. She believes lies and has embraced falsehoods about God, and, by implication, so in the end does Adam, her husband and head. Thus Francis Turretin does not merely see Adam as caught in neutrality. He believes something definite, and is not simply an agnostic. Turretin speaks of Adam's 'engendering a false faith from [Satan's] lies'.[38]

Here, though, we need to return to the question of the relationship between Creator and creature being correlative. Two propositions are in play: first, the point that in sin we have a false faith about God; the second, that our relationship with God is co-relative. If both these things are so, then our false faith about God means we have a false faith about ourselves. Second, lying about God will mean lying about ourselves and lying about ourselves will mean lying about God. In more systematic terms, anthropology and theology are so linked that false statements in the one topic entail false statements in the other.

Idolatry as the *sin*

At this stage in the argument we must ask whether idolatry is just a sin, one among many. The point made in such a statement is that while all of us can and do sin, Jesus excepted, the particular form sins take varies between persons. Some may commit idolatry, some dishonour their parents, and so forth. It is certainly true that particular sinful acts are prohibited, and that idolatry is listed alongside such sins. Thus the Ten Commandments have specific prohibitions both on the acts of adultery and making a graven image. This is relevant in our present discussion because it could suggest that too much weight is being rested on the idea of idolatry.

However, while it is clear that there are specific prohibitions, such as the making of an idol for worship, idolatry does seem to be a fundamental concept. Thus Paul's discussion in Romans 1:18–32 envisages the specific sins of immorality in verse 24 as God's judicial response to idolatry. God 'gave them up', and the cycle of sinful conduct that ends in the ethical reversals of verse 32 in which humans approve what is bad is seen as the result of the idolatries of verses 21–23, not simply as another set of instances of sinfulness.

---

[38] Turretin 1992–7, 1: 9.q.6.ix (605).

Tertullian puts this line of thought well: that specific sins are connected to idolatry and, as it were, outworkings of it:

> The principal crime of the human race, the highest guilt charged upon the world, the whole procuring cause of judgment, is idolatry. For, although each single fault retains its own proper feature . . . yet it is marked off under the general account of idolatry.[39]

I referred earlier to the way J. Green envisages repentance in Acts both for Jew and Gentile as relating to idolatry. It is worth expanding this thought with regard to both groups of people.

For Israel, the covenant people, idolatry proves a consistent problem in their life in the Old Testament. It is, after all, finally their sins of idolatry that are specified as calling down God's judgment in the conquests by Assyria and Babylon (2 Kgs 17:7–23). And the presentation of the Jews of Jesus' day does not, on reflection, show idols are lacking. The Pharisees are associated with both love of wealth (e.g. Luke 16:14) and love of social prominence (e.g. Luke 11:43). These may not be graven images, but they are things of this world, creaturely things, and are 'loved'. The use of the terminology of love is striking because, of course, the summary of the law (Luke 10:27) is in terms of love: love of God and of neighbour.[40] In loving and pursuing these things rather than God, the Pharisees have in Tertullian's terms stood them in front of God.

As for Gentiles, idolatry helps us see why repentance, an idea which presupposes that a law has been broken, applies to them. Though outside the terms of the covenant in its Mosaic form, they are still creatures of God.[41] For the Creator–creature relation is, among other things, one that brings law and obligation with it: the Creator legitimately legislates for his creature, and Genesis 2:17 is an instance of this. Being in a creaturely relationship is inevitable for Gentiles as it is for Jews, and a Gentile's obligation to God does not arise by contingent

---

[39] Tertullian, *On Idolatry* 1. Idolatry is a stock reference point in Justin Martyr (e.g. *First Apology* 9) and the Greek apologists. Athanasius devoted a monograph to it and the tradition is continued to some extent in Augustine's *The City of God*.

[40] Luke 10:27 uses *agapaō* of love of God and neighbour. Luke 11:43 records Jesus' stating the Pharisees 'love' (*agapaō*) the seat of honour, while Luke 16:14 describes the Pharisees as *philargyroi* (lovers of money); but earlier (Luke 16:9–13) Jesus has spoken of loving a master (*agapaō*) in his challenge to love God not Mammon.

[41] Gentiles are indirectly beneficiaries under the Abrahamic covenant in view of Gen. 12:3 (all the families of the earth shall be blessed), construed in Acts 3:26 as blessing in terms of God's turning people from their wicked ways and granting forgiveness. But by birth they are strangers to the covenants of promise (Eph. 2:12).

circumstances, such as deciding to conclude or accept a contingent covenant with God. Thus it is as a creature that a Gentile of Paul's day, born outside the covenant and a stranger to its terms, can be said to be a law-breaker. The same is equally true, of course, of those outside Christian circles today: it is not enough for them to say they have not consented to, say, Christian moral laws forbidding deceit. Creaturely existence itself brings its obligations.

Idolatry as world view

We must now try to relate idolatry to a contemporary apologetic concept, and some recent basic discussion surrounding it. In the previous chapter we noted how Peter describes the sin of murdering Jesus in terms that emphasize the gulf that lies between the view of God, so to speak, and the values with which he is associated, namely life, and the values of the Jews, which are associated with the antithesis of life, death (Acts 3:14–15). We also saw how pervasive idolatry was in Athens in Luke's account (Acts 17), so that the sin of which the Athenians must repent is visible and present everywhere. Given this fundamental and pervasive nature of the sin of which people must repent, it is fair to relate this to the contemporary idea of world view, and think of idolatry as a world view.

J. Sire speaks of a world view thus: 'A worldview is a set of presuppositions (assumptions which may be true, partially true or entirely false) which we hold (consciously or subconsciously, consistently or inconsistently) about the basic makeup of our world.'[42]

Thus the Athenians in their idolatry have an entire world view in their supposition that God dwells (in some sense) in houses made by hands and needs the services that humans provide. This is how they view their gods and, given the place serving the gods evidently has, this shapes the world for them. After all, conceptions of how humans relate to the divine very plausibly shapes world view.[43]

However, in analysing a world view, as Sire himself points out, we deal not just with the intellect but also with the affections and the heart. The spectacles through which we see the world are not simply the product of a series of purely philosophical propositions, but of heart-felt affection. Luke signals the power of idolatrous affection quite clearly. It emerges starkly in the riot of the silversmiths in

---

[42] Sire 2004: 19.
[43] In this connection note the shape A. Kuyper envisages for a *Weltanschauung*, a world view, that it must deal with 'the three primary relationships that make up human existence: to God, man, and the world' (Naugle 2002: 20, citing Kuyper's *Lectures on Calvinism*).

Ephesus in Acts 19:23–41. It is true that the riot may start with the self-interested silversmiths of Demetrius's group, but the affections of the crowd are also engaged and with great passion, judging by the fact that chanting continued for two hours (Acts 19:34), in a, to a modern mind, surprising fashion (but then we have different idols).

This affects our engagement with an idolatrous world view, because we encounter not just ideas and arguments, but positions held with affection and passion.[44]

The second point we should make about world views again reflects on the way a world view is not just a set of propositions. A person's world view normally, perhaps inevitably, has a narrative dimension. That narrative may take place on several levels: one may have a story about the origin of the world, or the history of one's nation, and this helps establish identity firmly just as do the more personal and individual aspects of someone's narrative. Thus one's world view may be shaped by narratives that depict one's nation as brave but struggling against insuperable odds, and one's own life as a particular instance of this.

One might say that the UK and possibly other Western cultures love 'before and after' narratives. The 'before' for many of the enlightened in Europe would run that once we believed in God, while the 'after' is that now our cultures have matured and grown up, we no longer need this story. One might say this is the great Enlightenment cultural narrative. Thus Immanuel Kant wrote of the Enlightenment, 'Enlightenment is man's emergence from his self-incurred immaturity [*Unmündigkeit*].'[45] But this puts the Enlightenment, which is characterized by its refusal to accept things on authority,[46] in a narrative form: once humanity was immature; now it is mature. This account is rendered the more plausible by technological advance, and forms a key part of Western culture's self-image. This cultural story is also the individual story for some, that once they believed but now they do so no longer.[47]

---

[44] Although this is not, of course, an argument for never using argument and ideas in meeting world views held with passion and affection.

[45] In his essay 'An Answer to the Question: "What Is Enlightenment?"' (Kant 1996: 17), Gregor translates *Unmündigkeit* with the less usual 'minority'.

[46] Kant continues in the same essay, 'Immaturity is the inability to use one's own understanding without the guidance of another.' (Gregor translates 'guidance' as 'direction'.)

[47] Darwin is seen as especially significant in creating a pre- and post-Darwin narrative, in which pre-Darwin religious belief was possible, but not so after *The Origin of Species* was published.

The significance of such narratives is the force that becomes attached to them. Discussing faith and repentance with someone whose story is that he or she has moved on and matured is rather different from simply pointing out the intellectual flaws in his or her approach. Obviously, there will be emotional investments, investments of personal identity, as well as the simple sense of 'There are more arguments than I realized.'

Idolatry as narrative

Let us pursue this idea of 'before and after' narrative. The 'after' part of the modern Western narrative just described is in some ways the happy ending, or at least a happy step forward on the road. But, put differently, it is the story of a culture or individual discovering or finding or, better still, choosing its idols. We may say that choosing is perhaps the best way of describing this because choice has become such a central part of modern culture, as sociologists such as Peter Berger have argued.[48] But this choice is part of an individual's (or a culture's) developing narrative about himself or herself. Pastorally, this seems important. If we wish to be able to speak to the point to a group or an individual, it will help enormously to name rightly the idols held, and in order to understand those idols rightly we shall be well advised to see them as part of a developing narrative of the sinful choice of idols. After all, Romans 1:18–32 itself describes a succession of particular sins to which people become progressively prone.

Idolatry as addiction

The idea of progression in idolatry is again illuminating. Beale rightly highlights that idolatry has its effects on those who practise it. His central contention is that 'we resemble what we revere',[49] and notes that idols are consistently portrayed as blind and deaf. It is, therefore, a working out of this resemblance dynamic that means idolaters are 'deaf' and 'blind'.[50] This language readily suggests inability to understand or grasp or respond to God (strongly hinted at in Isa. 44:18–19).[51]

---

[48] See in particular Berger's influential *The Heretical Imperative* (1979).
[49] Beale 2008: 22.
[50] Ibid. 41–49, citing Isa. 42:17–20; 43:8–10; 44:18–19. He exegetes Isa. 6:1–13 in this light, and stresses what he calls the 'sensory organ malfunction' language that surrounds the idolater.
[51] Hence Meadors stresses (e.g. 2006: 174) the way that idolatry calls forth a hardening of the idolater's heart by God in judgment.

However, the question then arises whether 'blindness' and 'deafness' exhausts the effects of idolatry. We should remember here another range of description employed in the Old Testament, that idolatry can be depicted as harlotry. Physical adultery or sexual immorality parodies marriage, for gifts God intended for marriage are twisted to other ends, but not without consequences. Spiritual harlotry likewise parodies holy marriage as Israel became embroiled with other gods. In Hosea 2:5 Israel shows a quasi-marital devotion to them. However, the sexual imagery (e.g. Ezek. 23) suggests the idolatrous relation is compulsive, carrying insatiability and addiction. But further, there is the developing conformity between worshipper and worshipped: in Ezekiel 22 Israel's standards are increasingly those of the idols they have constructed. A people become like their gods, predictably, given the addictive, compulsive nature of the relationship, as Psalm 115:8 indicates. Vinoth Ramachandra works through some examples of this resemblance dynamic:

> [I]t is not surprising that those who worship technology eventually develop machine-like personalities: emotionally under-developed, shallow in their relationships, driven by a desire to control and quantify every human situation, unable to appreciate beauty and value in anything outside the artificial. Those who worship sex, on the other hand, are incapable of trust and commitment in their human relationships and hide a lonely existence behind a mask of superficial 'adulthood'.[52]

This resemblance dynamic need occasion no surprise. For idolatry parodies the mutual relationship to which Calvin points, that knowledge of God and knowledge of humanity are closely bound together.[53] For humanity stands in relation to God as creatures, and in a special relationship as the only creatures made in his image and likeness. In that sense there should be a dynamic in which humans come to resemble their God. This is part of our createdness. This dynamic is twisted to disastrous effect in idolatry.

There is, though, something paradoxical in this resemblance dynamic. The paradox arises in this way. Idolatry involves a parody of the real relation between creature and Creator, in which the idolater takes something within creation as of ultimate value, or defines God

---

[52] Ramachandra 1996: 115.
[53] Calvin 1960: 35 (*Inst.* 1.1.1).

REPENTANCE: IDENTITY AND IDOLATRY

on his or her own terms. There is an exercise of power here, for the idolater chooses or designs his or her god. At one level, then, idolatry seems to establish us as masters, for we are creators of values for ourselves, just as Nietzsche advocated. This is even more apparently the case if we regard ourselves as creating not just values but even ourselves, as Stirner advocated.[54]

However, the image of harlot Israel insatiably craving her adulterous lovers does not speak of idolater Israel as master, but rather as mastered. The apparent master status of the idolater proves to be a gateway to something else, to a slavery.[55] If an idolater acts as the Creator by fashioning his or her own gods, then the final result may not be a straightforward enjoyment of liberty but that the idolater is imprisoned by his or her creation.[56] There is no little irony in this, given what the idolater has done, or tried to do, to his or her real creator.

In the biblical account of idolatry this captivity that results from idolatry cannot be divorced from the way idols are linked to the demonic, notably 1 Corinthians 10:20–21.[57] This is not to say that idolatry is demonolatry in a conscious and aware sense. That treats the conscious awareness of, say, the worshippers of Aphrodite and Apollo at Corinth in too reductionist a way. But Paul certainly opens the way to understanding idols as vehicles for demons through which influence can be exercised.[58] The Athenians do not know what they worship in their idolatry in more ways than one.[59]

This naturally suggests several things. First, if idolatry has this kind of power to bind, then repentance is no easy act of self-generated will.

---

[54] Stirner 1907.

[55] Ramachandra (1996: 111) notes we can become 'possessed' by our idols, citing in particular the ideologies that we construct. These and the organizations that enforce them acquire a scale that dwarfs and means 'No one is any longer in control' (ibid. 112).

[56] In this respect it is intriguing how prevalent in popular entertainment is the theme of our technological creations becoming, or attempting to become, our masters: the computer HAL in *2001: A Space Odyssey*, and more recently the *Terminator* cycle and the *Matrix* trilogy.

[57] Fee (1987: 472) suggests that, faced with the 'power' of pagan gods, Israel saw this power as necessarily demonic, since it could not be God.

[58] Clearly, some would argue that the 'demonic' is not to be understood in terms of personal opponents of human beings, but rather as forces, especially within the social structures, bureaucracies and ideologies humans create. Without wanting to dismiss the oppressive trajectories of institutions, the biblical evidence does also suggest personal and consciously directed malevolence at human beings: the prime examples are the synoptic exorcism narratives.

[59] This point is heavily developed in patristic accounts of the nature of idolatry; e.g. Tertullian, *On Idolatry* (Roberts and Donaldson 1980, 3: 61–76).

It will indeed be a gift. Second, if idolatry does not represent liberation from our Creator, but involves bondage, then repentance is rightly associated with liberation and deliverance, as Paul says in his account of Jesus' charge to him in Acts 26:18. Third, if idolatry is associated with the demonic, then the liberation Paul links to repentance is quite properly seen as liberation from the power of Satan (Acts 26:18). Fourth, given the pervasiveness of idolatry in human life, repentance will indeed be lifelong. Some of the recovery programmes from substance abuse stress that one does not say, 'I used to be an alcoholic,' but rather, 'I am an alcoholic who has gone two years since a drink,' or whatever it may be. Understanding the power of idolatry underlines the thought that repentance will be a sustained dealing with these affections.

Idolatry as identity

We need now to draw together some of the threads from this discussion of idolatry, relationship and world view.

Idolatry as false identity

To begin with there is the question of identity. If idolatry relates to the parodying of our fundamental relationship, and represents the grid or the spectacles through which we view the world, then idolatry becomes constitutive of our identity. One can see it as the story one tells, not necessarily consciously, to establish and buttress one's place in the world, and so it becomes the identity one seeks, consciously or not, to establish for oneself.

The problem is, given that idols are false, then this identity is false too. It is an alienated self-consciousness, to borrow the Marxist rhetoric of an earlier generation. For as a creature, a human being has an identity, but one that the fictitious identity of idolatry obscures. Buber writes, 'This selfhood . . . steps in between and shuts off from us the light of heaven.'[60]

Repentance as self-knowledge

All this, though, casts an intriguing perspective on repentance. We have seen the stress laid on repentance from idolatry, and we can now see that repenting of idolatry means not only repudiating our false faith about God, although that is certainly true. Rather, as we

[60] Buber 1953: 129.

repudiate false faith about God, we repudiate the false identities our idolatry has fostered, established and supported.

Søren Kierkegaard reflects on the practice of repenting in confession of sin to God. Why do this? God does not need the information, since he is all-knowing. Kierkegaard observes, 'the all knowing one does not get to know something about the maker of confession, rather, the maker of the confession gets to know about himself'.[61]

One can, though, put this even more sharply: repentance and confession involve a twofold recognition of identity: a recognition of God and a turning to him as the true God; and a recognition of self in which a human knows himself or herself from God's view, an acceptance that God knows us as idolaters. In I–Thou terms, the first recognition accepts God as he discloses himself to us.[62] In the second recognition we accept the view held about us by the Thou one meets,[63] and derive identity and self-understanding from that. Both recognitions accept that God addresses us as Lord. Thus the unrepentant Pharisees of Luke's Gospel are those who do not know themselves as they truly are, sinners who do not love God, but love the things of this world instead. The lost son, however, comes to a true valuation of himself, as does the tax collector in the parable of Luke 18.

We should stress again how different this structure of identity is from current discussion in the cultural West. D. Oyserman remarks that 'feeling good about oneself, evaluating oneself positively, feeling that one is a person of worth, have been described as a basic goal of the self-concept, a basic human need, akin with the pleasure principle'.[64]

To begin with, repentance does not involve an evaluation of oneself simply by oneself, but acceptance of another's valuation.[65] Second, the evaluation of the self in repentance is not positive, but an acknowledgment or recognition of profound wrongness. This in particular represents a strongly countercultural account of self, where, as Oyserman underlines, positive self-esteem can be put in the striking terms of a 'fundamental human need'.[66]

---

[61] Kierkegaard 1956: 50–51.
[62] Cf. Barth (1960: 252–256) and the notion of self-disclosure in being in encounter.
[63] Cf. ibid., and the stress on allowing ourselves to be addressed in being in encounter. This reaches the point of being addressed by the Thou about ourselves.
[64] Oyserman 2004: 9.
[65] Oyserman (ibid. 14) tellingly notes that 'current theories about personality . . . and well-being . . . imply an autonomous goal-orientated self . . .'.
[66] Ibid. 9. Campbell and Baumeister (2004: 79) comment on the wide acceptance of the idea that 'self-love' (which includes positive self-esteem, 81) is necessary in order to love others, but conclude there is a paucity of evidence to support this (92).

In a rough and ready way this helps us see something distinctive about repentance in comparison with faith. Faith in the New Testament sense readily focuses on belief about another, while repentance necessarily has as a major element a new belief about oneself, although in the context of relation with another.

Idolatry, agnosticism and atheism: objections to using the idea of idolatry

There is, though, an obvious objection to the idea that repentance relates to idolatry. It may be said that repenting of idolatry makes good sense in an Athens steeped in such superstitions, but has little to say to a modern country, where agnosticism and atheism are so prevalent.

Personal and impersonal, big and small, gods

One Christian apologist of an earlier generation used to respond to convinced atheists by asking who the God was they said they did not believe in. His point was that often their ideas about the Christian God were so wide of the mark that he could quite properly reply that he did not believe in that God either, and then proceed to something fruitful. It is certainly true that much depends on how one defines God. Western cultures, to their great benefit and also to their great responsibility, have been so steeped in Christian thought that various attributes of the Christian God are readily assumed into a definition, so that a belief in God is associated with omnipotence and incorporeality and love. Thus within this tradition one might say the Greek god Zeus is not really a god because while in Greek mythology he is immortal he nevertheless had a beginning: he is not uncreated and eternal.

This bears on the present discussion. People pleading into this tradition of thought may well be confessional atheists in the sense of denying the Christian God. But their definitions may blind them to the way gods, or idols, are present in their lives using other definitions. So, let us think about what even the atheist media classes look like if you eliminate one part of the Christian definition of God. Suppose we take it that a god does not have to be personal and does not have to be big and omnipotent. At that point the descriptions of an op-ed writer about the appetites he or she has for wealth, sex, Pulitzer Prizes and personal supremacy start to look like descriptions of impersonal forces, which on a micro-level drive this individual. Such 'small' gods are close and accessible, or 'near', in R. Keyes's terms.[67] Although 'small' in one sense (for Pulitzer Prizes are not necessarily even of interest to many), such idols can nevertheless exercise profound influences over their devotees.

Equally, the sense of vast forces of economics or nature that bring about banking collapses or tsunamis sound curiously like the fatalistic and resigned descriptions of the blind Fate or Heimarmene of Hellenistic times. Here one might well call these gods 'big' simply because of the scope of influence they are seen as having. In Keyes's terms these are 'far' gods.

For these reasons, we can see our atheist and secular culture as steeped not in a big personal God, but in many impersonal ones, some big and some small.

Agnosticism and the God who cannot

As for agnosticism, the point is often made that ultimately this collapses back into some kind of atheism, but, we need to add, specifically atheism in the sense of disbelief in the Christian God. For the Christian God is one who reveals himself to humanity, and in the Person of Jesus the Son took flesh and was seen, heard and touched by human eyes, ears and hands (1 John 1:1–3). Strong agnosticism, along the lines that one cannot know about God, is obviously a denial of the incarnation. Equally obviously, this too is a position of faith: it asserts what God cannot or has not done. God must be, as it were, like this. At that stage idolatry is a very good description of such strong versions of agnosticism, for God is defined according to the imagination of human beings: just what Paul forbade in Acts 17:29.

Nor does it seem possible to salvage a weaker form of agnosticism, along the lines of 'I personally do not know, because God has not told me personally; although he may have told others.' Such an approach insists, albeit in polite terms, that God has not spoken to one. Yet Romans 1:18–20 is clear that he has, and that the problem is not of God's not speaking, but of humanity suppressing the truth. Again there is a shaping of what God can or has done.

---

[67] Keyes (1992: 37) contends that idolatry comprises two kinds of idol, one ('near') counterfeiting God's immanence, the second ('far') counterfeiting God's transcendence. Keyes's stress on idols in pairs helpfully opens the door to considering the drift to polytheism.

Idolatry and idolodoulia

The obvious supplementary objection is now that in secularism and atheism there is no worship. There is no equivalent, for example, to the liturgical service of the 1662 *Book of Common Prayer*. One must be wary of confusing several things here. To begin with, the humanist organizations in the UK do from time to time try to produce rites of passage; especially for funerals. Similarly, civil weddings have a formal element and a liturgy in that sense; just, some might say, not a very good one. But the point remains, it will be said, that the humanist funeral is not a service of worship.

Here, of course, it all depends on what one means by 'worship'. In the sense that a humanist funeral service does not contain personal addresses to God, whether of petition, protest or praise, in prayer or song, it is not a service of worship. But it is worth asking whether worship can be put so restrictively. For example, some magic rituals may not involve such personal addresses, but are rather ways of making impersonal supernatural forces do one's bidding.[68] Yet the association between idolatry and the demonic suggests occult practices can rightly be called 'idolatry'.[69] Further, critically, the attempt at control that is such a feature of 'magic' does not differentiate it from idolatry, for the idolater 'shapes' or controls his or her god. To that extent the core ideas of idolatry are not confined to the more obviously 'religious' practices.

Some rather more sophisticated analysis is called for, as Calvin provides in his discussion of honouring saints and images. The medieval defence for that was that such honour was only *doulia*, not *latria*: 'service', not 'worship'. Calvin's protest was that this distinction is specious. He writes, 'Let us drop fine distinctions and examine the thing itself.'[70]

The *doulia–latria*, or service–worship, distinction was misleading, Calvin argued, because *doulia* transferred to the creature honours that belonged to God. He continued, 'For by his law it pleases him to prescribe for men what is good and right, and thus to hold them to a sure standard that no one may take leave to contrive any sort of worship he pleases.'[71]

---

[68] Arnold (1992: 19) stresses the way magic is the 'management' of supernatural powers and comments, 'In religion one prays and requests from the gods; in magic one commands the gods and therefore expects guaranteed results.'

[69] Arnold (ibid. 27) argues that the cult of Ephesian Artemis was 'closely linked with magical practices and beliefs'.

[70] Calvin 1960: 119 (*Inst.* 1.12.3).

[71] Ibid. 120 (*Inst.* 1.12.3).

This focuses the question on matters that relate to God's sovereign prerogatives: honour, obedience, prizing. At this level of analysis it makes good sense to see atheism as idolatry, for characteristically something is prized and sought after, or honoured.

The great atheist systems of the twentieth century such as communism, or, in some forms, fascism, were religious in this sense. What was prized may have been a distantly future utopia. But in the case of Marxist-Leninism this distant socialist utopia was 'honoured' with the lives and deaths of millions of people. If one thinks of Stalin's activities in the Ukraine in the 1930s, it is appallingly accurate to speak of people being sacrificed for the sake of these ideas.[72] On a very different scale we live in a culture that prizes sexual satisfaction so highly that it sacrifices other things for the sake of it. Of course, it may not be wrong to prize a future, nor to prize the gift of sexuality, but when these things are prized above what God says either directly in his word or indirectly through the promptings of common grace in the conscience, then God's sovereign prerogatives are obviously displaced.

Atheism and polytheism

This brings forward the objection that while it may be true that the great political-ideological metanarratives of the twentieth century did lead to sacrifices and can be represented as religious, the culture in which we now live characteristically has no grand metanarratives, and individuals do not have unified, monistic world views in which values are arranged hierarchically.[73] Sometimes one is preferred; sometimes another. This takes us to the question of atheism as against polytheism and the relations between the two.

The church fathers, of course, envisaged polytheism as tending to atheism, for they reasoned that a world of many gods ultimately meant a world with no gods. Thus Gregory of Nazianzus writes:

> The three most ancient opinions concerning God are Anarchia, Polyarchia, and Monarchia. The first two are the sport of the children of Hellas, and may they continue to be so. For Anarchy is a thing without order; and the Rule of Many is factious, and thus anarchical, and thus disorderly. For both these tend to the same thing, namely disorder; and this to dissolution, for disorder

---

[72] Ramachandra (1996: 106–135) rightly speaks of the 'violence' of idols.
[73] The seminal work here is Lyotard 1984.

is the first step to dissolution. But Monarchy is that which we hold in honor.[74]

Similarly, Athanasius argues that if polytheism is true, so that another God exists beside God, then neither is truly God.[75] Polytheism is ultimately atheism. But this depends on a particular conception of God, namely one who is supreme. Athanasius' point is that there cannot be two supreme beings, and there are not two gods, in his definition of God.[76]

However, we might also reverse this and suggest that if polytheism collapses into atheism in one sense, atheism also degenerates into polytheism in another sense. Why might this be so? Even in cultures that have embraced atheism, virtues and values do not disappear entirely. Faithfulness and truthfulness are clearly found among atheist communities too and can be prized and recognized as God's common grace. It is, though, no longer easy to find a way of integrating these virtues. G. K. Chesterton remarked with considerable foresight:

> The modern world is full of the old Christian virtues gone mad. The virtues have gone mad because they have been isolated from each other and are wandering alone. Thus some scientists care for truth; and their truth is pitiless. Thus some humanitarians care only for pity and their pity (I am sorry to say) is often untruthful.[77]

However, this isolation of virtues from each other is actually celebrated by the influential Oxford philosopher Isaiah Berlin. Berlin articulates a powerful and prominent view that values or virtues are incommensurable with each other. You cannot compare the value of, say, freedom with the value of equality. He wrote of 'the fact that human goals are many, not all of them commensurable, and in perpetual rivalry with one another'.[78]

---

[74] Gregory of Nazianzus, *Third Theological Oration: On the Son* 2 (Schaff and Wace 1983, 7: 301).
[75] Athanasius, *Against the Heathen* 6 (Schaff and Wace 1991, 4: 7).
[76] Ibid. Athanasius works from two biblical propositions: (1) that the lord God is one; and (2) that God is lord of heaven and earth. This latter proposition (drawn from Matt. 11:25) makes God's universal sovereignty central to who he is.
[77] Chesterton 1909: 51.
[78] Berlin 1958: 241.

In Berlin's view this incommensurability of values is to be celebrated as a good and inevitable development.[79] It means one must say that my estimation of the value of, say, chastity, cannot be compared with your value of personal fulfilment. My good is mine; yours is yours. This, though, describes a world in which there is no supreme common value and to that extent no supreme God, even an impersonal one. But it also describes a world in which particular values to particular people are prized, sought and honoured, and are sought sometimes without check or restraint, because commensurability between values is not possible. These isolated values and virtues challenge the sovereignty and supremacy of God precisely because they are prized and sought without check or restraint, at least in their own little domains. Berlin envisages we stand for our isolated values and virtues 'unflinchingly' because they are still 'sacred'.[80] Values in Berlin's scheme function as absolute, as gods.

In this way we can envisage a reciprocal relationship between atheism and polytheism in modern, or postmodern, Western cultures, like this:

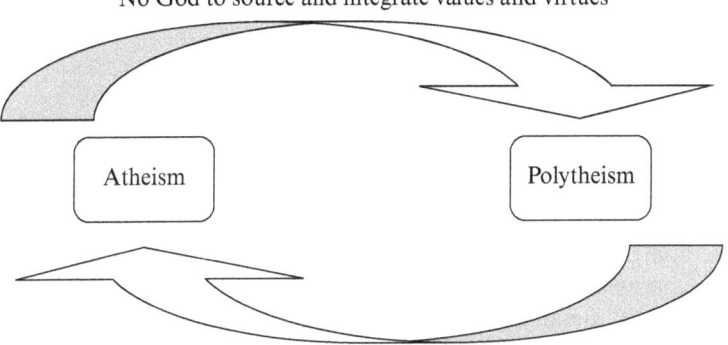

No God to source and integrate values and virtues

Many competing, disintegrated virtues deny God's overarching rule

Thus much of our characteristic modern idolatry has an ambiguity. Viewed one way it is atheist, in the sense of denying a personal, supreme God, but viewed another way it is functionally polytheist at the level of competing impersonal values and forces that are lauded and pursued.

---

[79] Berlin traces the development of this idea through Niccolò Machiavelli, Giambattista Vico and Gottfried von Herder. Berlin is a subtle and profound historian of ideas, but it is not clear that the line of development is quite this neat or his construals beyond doubt on this point.
[80] Ibid. 242.

We need to raise here the question of what impact a polytheistic world view has. Given the resemblance dynamic by which we are shaped by the gods we have created, and given that these gods, whether 'big' or 'little', are in isolation from each other, it seems plausible that one mark of this polytheistic outlook will be fracture. Fracture at an individual level, because an individual has several idols battling for dominion in different areas of life. Fracture at a social or collective level, because, especially with the propensity for 'little' gods to multiply, people will not have gods in common. Of course, one of the difficulties this brings in addressing a person is knowing which aspect of them one is addressing. For example, the professional who has a high set of standards for speech in the office, fuelled by reverence for professional standards, may behave very differently outside the office setting. When talking about the seriousness of deceit, there may well be a premium on making sure one addresses that person in his or her professional rather than private aspect. With a polytheist, part of the apologetic and evangelistic challenge is no doubt to find a way of addressing the most helpful aspect of that polytheist's world view.

Communicating idolatry

With this in mind, it is worth thinking about how this understanding of idolatry may affect our calls to repentance.

To begin with, it suggests particular sins can very profitably be understood as symptoms and presented as such. A particular sin demonstrates, as it were, something behind or underneath it. It discloses the disruption and distortion of the most fundamental relationship a human being has: that with the Creator.

This matters significantly in a culture that to some extent adopts a functionalist attitude to ethics and can, for example, condone lying and immorality if there are only limited consequences. Relating a particular sin like lying to something as fundamental as the relation between creature and Creator gives a perspective of the seriousness of sin. It no longer seems so trivial that it is not worth humbling oneself.

As well as perspective, seeing particular sins as outworkings of the problem of idolatry establishes a certain equality between sins. Of course, some sins have more obvious and serious consequences in this life. Manipulative behaviour at work normally has less tragic consequences than murder. And this undermines two characteristic objections a hearer has to the call of repentance for his or her specific sin. One objection is that one's own sins are being singled out as if they were the only ones. This is, in effect, one of the specious objections heard in the current debates within the Anglican communion on same-sex sexual relations. But the stress on the idea that, in the old principle, commandments two through ten are broken only by breaking the first, indicates a fundamental equality of sins. The second objection is that one's own sins are trivial, understandable and so much less bad than examples of genuine evil. Again the principle that particular sins are outworkings of something deeper assists us. It would be like congratulating oneself one has only the sneezing symptom of bubonic plague rather than the more painful symptom of swelling buboes. It does not alter the underlying problem of having a fatal disease.

This means, I think, that in calls to repentance and the explanation of sin we can and should teach on specific sins. This seems good and wise in an age that has become simply ethically ignorant that malice and gossip, as well as gross sins of violence, are forbidden. Rhetorically, this adds proper relevance and immediacy. But the perspective must be that these are symptoms of something deadly serious, and as such just cutting out, say, adultery and drunkenness, is only a way of treating symptoms. This opens the way to the principle of salvation by grace alone, rather than moralism.

Second, teaching repentance at this stage involves a focus on who we are. There is an apologetic priority on anthropology and the question of what a hearer thinks a human being is, and specifically who the hearer thinks he or she is. The call for faith rightly involves a strong focus on who Jesus is and what he has done. That is perfectly right. But this is an age that does not simply ask, 'Is this true?', but more, as Tim Keller puts it, 'Does this work for me?' In those circumstances the account one gives of who I am, both in the sense of personal individual identity and in the sense of identity as a human being, affects what counts as working for me.[81] Repentance and repentance of idolatry take us exactly to Calvin's point that knowledge of God and knowledge of ourselves are related.

Third, consistently in the background in this discussion of the teaching of, or call for, repentance, is the idea of creation: that a human being is a creature and there is a Creator. We may not want

---

[81] Two lurking philosophical questions here for a culture given to hedonism are (1) whether a pleasure can be bad, and (2) whether there can be 'false' pleasures – things one thinks are pleasures but are not.

or need to teach the doctrine of humanity as created every time we stand up, but I suspect we must presuppose it and be ready and able to defend it every time we speak. If we do not, the fundamental reversal of relationship between Creator and creature that John Stott speaks about will remain unchallenged, and there is no idolatry in the mind of the hearer of which to repent. For this reason, the evangelistic tract *Two Ways to Live* was theologically spot on to begin with creation.

This means for many of us familiarization with some demanding apologetic questions and a willingness to engage on some intimidating questions about what we make of evolution or the origin of life. It is not, of course, that we would rather talk about the issues of six-day creation than the cross, but that we may talk most effectively about the cross when we remind our hearers that he whom humanity murdered at Jerusalem is its maker.

Fourth, there is the death and resurrection of Jesus. We have seen how the death of Jesus functioned to show not just that the people in Jerusalem sinned but also the depth of their estrangement from God. It is no doubt true that Jesus was a victim of oppression and miscarriage of justice, as so many have been in human history; nevertheless, the unique qualities of his death underline something about his murderers.

As important as the calls for repentance is Jesus' resurrection. Naturally, this functions in Jerusalem as a guarantor of Jesus' identity as the Messiah, and is also implicitly a refutation of the Sadducees. But by the time Paul speaks in Athens it is a guarantor of judgment. In his novel *That Hideous Strength* C. S. Lewis imagines a technology that can raise someone to at least a kind of life from the dead. It is a terrifying moment to hear one of the characters observe, 'They cannot refuse the little gift.'[82] It is terrifying because of the thought that one cannot escape these people even by death. Throughout Acts the resurrection is stressed as a sovereign act of God. And the implication is that if he can raise this man, then he can raise anyone; and the upshot therefore is that all must face whatever judgment God determines. Bertrand Russell famously observed, 'When I die I rot.' In the light of the resurrection, Russell's quip emerges as wishful thinking. The resurrection of Jesus is, of course, something of tremendous hope, but also a sobering demonstration that God's sovereignty is inescapable, even by death.

---

[82] Lewis 1945: 176.

Conclusion

We have been thinking about repentance in the context of repentance from idolatry. The connection with idolatry highlights that repentance is not a mere moralism, but deals with who we are and who God is, ultimately in the context of our relationship as creatures with Creator. Idolatry represents a parody of that relationship and can occur in diverse ways, so that even atheism is a form of idolatry; notably, in our time, a functionally polytheistic idolatry. In this parody idols, apparently a manifestation of human control, in fact become instruments by which we are controlled, for there is a dynamic at work by which we come to resemble what we worship.

Within this framework of thought those who are repentant are those who have recognized their dislocation and estrangement from God, not necessarily articulately. Recognition of such dislocation is relational and personal, and the repudiation of that dislocation and estrangement is a seeking to be brought back into relationship and integration with God. This is rightly associated with liberation from the dominion that idolatry brings, and this underlines why repentance and forgiveness are occasions for joy.

The unrepentant by contrast emerge as those persisting in relational dislocation. Because of the centrality of the Creator–creature relationship this represents a disintegration. This disintegration comprises both false faith about God and false understanding of who one really is. To be unrepentant is an awful thing, and woe betide us if it does not excite compassion.

Chapter Five

Repentance: faith and salvation

Bricks without straw?[1]

Recap

In chapters 2–4 we examined how the call for repentance becomes universalized. Thus in Luke's Gospel the imperative for repentance is applied not just to such obvious candidates as tax collectors and sinners, but also to Pharisees, who are progressively shown to share the same nature as the tax collectors and sinners they so despise. In Acts that universalization is shown in the extension of the call to repentance from the inhabitants of Jerusalem, who have committed a gross and obvious wrong in the murder of Jesus, to pagan Gentiles too.

Repentance involves an acknowledgment of wrongdoing, and as such presupposes that a law has been broken. So if Gentiles are called to repent, this necessarily implies that they too are bound by a law of God, even though they are not parties to the Abrahamic covenant and the commands given at Sinai. I have argued that the law in question relates to the fundamental, inevitable relationship that a human creature has with his or her Creator. As creatures we are bound to offer God right honour and worship. In our idolatry we refuse, either explicitly or implicitly, to do this.

Repentance can then rightly be said to be a turning from idolatry. What is more, since idolatry has a relational dimension in that it parodies true relationship, it means that when we repent of it, we begin to acknowledge our true relational location. Repentance is a double recognition or *anagnōrisis*. It acknowledges who God or Jesus is, and implicitly affirms God's character as forgiving, but also admits who we are and the wrongness of who we are in relation to God. Repentance 'locates' us, and does not merely acknowledge Christ. This brings us to the question of repentance and faith and whether and how they are related.

---

[1] Exod. 5.

The relation of repentance and faith

There are several logical possibilities for the relationship between faith and repentance. First, it may be that repentance is prior to faith, whether logically or temporally, so that faith arises only when there has been repentance. Second, it may be that repentance and faith are completely mutually independent, so that the presence of one neither guarantees nor denies the presence of the other. The third possibility is that repentance may be consequent upon faith in some way, either logically or temporally.

This issue could very easily savour of being purely technical and scholastic, and therefore be dismissed as a classic question of the type 'How many angels dance on the head of a pin?' In fact, despite the technical sound (and just like the angels on a pinhead) it matters considerably. The reason is that two very different accounts of the *ordo salutis*, the order of salvation, are at stake. And inevitably our understandings of the *ordo salutis* will affect both how we proclaim the gospel and also how we pastor and minister within our churches. The two different accounts of the *ordo salutis* are as follows:

- Repentance and faith are mutually independent.
- Repentance and faith are mutually connected.

We must develop each briefly.

Repentance and faith mutually independent

This version of the *ordo salutis* can be diagrammed thus:

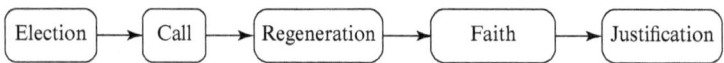

This version preserves some Reformation distinctives because of the priority it places on election and call. Regeneration, the third stage, is not something we do by ourselves or contribute to, but depends on election and call, which are acts of God. Accordingly, this version of the place of regeneration gives no place to either Pelagianism (understood as autonomously generated faith) or Semi-Pelagianism (understood as synergistically generated faith). Similarly, faith is not a work, because it arises from regeneration, and it leads to justification, understood in conventional terms as the imputation of Christ's righteousness and the consequent judgment of innocence that that entails.

It is, though, an account that envisages justification occurring without repentance. Repentance is not logically required, either as a ground, or as a co-requisite of faith. In this version faith might be saving but it is void of repentance, which gives it at best an anaemic character.

Repentance and faith mutually connected

This version of the *ordo salutis* can be diagrammed thus:

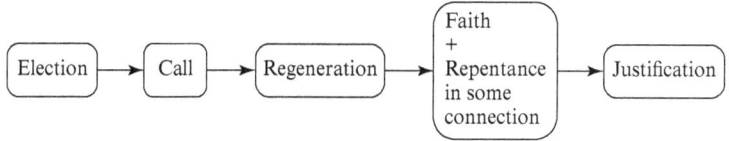

This equally preserves the priority of election and call, and has a place for regeneration that is similarly not open to Pelagian or Semi-Pelagian handlings, but because it places faith and repentance in some kind of connection, this means that justification and the other aspects of salvation are not disconnected from repentance. This means that faith and repentance in effect flavour each other. The kind of connection is not at this point the issue. The connection between faith and repentance may be that one produces the other, or that both are sides of the same coin, but the net effect is that in an individual a faithless repentance, or a repentanceless faith, may not be the kind of faith and repentance that lead to justification and forgiveness.

Naturally, a key point here is what we mean by 'faith' and to this question we now turn. We shall examine John Calvin's account of faith and repentance in some depth before detouring briefly to consider two writers from the emerging church movement, and then finally considering a great critical admirer of Calvin, Karl Barth.

Faith and repentance?

Calvin on faith

Calvin's extensive theoretical discussion of faith and repentance occurs at the start of Book 3 of his *Institutes*. In the course of his long criticisms of various medieval accounts of faith he writes:

> Now we shall possess a right definition of faith if we call it a firm and certain knowledge of God's benevolence toward us, founded

upon the truth of the freely given promise in Christ, both revealed to our minds and sealed upon our hearts by the Holy Spirit.[2]

One concern here is to provide an account of faith that has genuine cognitive content and does not merely collapse into the variety of implicit faith that says, 'Whatever the Church believes, that I believe.' He also, though, wants to assert an affective dimension. It is, moreover, Christocentric in that our knowledge of God's benevolence is not mere presumption but arises from Christ and the promises that surround him.[3] Faith is related directly to the incarnate Son and does not arise otherwise. God's benevolence is stressed, and this feature of Calvin's definition of faith will be important in his nuanced account of repentance.

However, the emphasis on God's benevolence does not mean that faith is a mere presumption that downplays other attributes of God. Thus Calvin also notes that a mark of true faith is a recognition of God's anger at sin,[4] and Calvin associates faith with a right fear of God that is not presumptuous.[5]

This means that faith involves a recognition of God that is grasped through Christ and the promises made through him, and also that understands both his benevolence and his holiness and consequent anger at sin. Both attributes, benevolence and holiness, are in view.

Of course, these attributes can be distinguished, but they are not to be understood as mutually contradictory or inconsistent. Rather, a classical doctrine of the simplicity of God would suggest that God's benevolence is holy, and his holiness benevolent: one cannot understand any attribute in isolation from the others. To this extent, faith's recognition of both attributes does not affirm a contradiction in the character of God.[6]

The mercy and goodness grasped by faith are thus set against the reality of divine judgment, and this is borne out by the account of faith in 1 Thessalonians 1:9–10, where Jesus is the one who delivers

---

[2] Calvin 1960: 551 (*Inst.* 3.2.7).

[3] Thus Beeke (2008: 278–279) stresses that faith rests on God's Word (for God's promises are found there) and therefore comes to rest on Christ, 'for the totality of the written Word is the living Word, Jesus Christ, in whom all the promises of God are "yea and amen"'.

[4] Calvin 1960: 557 (*Inst.* 3.2.12).

[5] Ibid. 568 (*Inst.* 3.2.22).

[6] For Turretin's sophisticated discussion of the simplicity of God, and the relation of attributes to each other and as they appear to us, see Turretin 1992–7, 1: 3.q.7 (191–194).

from the wrath to come. Thus the promise in Christ is a promise of deliverance against divine judgment. Salvation may be more than this, but is not less.

However, while Calvin is concerned that there be genuine cognitive content to faith, faith is also something that personally appropriates God's attributes of kindness and mercy, and sees them as applied to oneself. A. N. S. Lane writes, '[S]aving faith is faith in God's mercy to *me*';[7] and again 'saving faith is not an abstract general belief in the divine mercy without an application of it to oneself'.[8] In effect the definition receives a personalized or individualized emphasis: 'God's benevolence toward *us*'.[9] God's benevolence is put into a relational context with respect to us.

Calvin on repentance

Basic definition

Calvin moves on in *Institutes* 3.3 to discuss repentance. He repudiates the idea that repentance must precede faith,[10] although, as we shall see, his position on whether faith or repentance is prior is complex. His account of repentance runs as follows:

> The meaning is that, departing from ourselves, we turn to God, and having taken off our former mind, we put on a new. On this account, in my judgment, repentance can thus be well defined: it is the true turning of our life to God, a turning that arises from a pure and earnest fear of him; and it consists in the mortification of our flesh and of the old man, and in the vivification of the Spirit.[11]

This prompts several reflections. First, this account of repentance gives a strong relational location of us as humans with respect to God. We turn to him and repentance affects us in vivification and mortification. Second, whereas Calvin's definition of faith most obviously focuses on a sense of God's benevolence to us, here the stress is on

---

[7] Lane 1979: 32; emphasis original.
[8] Ibid. 551 (*Inst.* 3.2.7).
[9] Calvin 1960: 551 (*Inst.* 3.2.7); emphasis added. Lane's distinction between abstract general belief and personal application is important for seeing why, say, demonic understanding of the attribute of mercy is not saving. A further consequence is that faith and assurance become closely related, not separated, so that assurance is faith writ large (Lane 1979; Beeke 2008).
[10] Calvin 1960: 593–4 (*Inst.* 3.3.2).
[11] Ibid. 597 (*Inst.* 3.3.5).

the fear that God properly inspires; not any fear, we may note, but a 'pure and earnest' fear. Not all fear of God's holiness is a repentant fear, something that ought to be evident perhaps from the reaction of demons to Jesus during his earthly ministry. Third, the depth of repentance is hinted at in the idea that this involves a renewed mind. This takes one away from the view that repentance is merely a disguised moralism, one of the fears arising from medieval doctrines of penance. Fourth, Calvin introduces his twin distinctive marks of repentance, vivification and mortification. His account has several balancing elements, and, as we shall see in relation to Barth's criticisms, the question arises as to whether he has achieved an appropriate balance.

Calvin goes on to comment on three elements in his definition. He expands on the idea of repentance as a turning of life, and writes:

> First, when we call it a 'turning of life towards God', we require a transformation, not only in outward works, but in the soul itself. Only when it puts off its old nature does it bring forth the fruit of works in harmony with its renewal.[12]

This emphasizes that repentance is not a mere moralism and also starts to clarify the role of fruits of repentance. Renewal of nature is stressed and this tends to exclude the idea of a self-willed improvement by performing or refraining from various external actions: the point is internality, not externality.[13] One senses here perhaps a reaction against the abuse of penitence through ostentatious rites by some medievals. Moreover, while Calvin clearly does think in terms of changed actions in life, this is a result of change of nature, not a precondition for change of nature. In this way the fruits of repentance remain fruits of repentance, not the foundation or condition for it.

He does, though, envisage something as a precondition to repentance. He writes, 'For, before the mind of the sinner inclines to repentance, it must be aroused by thinking upon divine judgement.'[14]

Calvin is not here meaning to make repentance solely and exclusively a response to judgment. He is clear that repentance does arise with respect to the promise of mercy, and that this is one distinction between godly repentance and a repentance that is actually a species

---

[12] Ibid. 598 (*Inst.* 3.3.6).
[13] Cf. Beeke (2008: 295) for whom Calvin, in opposition to the Roman Catholicism of his day, underscores 'the inward aspects of repentance'.
[14] Calvin 1960: 599 (*Inst.* 3.3.7).

of despair. Nevertheless, the reality of judgment is insisted upon (as it is with respect to faith too). This immediately prompts us to reflect that a proclamation of the gospel of grace that seeks repentance as well as faith cannot describe God in such ways as to rule out judgment.

Lastly, we move to Calvin's explanation of mortification and vivification. He writes:

> Both things [mortification and vivification] happen to us by participation in Christ. For if we truly partake in his death, 'our old man is crucified by his power, and the body of sin perishes' [Rom. 6:6], that the corruption of original nature may no longer thrive. If we share in his resurrection, through it we are raised up into newness of life to correspond with the righteousness of God. Therefore, in a word, I interpret repentance as regeneration, whose sole end is to restore in us the image of God that had been disfigured and all but obliterated through Adam's transgression.[15]

Here Calvin has joined his account of repentance with faith union with Christ and the idea of regeneration. Once repentance as mortification and vivification has been linked like this to faith union, then it appears as something for the whole of the Christian life and not simply at the point of becoming a Christian. Insensibly, though, Calvin has also raised the stakes over repentance. If repentance is so closely linked to regeneration itself, then the absence of repentance prompts the most serious questions about the regeneration of someone who does not have a repentant life. It seems they may lack a mark of regeneration.

As with Calvin's discussion of faith, there is a strongly personal or individually appropriated element to his thoughts on repentance. This is present in the stress on interiority;[16] but, as with the stress on a sense of benevolence 'to *me*',[17] there is a stress on personal appreciation of God's anger. This aspect of personal appropriation will be developed below.

Repentance and forgiveness of sins
As well as seeing repentance in the light of regeneration, Calvin also takes repentance very closely with the forgiveness of sins. As we have

---
[15] Ibid. 600–601 (*Inst.* 3.3.9).
[16] Cf. Beeke 2008: 295.
[17] Lane 1979: 32; emphasis original.

seen, he envisages the gospel as having two elements: 'the sum of the gospel is held to consist in repentance and forgiveness of sins'.[18]

Two comments need to be made. The first relates to the biblical data. Calvin is surely right to note how repentance (certainly given Luke–Acts) is linked to the forgiveness of sins. This is what the risen Jesus commands to be proclaimed to the world in his name, and is Paul's summary to Agrippa of the mission that the risen Jesus gave him on the road to Damascus. It is, in fact, striking how frequently the apostolic proclamation in Acts to Jew and Gentile is framed in terms of the language of repentance rather than simply 'faith' or 'belief'.

The second consideration is the relation of forgiveness of sins to justification. At first hearing this sounds slightly obscure. The question, though, created by the New Testament data is this: Luke–Acts links forgiveness of sins with repentance, while Paul links justification with faith. This means there is a question not just about the relation of faith and repentance, but also a question about the relation between forgiveness and justification. So let us go back to the view that might see faith and repentance as fundamentally unconnected. The relevant diagram goes thus:

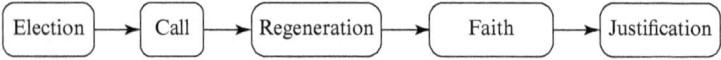

The diagram suggests the final box, justification, can be achieved, in effect, by faith alone, because, of course, repentance is not connected to faith. This, though, raises the question of whether justification takes place without the forgiveness of sins. If justification can take place without the forgiveness of sins, then the lack of a connection between faith and repentance is underlined. If, on the other hand, justification itself relates to the forgiveness of sins, then that implies connection between faith and repentance.

The idea of justification occurring without the forgiveness of sins seems highly problematic. Apart from anything else the parable of the Pharisee and tax collector (Luke 18:9–14) has a tax collector showing repentance and mourning for sin, who pleads for mercy and whose fate is described as being 'justified' (*dedikaiōmenos*). Here mercy for sin is related to justification, and that seems to connect forgiveness with justification.

---

[18] Calvin 1960: 592, 613 (*Inst.* 3.3.1, 19).

The obvious objection to this citation is that this may reflect Lukan rather than Pauline usage of justification language. However, Paul too relates justification to the forgiveness of sins. This takes a number of steps. First, Romans 4:1–3 discusses how Abraham was justified, and uses the 'reckoning righteousness' language of Genesis 15:6 to explain how he was justified. Reckoning righteousness and justifying are thus tied together. Second, Romans 4:6–8 describes the blessedness of those to whom God reckons righteousness. The blessedness in question, for those reckoned righteous, is the forgiveness and covering of sins. This links justification with the forgiveness of sins. This does not mean that justification is exhausted by the forgiveness of sins.[19] Forgiveness of sins may arguably be the most striking indication of what justification comprises, but may not exhaust it. Thus W. H. Griffith Thomas relates forgiveness of sins to pardon and writes that justification is more than pardon:

> A criminal is pardoned, but is not regarded as righteous. But Justification is that act of God whereby He accepts and accounts us righteous, though in ourselves unrighteous. The Christian is not merely a pardoned criminal, but a righteous man . . . Forgiveness is only negative, the removal of condemnation; Justification is also positive, the removal of guilt and the bestowal of a perfect standing before God.[20]

Yet Luke also discusses the blessing of forgiveness of sins under the Abrahamic covenant in Peter's speech in Acts 3:25–26. However, Peter has linked repentance to the forgiveness of sins in 3:19. At this point it is perhaps easier to reject the idea that Luke and Paul have two really quite different accounts of the *ordo salutis*, and rather see Luke's and Paul's envisaging a single *ordo salutis* in which, as justification and forgiveness of sins are indeed related, the notions of faith and repentance are also therefore connected with each other.

However, we must now return to the question of the priority of faith over repentance. We saw earlier that Calvin repudiates the idea that repentance is the precondition for faith and must be preached first.[21] Yet this priority is not simple. Calvin writes:

---

[19] This idea has been associated with, among others, Norman Shepherd.
[20] Griffith Thomas 1920: 186. For many, this is related to the imputation of Christ's 'active obedience'. On this point see VanDrunen 2006. On the question of imputed righteousness more generally see Carson 2004.
[21] Calvin 1960: 593–4 (*Inst.* 3.3.2).

> Now the hatred of sin, which is the beginning of repentance, first gives us access to the knowledge of Christ, who reveals himself to none but the poor and afflicted sinners, who groan, toil, are heavy-laden, hunger, thirst, and pine away with sorrow and misery.[22]

Here the hatred of sin appears as fundamental to knowing Christ. This occasions no surprise after Calvin's account of faith, in which the right fear of God is set alongside a trust in God's benevolence. But what emerges here is that the same conviction may play a role in both repentance and faith, and this underlines the intimate connections between the two ideas in Calvin.

We should add at this point that the hatred of sin that Calvin points to here helps in the appreciation of *forgiveness* for sins. The sinful woman at the feast of Luke 7:36–50 loves much because she has been forgiven much, and this rests in part on understanding the depths and hatefulness of sins. In this way elements associated with repentance are not merely the method through which forgiveness of sins is appropriated, but show a sharing of the perspective of God.

Repentance as gift
In his discussion Calvin has been at pains to avoid a framework for repentance that would undermine the principles of salvation by grace alone. Repentance is not a work any more than faith is. He discusses repentance as the condition for forgiveness in these terms:

> Yet we must note that this condition is not so laid down as if our repentance were the basis of our deserving pardon, but rather, because the Lord has determined to have pity on men to the end that they should repent, he indicates in what direction men should proceed if they wish to obtain grace.[23]

For him both faith and repentance as distinctively Christian phenomena involve the appreciation of God's mercy. We have noted how benevolence to us is part of the account of faith. He writes in connection with repentance, 'no one will ever reverence God but him who trusts that God is propitious to him'.[24] Thus a belief about God and his mercy becomes a presupposition of Christian repentance, but

---
[22] Ibid. 614 (*Inst.* 3.3.20).
[23] Ibid.
[24] Calvin 1960: 594 (*Inst.* 3.3.2), citing Ps. 130:4.

it is nevertheless a personalized concept, because it is a benevolence or mercy *towards us*. Commenting on Acts 3:19–26, he says, 'For as I said a short while ago, no man can be stirred up to repentance unless salvation is set before him.'[25]

However, an attitude to repentance that saw it as freely and spontaneously generated by a human being would sit uneasily with the priority that Calvin and others give to the content of repentance as an acknowledging of, and a rejoicing in, God's free grace. It is therefore not surprising to see Calvin's understanding repentance itself as a gift. He writes, 'Further, that repentance is a singular gift of God I believe to be so clear from the above teaching that there is no need of a long discourse to explain it.'[26]

Naturally, one does find such 'gift' terms for repentance or language in which God brings people to him ('turning' them) emphatically employed in Acts (Acts 3:26; 5:31; 11:18).

But besides this Calvin has linked repentance to regeneration, as something that comes from it. Regeneration is, of course, a sovereign act of God. This connection is drawn out as Calvin comments on Acts 5:31:

> 'Repentance is indeed a voluntary conversion, but what is the source of this willingness except that God changes our heart, making a heart of flesh out of a heart of stone, one that is pliable out of one that is stiff and hard, and, finally, one that is upright out of one that is crooked? And this happens when Christ regenerates us by His Spirit.' This must be increased throughout life.[27]

The upshot is that Calvin has an account of the relation of faith and repentance that does indeed strive to distinguish them, but in which they are undoubtedly, as he would say, inseparable. As well as inseparable, faith and repentance are highly personal, because the mercy and so forth of which they speak is individually appropriated.[28] The significance is that his account of faith and repentance upholds the principles of salvation by grace, and his extensive place for repentance does not threaten this.

---

[25] Calvin 1554: 101.
[26] Calvin 1960: 615 (*Inst.* 3.3.21).
[27] Calvin 1552: 149.
[28] The point that Lane and Beeke make about faith being an individualized appropriation is also applicable to repentance.

Repentance without faith

Inseparable? Faith-shaped repentance

We have just observed that for Calvin repentance and faith are inseparable. We need to pursue this a little further. The hostility Calvin expressly displays to the separation of faith and repentance is that it produces merely moral teaching. This is bad enough in itself, because it is fundamentally misleading, but in addition it finally leaves men and women without hope, precisely because Christian repentance is a repentance with the hope of salvation and forgiveness in view.

Calvin, of course, has been followed in just this approach. A faithless repentance is an impossibility in classic Anglican theology: '[T]herefore they, that teach repentance without a lively faith in our Saviour Jesus Christ, do teach none other but Judas's repentance'.[29]

The reference to Judas's repentance is telling, because Judas did indeed experience repentance as regret or remorse for his actions, but his subsequent suicide speaks of despair, including a despairing of God.

We need, though, to consider why repentance without faith is an impossibility. Two things are striking: faith and repentance have the same causes, and some of the same objects.

Thus, first, faith and repentance have the same cause in that both faith and repentance are depicted as gifts of God, not freely and spontaneously generated effects of a human being. Rather, they are outcomes of the sovereign work of regeneration, by which hearts of spiritual stone become hearts of spiritual flesh and live. William Ames summarizes: 'Repentance has the same causes and principles as faith, for they are both free gifts of God.'[30]

Second, faith and repentance have some of the same objects. Faith deals with God's benevolence, but Christian repentance likewise distinguishes itself by an emphasis on the possibility of forgiveness to which Christian repentance is repeatedly joined, and this depends on God's mercy. Faith has a place for God's sovereignty and reign, for it has a reverent fear of him, while repentance is joined to the certainty of judgment. Faith rests on the figure of Jesus who died and was vindicated in resurrection. Repentance is Christ-centred too, with the hope of salvation and the certainty of judgment both underlined by the resurrection.

---

[29] Homily 32 (Bray 2015: 503).
[30] Ames 1997: 159, 160.

REPENTANCE: FAITH AND SALVATION

This proximity and interconnection become clearer in the homily on faith, for here part of faith is that the repentant will be welcomed.

> [Faith] is also a true trust and confidence of the mercy of God through our Lord Jesus Christ, and a steadfast hope of all good things to be received at God's hand; and that, although we through infirmity or temptation of our ghostly enemy, do fall from him by sin, yet, if we return again unto him by true repentance, that he will forgive and forget our offences for his Son's sake, our Saviour Jesus Christ, and will make us inheritors with him of his everlasting kingdom . . .[31]

Where we might sketch out a difference between faith and repentance would be over the question of focus. Repentance, we have seen, involves an acknowledgment by a person of his standing in the context of his relation with God. It acknowledges sin and estrangement and relies on Christ to provide forgiveness. The focus, though, we might say, is readily on who the sinner is. A person's faith most naturally involves an acknowledgment of who Christ is, and God's promise of salvation to those who trust in him, and to the individual who has faith in particular. Here the focus most easily is seen as Christ and who he is.

Yet even though the focus for faith and repentance may appear to be in different places, they are indeed inseparably related, because both faith and repentance are set in relational contexts: faith is a person's faith in Jesus as lord and saviour in simple terms, but it consists not merely in assertion of the reality about Jesus but in the personal appropriation of it. Put very starkly, Thomas's acclamation of faith in John 20:28 is not just 'Lord and God', true enough as far as it goes, but '*My* Lord and *my* God.' Thomas's faith may focus on Jesus, but cannot be adequately explained without accounting for Thomas and who he is as well.

Similarly with repentance: repentance locates one relationally, a sinner who in idolatry was turned from God and now turns to God for forgiveness through God's Son.

We may at this point hear again John Murray's words: 'The faith that is unto salvation is a penitent faith and the repentance that is unto life is a believing repentance.'[32]

---

[31] Homily 4, 'A Short Declaration of the True, Lively, and Christian Faith' (Bray 2015: 32).
[32] Murray 1955: 113.

Murray is responding to the question whether faith or repentance is the logically prior category. However, his point is that saving faith is repentance-shaped, and repentance for the forgiveness of sins is faith-shaped. Murray's aphorism has much to commend it in view of the discussion so far. Its implications, though, are shattering for some of our present church contexts.

For if it is true that churches have been preaching faith without repentance, then the question must arise whether saving faith has been taught or called for at all. For Murray's point is that a 'faith' that is not a repentant faith is not biblical faith.

This must also be related to the point that repentance and faith have different foci: faith telling us who Jesus is, and us in relation to that, and repentance an acknowledgment of who we are and God and Jesus in relation to that. If the answer to the question 'Who am I?' is not a repentant answer, then inevitably it will affect how I construe and understand Christ.

Repentance redefined for a therapeutic culture?
The reason why this matter is pressing is that late twentieth- and early twenty-first-century Western cultures are rightly seen as having taken a strongly therapeutic turn. In this, one's misdoings are classified medically rather than morally, and one's self-perception is not infrequently that of victim rather than anything else. There is a very strong inclination to answer the 'Who am I?' question as 'I am the wronged one.' The risk is that this default position of victimhood is assumed as people hear a call to have faith, and the logic of Murray's comment is that the call to faith will be subverted by the unchallenged but powerful default answer to the 'Who am I?' question.

This is further complicated by the way some do retain the terminology of repentance but fill it with different content. Thus Brian McLaren, while he does envisage that humans rebel against God, does not seem to see this in terms of offence and breach of legal obligation. Rather, his account of the human predicament focuses on three elements:

- a lack of justice
- sin against self
- systemic evil

It is naturally indisputable that lack of justice is a consistent human experience, and structures can be constructed that perpetuate and accentuate suffering and injustice, and McLaren rightly sees this. Yet what is striking about McLaren's three categories is how easily they fit into a therapeutic, victim-based outlook. It is inevitably tempting to see lack of justice and systemic evil most clearly in cases where one feels oneself the victim. As for sin against self, McLaren is undoubtedly right to describe things like egotism, hedonism and consumerism as 'fruitless ways of life',[33] but this falls short of the apostolic perspective that judgment awaits those who persist in these idolatries and do not repent. 'Fruitless' is simply not an adequate euphemism for hell, not least because it tends to make the question 'Does hedonism work for me?' the key issue. The fruitlessness or otherwise of a particular habit or way of life is not an irrelevant question but it tends to draw the issue of hedonism away from whether it pleases God to whether I find it profitable, so that I am once again the reference point. Yet one of the features we noted about the relational impact of repentance is that it involves my accepting God's account of who I am, rather than continuing to construct my own identity. The question of fruitlessness is not sufficiently searching. One might say it leaves one's non-Christian identity intact, and since I have argued that identity is fundamentally false, this is a critical shortcoming.

With the human problem set up in this way McLaren defines repentance in these terms. It is

> [l]ooking at every facet of your life again . . . from the way you think about God to the way you treat your spouse, from your political affiliations to your spending habits, from what makes you angry to what makes you happy . . . It involves a deep sense that you may be wrong. Wrong about so much, along with the sincere desire to realign around what is good and true.[34]

There is much here to agree with. Clearly, it is laudable to have a sense of openness to having made mistakes and the need for self-examination, and a sense that such mistakes may have been made on a wide scale across the patterns of one's life. But the language of 'you may be wrong' raises, perhaps unexpectedly in an emerging church leader, a slightly intellectualist feel: that people have made mistakes about what will constitute fruitful lives.

---

[33] McLaren and Campolo 2003: 25.
[34] McLaren 2006: 105.

This intellectualist feel is reinforced by McLaren's translations of important passages calling for repentance in Acts. Thus Acts 5:31b is taken by McLaren as 'God has lifted Him high, to God's own right hand, as the Prince, as the Liberator. God intends to bring Israel to a radical rethinking of our lives and to a complete forgiveness of our sins' (VOICE).

While Acts 2:38 becomes, 'Reconsider your lives: change your direction. Participate in the ceremonial washing of baptism in the name of Jesus God's Anointed, *the Liberating King*. Then your sins will be forgiven, and the gift of the Holy Spirit will be yours' (VOICE; emphasis original).

In both instances McLaren has retained the connection between repentance on his terms and forgiveness of sins. But the vocabulary of the account of *metanoia* is cast in intellectual terms ('reconsider'; 'rethink').[35] This clearly risks removing repentance from some of the affective dimensions associated with it: joy at forgiveness, love in gratitude, sorrow for sin and the offence it has caused. It is difficult not to feel that McLaren's repentance does not necessarily include a sense of contrition. This is underlined by the way that Peter's call of Acts 2:38 is preceded by the statement that the people were 'cut to the heart' (Acts 2:37). Again the terminology is interesting: Calvin, following his connection between repentance and regeneration, and some of the biblical data, talks of the heart, while McLaren takes us to the intellect and its considerations of what is and is not fruitless.

At this stage one realizes McLaren may be returning a different answer to the question 'What is a human being after the fall?' And while he rightly envisages the way sin goes across every aspect of life, it is not clear that the depths of the disruption of relationship between humanity and God are fully appreciated. And that can only lead not merely to an attenuated account of repentance, even while the term is retained, but also, on Murray's logic, to an evacuated account of faith. Jesus may be called the Liberating King, but it is not clear that he is the one who saves from the wrath to come.[36]

The question of who we are also affects another emerging church leader, Steve Chalke. Chalke writes of Jesus' call to repent and believe:

---

[35] It would be an etymological fallacy to infer that, since *metanoia* is formed from a root featuring knowledge, mind or thought (*nous*, etc.), *metanoia* itself must be intellectualist.

[36] 1 Thess. 1:9–10.

'Start living your life differently; do it my way! Your way won't work. Choose mine instead!' That's precisely what the people heard – a call to a new agenda, a different way of doing life, a bigger and better vision for life than anyone else had previously articulated.[37]

Chalke decries the attempt to make people feel guilty by a recitation of particular sins and the negative air of 'Don't do that.' He goes on:

> The world is full of people who have been told, time and again by the Church, what not to do. What they long to hear about is what God wants them to do. People are desperate for a message that they can buy into, that they can see will make a difference to them and to the world in which they live.[38]

He expands on the negativity he envisages in the traditional accounts of repentance as he describes what religion should be at its positive best:

> It [religion] is about a calling *to* something rather than *away from* something; about putting God's agenda at the centre of your life, and in doing so being good to yourself and bringing goodness into the world. All this is precisely what Jesus meant when he used the word *repent*.[39]

On this basis Chalke speaks of the need to proclaim a message of hope. With this the traditional discussions of repentance would agree, at least up to a point. Calvin certainly does see a proclamation of repentance that is merely negative and condemnatory as defective. Yet he is insistent not merely that hope is held out in the proclamation of repentance, but also specifies what that hope is: forgiveness of sins.

The presupposition of Calvin's call to repentance is the future judgment which men and women cannot face but for the salvation Christ brings. That in turn means an acceptance and acknowledgment of guilt is implicit and indispensable. This dimension is absent from Chalke's discussion; and instead of lives that are guilty before God, Chalke speaks of the 'pointless' ways of life in which people are caught, and how they will see this pointlessness.

---

[37] Chalke and Mann 2003: 116.
[38] Ibid. 117.
[39] Ibid. 119.

THE FEASTS OF REPENTANCE

Chalke's account of repentance as we have seen invokes the idea of repentance and religion not as turnings away, but as turnings to. Again there is an important half-truth here. The biblical language does indeed feature the idea of turning to God positively. Paul describes his ministry in just these terms in Acts 20:21. But it is not the case that turning to precludes turning from. Chalke has presented the two kinds of turning as if they are mutually exclusive. Simply from a logical point of view this is problematic. Clearly, a turning to something may very easily imply a turning away from something else. It is not quite a strict necessity, but that is not necessary for Chalke's set of mutually exclusive alternatives to collapse. One only has to note that sometimes a turning to something will be a turning away from something else.

However, more serious than the logical observation is the glossing over of biblical descriptions about repentance and turning. For the biblical data demonstrates quite simply that turning to does involve turning from, as in Acts 14:15: 'we bring you good news that you should turn from these worthless things to the living God' (NRSV). Paul's account in Acts 26:18 before Agrippa is equally pointed. He tells of his commission from Jesus 'to open their eyes so that they may turn from darkness to light and from the power of Satan to God, so that they may receive forgiveness of their sins and a place among those who are sanctified by faith in me'. Again the pattern is of turn from something to something or someone else.

The disadvantage of never mentioning what one turns from is that one may lose sight of the plight Jesus outlines so graphically to Paul in Acts 26:18: Jesus tells Paul that those who do not know him are in darkness and under the power of Satan. To gloss over this state is to risk obscuring quite what the problem is. There is an anthropology at work here that certainly recognizes some aspects of the human condition, but fails to bring out the depth and seriousness of human failure and sin.

Chalke's vocabulary of 'pointlessness' is strikingly similar to McLaren's 'fruitlessness', and his fears that people lack adequate self-worth resembles McLaren's misgivings about sin against self. Both are true in their way, but not the most important thing to say. As with McLaren, there is a slightly intellectualist feel to the idea that Jesus was bringing in a 'new agenda', a term that does not capture the offence to God constituted by the old agenda and human complicity and participation in it. The most striking absence in Chalke's discussion in *The Lost Message of Jesus* is the connection between repentance and forgiveness of sins.

Of course, this discussion about repentance and its presentation among emerging church leaders takes place against a backdrop of criticism about the presentation of the work of Christ. Thus famously, or notoriously, Chalke has been associated with the repudiation of the doctrine of penal substitution, and the point has been made that this involves us in a different doctrine of salvation and what God has done for us through his Son the Lord Jesus. At its sharpest, such an approach gives a different answer to 'Who is Jesus?' because it gives a markedly different account of what he did and what kind of God stands behind those actions. These are questions of faith, in the sense of being focused on Jesus, his acts and his promises.

Yet this different soteriology is intimately connected with a different anthropology in which the language of turning and change provides a different answer to what the human plight is, and this rests on a different account of who a human being is after the fall. The tax collector of Luke 18 and the penitent thief of Luke 23 both acknowledge guilt before God, and appropriate for themselves the status that God places on them for their deeds, namely guilt. They accept God's verdict on who they are as individuals, and allow identity to be determined by him. It is difficult to see how this acceptance of identity and status features in McLaren and Chalke. Accordingly, Murray would remind us that it is entirely predictable that, in differing from more traditional presentations of the gospel in either faith or repentance, they will differ on the other as well. This does not, we should note, mean that a presentation of the gospel that follows the lines these writers have advocated will never produce saving faith. The situation is more complex than that, but I shall defer discussion of the complications in this area until after we have considered the contribution of Karl Barth.

Barth on repentance

As one might expect Karl Barth's thoughts on repentance and conversion are stimulating and, at points, controversial.

Barth underlines the strength of conversion in the metaphor he chooses: 'The first thing that we have to say is that Christians (and therefore those who are sanctified by *the* Holy One) are those who waken up.'[40]

Such language finds a basis in Ephesians 5:14, but Barth makes imaginative use of the idea of conversion as awakening. First of all,

---

[40] Barth 1958: 554; emphasis original.

such awakening is an awakening from 'sloth', as he calls it: '[T]he sleep from which they [Christians] awaken is the relentless downward movement, consequent upon their sloth. Like all others, they participate in this movement, in many beautiful or bad dreams, but not really knowing what is happening to them.'[41]

The reference to dreams implies a life that has an illusory perspective to it, of which those living it are largely unaware. When one awakens from a dream one returns to reality and to who one 'really is'. The identity one has in a dream not infrequently has a fictitious, misleading quality to it. This notion of dream and awakening coheres readily with the argument made in the last chapter to the effect that the identity we have as idolaters is a false and alienated identity that is fundamentally fictitious, and that repentance involves recognition of real, true identity.

However, Barth also pursues another dimension to awakening: it is an awakening from death. This is, of course, the way Paul uses the awakening image in Ephesians 5:14: the command to awake stands with a command to rise from the dead. Death language has, after all, been used emphatically for the preconversion state of a human being in Ephesians 2:1, 5. Such language of awakening from death naturally means this is not a spontaneous, self-generated act of the human individual:

> But from the sleep of covenant-breaking humanity, of the world in conflict with God, there can be no awakening, not even by the greatest catastrophes, by the crashing in ruins of whole cities, by the imminent threat of the worst personal evils, by the thunderous voices of the very greatest prophets. Certainly none of us can of himself supply the jolt which will awaken from this sleep.[42]

Unsurprisingly, therefore, repentance/conversion is linked to regeneration and new nature,[43] and involves the bearing of the fruit of repentance on the basis of a radical inner change.[44] This is in response to God's revelation: 'We may sum up as follows. By the revealed truth that God is for him and he for God, the whole man is set in the movement of conversion.'[45]

---

[41] Ibid. 555.
[42] Ibid.
[43] Ibid. 563.
[44] Ibid. 564.
[45] Ibid. 570.

The response, though, is both a halt and an advance, a halt from the direction in which one has been going and an advance in the direction God stipulates.[46]

Given Barth's stress on the fruits of repentance and the responsibilities that go with being awakened, he must inevitably see repentance and conversion as ongoing in the Christian's life. His depiction of this life is that of conflict between two total men within each of us: two men 'who cannot be united but are necessarily in extreme contradiction'.[47] This way of describing the Christian life, that it features an internal 'quarrel', is powerful and vivid.[48] This depiction of the inner life as one of quarrel and contradiction strongly resembles traditional readings of Romans 7.

This bears clear similarities to the kind of classic Reformation presentation we have seen with Calvin, especially in the connection with regeneration, the priority of God's action and the insistence that repentance and conversion do not arise merely from a proclamation of law, but of 'God for us'. Not for the first time, Barth's choice of metaphor is striking and valuable: the implication of conversion as an 'awakening' from a dream helpfully counterbalances and critiques the feeling that the unconverted, unrepentant life is more 'real' and Christian life dreamlike. Rather, awakening is a return to, or recognition of, real identity. But what is less obviously apparent is the connection of repentance with the forgiveness of sins, which is so strongly emphasized in Calvin. We must turn now to Barth's criticism of Calvin, from whom, clearly, he has taken so much, and also one of his more distinctive contributions to the repentance discussion.

Barth's criticism of Calvin

Barth launches at least two major criticisms of Calvin's position: first, that actually he has two accounts of repentance, and second, that he overstresses mortification in Christian living.

Two accounts of repentance

For Barth, Calvin has two accounts of repentance.[49] One, which he applauds, is rooted properly in faith and the true liberating grace of the gospel. He refers here to that element of Calvin's thought on repentance

---

[46] This double aspect of halt and advance stands at odds with Chalke's idea of repentance as only a turning towards (Chalke and Mann 2003: 117).
[47] Barth 1958: 571–572.
[48] Ibid. 573–574.
[49] Ibid. 580.

which distinguishes Christian repentance from mere remorse on the grounds that the repentant comes to God convinced of his mercy.[50] However, Barth also sees an alternative account in Calvin, one rooted in the fear of God and impending judgment. He continues:

> In so far as Calvin's teaching is shaped by these considerations, finding the *principium poenitentiae* in fear of God and its primary fulfilment in *mortificatio*, and thus acquiring a predominantly sombre character, we can only say that, contrary to his own initial statements, he developed his doctrine in the light of the concept of law which cannot be regarded as identical with the law of the spirit of life.[51]

This alternative root he deplores as inconsistent with the free, liberating grace of the gospel.

Three considerations arise here. First, if it is indeed true that the fear of God is not part of repentance, and not properly part of what God reveals and engenders, then this would equally be a problem for Calvin's account of faith. For, as we have seen, while he stresses God's benevolence, he also sees fear of God as part of faith. Second, while Barth may be right that repentance features for Calvin both fear at God's judgment and hope in his mercy and salvation, it is not clear that this amounts to inconsistency on Calvin's part, rather than depicting a complex set of factors. This takes us to the third point, which is that these two elements simply seem to be present in the source data of the Bible. Notably the Acts 17:30 call to repentance is predicated precisely on impending judgment. It is true that the constant conjunction of repentance with forgiveness of sins offers hope, but it may be said that the very concept of forgiveness implies the possibility of full justice being exacted. It is worth underlining that mercy and justice are not necessarily contradictory notions. After all, mercy relies on the presence of law, for it is exercised towards one who has broken a law and merits justice exercised against him or her. As such Barth's criticism here seems overstated, and we pass to his second objection.

An overemphasis on mortificatio

Barth contends that Calvin has an overemphasis on *mortificatio*,[52] and envisages this as arising from Calvin's misguided reliance on the

---

[50] Calvin 1960: 594 (*Inst.* 3.3.2).
[51] Barth 1958: 581.
[52] Ibid.

fear of God. For Barth this breeds a certain joylessness in Calvin's handling, and he observes, 'Why did he so morosely argue that *vivificatio* is not to be regarded as a joy?'[53] It is, perhaps, fair to observe that much of Calvin's discussion does indeed focus on the deeds of mortification and issues such as the ongoing presence of sin. To that extent this point of Barth, which does not simply arise from his first criticism, is much more convincing and rightly re-emphasizes a biblical perspective. For the biblical material, while it does stress sorrow for sin also provides strong festal associations for repentance and heaven rejoices at the repentant, and expects us to do so as well.

Christ as the representative repentant

For Barth, the New Testament descriptions of conversion, if we apply them to ourselves, 'smack of hyperbole and even illusion'.[54] This is a striking observation, for it compels us to ask whether our accounts, or even experience, of repentance have not become anaemic, in contrast to the full-bloodedness of Zacchaeus or the woman at Simon's feast. Barth's solution, though, is not to ask whether we have in fact truly repented, but in effect to suggest it is not directly us who repent.

> [E]verything is simple, true and clear if these statements are referred directly to Jesus Christ, and only indirectly, as fulfilled and effectively realised in Him for us, to ourselves. It is to be noted that they are indirectly, and therefore genuinely, to be referred to us: in virtue of the fact that He is the head, and we the members; in virtue of being in and with him; in virtue of the fact that by His Holy Spirit He has clothed us with that which properly He alone is and has; in virtue of the fact that he allows us to have a share in that which belongs to him . . . It is in *His* conversion that we are engaged.[55]

In this way Christ repents representatively and we are converted through his conversion. He is the head, and in him we repent and are converted. This, though, raises some considerable problems. To begin

---

[53] Ibid.
[54] Ibid. 582.
[55] Ibid. 583; emphasis added. Cf. p. 582, 'we ask who is the man of whom we have spoken continually as one who is engaged in conversion. And the answer is simply that in the true sense it is he alone. It is not he without those to whom he is revealed as such in the power of the holy spirit. It is he as their head. But it is he, and he alone, as the origin and basis of the conversion of the many.'

with there is the question of how Christ is our head and we come to have him as our representative. The language of being 'in' Christ is normally taken as faith-union, and thus Barth's account apparently presupposes faith-union as the basis of conversion/repentance.

At this, however, a striking difficulty emerges in that the argument seems to require that such faith is a repentanceless faith, for on this argument faith-union must take place without it. The question would then be what kind of faith it is in this *ordo salutis*. We have, moreover, seen how in Calvin faith and repentance are distinguishable yet inseparable, while here though one may lead to the other, they are scarcely inseparable in the way Murray observed: that faith is repentant and repentance faithful.

With this apparent disjunction between faith and repentance comes a further problem: faith is strongly associated with justification in the New Testament data, and repentance with the forgiveness of sins. We have seen how a connection between faith and repentance entails connection between the language of justification and forgiveness, but this connection also comes under pressure if the faith–repentance nexus is lost. For these reasons it seems unattractive to speak of a representative conversion.

We should not, though, lose sight of Barth's point of departure for his discussion of representative repentance, which is that biblical language of repentance seems hyperbolic when set against our experience. This remains an acute observation and quite conceivably reminds us that we resemble Simon rather than the woman of Luke 7, and that we love little because we think we have been forgiven little.

'Faith' without repentance: some pastoral implications

We should now move to think about the pastoral implications of separating faith from repentance. I shall in this chapter and the following mention three: lack of self-understanding; lack of love towards God; and lack of love towards neighbour.

Lack of self-understanding

To begin with, lack of repentance inhibits or removes our self-understanding. The risk is that if we do not locate ourselves rightly as those turned away from God in idolatry and therefore in darkness and under the power of Satan, we do not understand ourselves as saved creatures. Repentance, after all, locates us relationally. We shall turn to the consequences of this lack of relational location presently. Before we do, we should note that the argument is not that lack of explicit mention of repentance necessarily negates saving faith. Nor is it suggested that those who come to faith under schemes and outlines that lack strong places for repentance are necessarily not saved.

For a distinction has to be drawn. The distinction rests on the difference between two claims. There is, on the one hand, the claim that someone has saving faith but has very definitely and knowingly refused to repent; and the claim, on the other hand, that people have saving faith and have repented, but have no self-awareness of the latter. In this second case, a person may have a faith that is, as it were, consistent with repentance and in fact logically demands it. Repentance is implicit in such faith. However, the logic of the position we have been looking at, articulated so clearly by John Murray, suggests the former case is non-existent. One cannot have a saving faith that precludes repentance. If one could, then forgiveness of sins would not flow from repentance, and the demands we find so insistently put by Peter and Paul in Acts would be superfluous. Moreover, repentance would hardly be a lifelong feature of Christian life as Calvin and others envisage, if it has no place from the very beginning.

It is, though, the second case, having a genuinely saving faith but where repentance is only implicit, that concerns us now. Paul Helm comments:

> To stress that justifying faith is accompanied by the conviction of sin and by evangelical repentance is not to promote these to the status of meritorious works. Rather, it is to fill out in a little more detail what justifying faith *is*.[56]

Helm's point is not simply calling into question the validity of a gospel message that does not deal with repentance, the first case. He is concerned for those who have experienced faith and repentance but have not been provided with the vocabulary to express it or understand it. He continues:

> An evangelistic proclamation of the faith which dispenses with the elements of conviction of sin and penitence, whose essential message is 'Jesus loves us – Come to Jesus' will produce converts

---

[56] Helm 1986: 85; emphasis original.

whose experiences of conviction of sin and of penitence are either smothered or explained away.[57]

Helm's remarks are perceptive. If faith and repentance are inseparable, though distinct, then it makes good sense to think of an authentic gift of faith, with an inarticulate sense of repentance, but whose presence makes no sense to the one perceiving it, and who cannot therefore perceive it as integrally related to faith. The urge to explain away what appears to be an irrelevant sensation may be very strong where the message that Helm slightly satirizes ('Jesus loves us – Come to Jesus') is combined with an anthropology that affirms us as sinless, or, more subtly, obscures our sinfulness by depicting us primarily as victims.

If my argument is correct, this smothering or explaining away will not make for spiritual health over time. After all, I have been arguing that repentance provides us with relational orientation and location by telling us who we are in relation to God: sinners deserving judgment for our idolatry, who recognize the evil and horror of that and who nevertheless turn to God for the mercy he has promised in his Son. That sense of who we really are in relation to God is attenuated without repentance. It is not surprising if Christians who lack the identity and relational orientation that repentance gives remain uncertain and unstable in their Christian identities, looking for and perhaps vulnerable to new winds of teaching. Is it entirely surprising that an era that in the West sits light to repentance is marked by a spiritual faddishness? It is no doubt true that the cultures in which we are placed are themselves in some ways unstable and prone to following the winds of fashion. Even so the readiness to seek the next celebrity Christian leader or the next must-have spiritual experience or technique does not seem to speak of a deep rest and security.

We need, finally, also to remember that Luke does provide us with examples of people who are genuinely religious and yet have no place for real repentance, and that is the character group of the Pharisees. They are, however, scarcely an encouraging example, given their lack of love, both for God and others.

Lack of love towards God

It may well seem scathing in some contemporary movements to pose the question of love for God. We have noted some examples from the

---

[57] Ibid. 125–126.

emerging church area where repentance is redefined and seems shrivelled compared to its presentation in Luke–Acts, yet there is scarcely a lack of talking about God's love for us and our love for God. Nevertheless, one is driven back to Luke's presentation of the woman at Simon's feast in Luke 7. She does stand in contrast to Simon, who is the unloving one (certainly at that stage). The love that the two characters have or do not have centres on forgiveness and an awareness of it. Simon's lack of awareness of sin and the consequent value of forgiveness leads him to love, it seems, but little, if at all.

It is love for God in this distinctive quality of gratitude for sins freely forgiven that repentanceless understandings of Christian life and the gospel seem to lack space for. This is not to say that this affect will necessarily be absent in these settings, but, as Helm hints, it may be incomprehensible, and seem irrelevant. No doubt there is an element of rashness in trying to foretell what the result will be of a spirituality that lacks this dimension of love for God, but two fears readily spring to mind in the light of the example of the Pharisees in Luke's Gospel.

First, there is the possibility of presumption, an attitude that is unaware of the depth and horror of sin and therefore lacks appreciation of the wonder of redemption, and the nature of God's mercy. Again, in a culture that has come to prize in some respects a chummy informality in so many areas, presumption can breed easily.

Second, as a related matter, there is the issue of pride. Repentance does humble, as the parable of the tax collector and Pharisee shows. With pride comes the possibility of imagining one contributes to one's salvation, and this in turn can create significant turbulence in our attitudes to others.

Again the argument must not be misunderstood: it is not being suggested that wherever a repentanceless faith is taught these spiritual maladies will always be there and present everywhere. As Helm notes, the pastoral reality is more complex than that. Nor is it suggested that presumption and pride do not arise where repentance and faith are proclaimed together in a perfectly orthodox way. Even so we can see that teaching faith without repentance can create excellent conditions for these maladies.

Lack of charity towards neighbour

We have touched at several points on the question of how repentance affects our treatment of others. This is such an important matter that it forms the bulk of the next chapter.

Conclusion

We have looked at the relation of faith and repentance in the context of a relatively standard *ordo salutis*. A consistent theme is that an account of faith is defective if it has been so constructed as to rule out repentance. This means that a call to faith in Jesus needs to be formed in a way that leaves open the call to repentance even if, for some reason, it is impossible to make that call explicitly on the same occasion. Repentance, apart from anything else, is needed to orientate us in relation to the claims of Christ. It locates us. The example I used in a previous chapter of the proclamation of Vespasian's accession to the purple illustrates this. The hearer of that proclamation must locate himself in relation to it, knowing whether it concerns him as an ordinary Roman, as a visiting German or as a commander who backed the wrong man in the war Vespasian has just won. Similarly, repentance locates us in relation to the proclamation of Jesus, and tells us we correspond to the commander who backed the wrong man. It is of no little significance to know this.

We have also seen that because of the connections between faith and repentance, the lack of the repentance dimension to faith will stunt faith itself. It will tend, unfortunately, to an attenuated spiritual life, not least because this will remain a spiritual life where there is lack of clarity about who we are and our identity as redeemed sinners.

Chapter Six

Repentance: forgiveness and the people of God

The Church: 'a positive hotbed of charity and humility'?[1]

Preliminary

In previous chapters we have been moving through biblical studies to more systematic theological questions, and we now move to matters of pastoral theology as we think further about identity. Thus the biblical material shows the universalization of repentance as the call to repent of idolatry. Idolatry is a double lie about identity: a lie about oneself and a lie about God. It misrepresents our relationship with God, revolving around a denial or reversal of the essential human relationship: that of creature with our Creator. From there we have examined repentance and its relation to faith in the *ordo salutis*, noting in particular John Murray's thought that faith is repentance-shaped and repentance faith-shaped.

We have seen repentance as a narrative about oneself, that locates us in relation to God and Jesus, telling a story about us as those who were turned from God, either explicitly or implicitly, and in darkness and under the power of Satan, but who now turn to God and his Son in view of the promise of forgiveness of sins. In this narrative we surrender the fictitious identities we have constructed for ourselves, or perhaps have had constructed for us, and accept the identity God sees in us and confers upon us. Naturally, this question of identity conferred by God must be related to his adoption of us as his children.

Miroslav Volf, in meditating on questions of identity, writes of what a Christian should be in terms of what he calls a catholic personality. 'A truly catholic personality must be an *evangelical personality* – a personality brought to repentance and shaped by the Gospel and engaged in the transformation of the world.'[2]

---
[1] Lewis 1942: 85.
[2] Volf 1996: 52; emphasis original.

In this way he endorses the idea of an identity that is shaped by something external to ourselves: in his view, the gospel. Volf opens up some searching avenues of enquiry. First, most obviously, the idea of an identity or personality that is so shaped by another or by something external sits very uneasily with the norms of both modernism and postmodernism.[3] We have already recalled Kant's famous words 'Enlightenment is man's emergence from his self-incurred immaturity. Immaturity is the inability to use one's own understanding without the guidance of another.'[4]

Here his sticking point is precisely the influence of an externality. The influential prophet of the postmodern mood, M. Foucault, asks rhetorically, 'Shouldn't one therefore conceive all problems of power in terms of relations of war?'[5] Thus the exercise of influence or shaping by an externality, a species of heteronomy, is analysed fundamentally as a hostile and bellicose act. This does not mean that the postmodern or modern self does not in some respects need others who are external to itself. Thus C. Lasch, among others, contends that one of the marks of current Western culture is that it is both therapeutic[6] and narcissistic.[7] For Lasch one of the features of a narcissistic outlook is the need it has of others to supplement and maintain an otherwise fragile sense of self.[8] In this way a distinction must be drawn about different attitudes to an externality. First there is an externality that one cannot have, so to speak on one's own terms, for one's own purposes, but that shapes oneself. This kind of externality is unacceptable to a modern or postmodern self because it infringes one's autonomy. But second, there is an externality that serves one to maintain one's own self-image. This does not threaten autonomy in this way, and this kind of externality is a resource the narcissist in some respects needs to exploit.

---

[3] Cf. the comments of Oyserman (2004: 13) on the individualistic formations of the modern self.

[4] Kant 1996.

[5] Foucault 1977: 122–123.

[6] Lasch (1979: 7) says, 'The contemporary climate is therapeutic not religious. People today hunger not for personal salvation, let alone for the restoration of an earlier golden age, but for the feeling, the momentary illusion, of personal well-being, health and psychic security.' Such an outlook can create great pressures to redefine salvation and sin.

[7] Ibid. 31–55.

[8] Lasch (ibid. 38) speaks of a recognizable psychological type: 'facile at managing the impressions he gives to others, ravenous for admiration but contemptuous of those he manipulates into providing it; unappeasably hungry for emotional experiences with which to fill an inner void; terrified of aging and death'.

This means Volf underlines how profoundly countercultural Christian repentance is, for the shaping externality of the gospel does undo simple autonomy. Moreover, while the gospel and the repentance that marks it do bring identity, they do not simply maintain a narcissist in his or her narcissism, for the gospel is not a resource to exploit in this way.

Second, Volf obliquely raises the matter of shaping factors other than the gospel. One of his pressing concerns is the construction of identity by social and ethnic factors in the Balkans, and what makes or shapes a person as a Serb or Croat. The challenge this presents is the extent to which other external factors continue to shape us even after conversion, or whether they are allowed to coexist with one's repentant turn to God. Writing of the ethnic factors that shape identity in the Balkans, Volf rightly sees that repentance and the owing of 'ultimate allegiance to God' mean that there is a proper distance for Christians from the cultures in which they live.[9]

Of course, what Volf calls a 'shaping' factor at some point touches on the earlier discussion of idolatry. For, as argued above, while an idol is in one sense shaped by human art and imagination, it also shapes those who worship it. Where the shaping factor of, for example, ethnicity, is so powerful as to repeal or lead one to disregard the laws of God, then it is right to see it as idolatrous.

Third, Volf envisages transformation within the world arising from the way the gospel shapes us. Naturally, this is a much-contested area, for accounts of what are right political and social organizations for Christians differ hugely. The scope here in this chapter is more tightly focused. Volf has raised the matter of corporate and human–human dimensions to the repentant, gospel-shaped life of Christians, and this chapter develops that particularly in relation to the life of the people of God. Does the repentance of the individual impact our corporate life before the return of Jesus Christ, and what shape does repentance give to Christian life together after the individual comes to faith and repents?

To consider these we look first at the impact of being unrepentant on corporate life and then the impact of being repentant.

The unrepentant

We must return to the abundant characterization of the Luke–Acts material. We recall how in his Gospel Luke envisages the Pharisees as

[9] Volf 1996: 51.

beset by greed and prone to idolatry in serving Mammon rather than God, appearances notwithstanding. However, two other characteristics vitally affect their relations with others: self-righteousness and pride, on the one hand, and hypocrisy, on the other.

Self-righteousness and pride

Self-righteousness and pride are laid before the reader in the parable of the Pharisee and the tax collector of Luke 18:9–14. Confidence in one's own righteousness is diagnosed by the authoritative voice of the narrator in verse 9, while Jesus speaks of those who exalt themselves in verse 14. We need to develop these traits in two relational directions, with respect to God and with respect to others.

In relation to God
One of the motifs of Luke's Gospel is reversal. There is the glorious reversal contemplated in Gabriel's words to Mary, which John the Baptist initiates, that people will be returned to God (1:16). Mary's song in 1:46–55 continues this theme of reversal as she rejoices in the humble being lifted up and the hungry fed (1:52–53). But at the same time, another reversal is contemplated, whereby the proud are scattered and the rulers brought down (1:51–52). The reversal contemplated in Luke 18:14 at the conclusion of the parable of the Pharisee and the tax collector is part of this sequence.

Narratively, the humbling of the proud is indeed what happens. This humbling crucially includes humbling in respect of the claim to one's own righteousness. Progressively, the pride and self-righteousness that characterize the Pharisees are exposed and criticized. From a character group who in chapter 5 are plausibly concerned for the honour of God and his prerogatives, they are gradually shown to be motivated by other things than God's glory. They want to find Jesus guilty of something (6:7), they resist God's purposes (7:30), one of their representatives does not treat Jesus with due honour and love (7:36–50), they are unclean and do not love God (11:39–43), are hypocrites (12:1), do not share heaven's values (15), and are lovers of money rather than God (16:14). For the reader, the proud Pharisees are very much cast down, and the sign of how complete this is comes with the resurrection, which in Acts is presented as a sign of power that both vindicates Jesus and condemns his opponents.

This narrative of reversal creates enormous discomfort for the reader faced with Pharisaic self-righteousness and pride. The discomfort lies in the way the values and outlook of the Pharisees are not merely so clearly at odds with Jesus and God (Jesus comes to bring repentance to sinners, 5:32; and God rejoices at the repentant, 15:7, 10), but are so clearly destructive of relationship with God. And, as always, the reader is implicitly challenged as to whether he or she shares these tendencies with the Pharisees.

In relation to others
However, these attitudes are equally corrosive of relationships between one human being and another. The Pharisaic attitude to others is a curious mixture of both contempt and unhealthy need.

We begin with the question of contempt. The connection between contempt for others and self-righteousness is made in the introduction to the parable of the Pharisee and the tax collector (18:9), and is made manifest in the prayer the Pharisee goes on to make. In 18:11 he draws a sharp distinction between himself and others, notably the tax collector. A division exists in his mind. The nature of that division has been put before the reader at several points in the Gospel. The Pharisees feel Jesus should not associate with sinners and tax collectors at numerous points, and the implication is that such people should be excluded from fellowship and acceptance. There are consistent attempts at exclusion by the Pharisees.

We do well to return here to the parable of the lost son and the attitude of the elder brother (15:11–32). It seems strongly that the elder brother's view is that the lost son should be excluded from the father's household (15:28). Given the context of 15:1 into which Jesus speaks this series of parables, it seems that what is at stake is an attitude that God's favour should not rest on others, or on another particular group. These others should be excluded from God's favour. There should be no feast held for their repentance, nor should heaven rejoice at their repentance (note 15:2, which prompts the sequence of parables in 15:4–32).

There is, then, a sense that this group sees a difference between themselves and others of a most entrenched and disturbing variety. Luke 7:30 indicates that the Pharisees in their unrepentance are obstructing the purposes of God, but the self-righteousness that prompts their own unrepentance also causes, it seems, a view that repentant others who are sinners still should be excluded. This sets them clearly as doubly opposed to the ministry of Jesus, which is to bring sinners to repentance. But their opposition seems to spring from two different grounds: they oppose Jesus' ministry for themselves because they view it as unnecessary, it seems. For others they apparently regard it as futile, because the others are, it would seem, so bad and contemptible (note that 18:9 describes the group to whom Jesus speaks as *exouthenountas tous loipous*; 'treating others with contempt').

Along with contempt comes envy. Thus in Acts we find that one of the motivations of the authorities is their envy at the apparent success of the apostles (Acts 5:17). Envy is not necessarily inconsistent with contempt, either for the apostles or for the crowd, but it also readily fits with another need associated with the unrepentant: the good opinion of men. There is, though, a twist to envy in this respect. It is not simply that the authorities in Acts want the good opinion of the Jerusalem crowd; it is that they want, as it were, to monopolize prominence among the crowd. They do not want good opinion shared. Further, as with contempt, envy attempts to block the proclamation of repentance and forgiveness. In that sense envy again readily leads to actions that in effect exclude.

We need at this point to turn to the question of exclusion more generally. Inclusion, of course, has become a central theme in the understanding of some within worldwide Anglicanism, and other denominations too. As such, actions or theological positions that exclude others are deemed fundamentally contrary to the Christian gospel. Hence the former Presiding Bishop of the American Episcopal Church, K. Jefferts-Schori, commented, 'It's what the Church is today. It is inclusive – even those who don't agree with the message, it includes them too.'[10]

I have freely criticized exclusionary practices and outlooks seen in Luke's Gospel. Does this mean the pro-inclusion Episcopal Church is right?

To answer this, the concepts of inclusion and exclusion perhaps need more careful reflection than Jefferts-Schori's sweeping statement. Volf tries to do just this, and key to his understanding of what counts as exclusion is his understanding of otherness: that there is an other. Exclusion occurs when the other is erased. Such erasure can occur through several strategies. Volf points out that some of these strategies of erasure of the other can be rather devious.

Naturally, there is the stark example of ethnic cleansing, very close to the surface in Volf's thought, which is indeed 'a world without the other'.[11] Yet, drawing on Michel Foucault's analysis, Volf notes that even the apparently inclusive modern personality can very easily

---

[10] Sermon preached at the start of the Lambeth Conference, July 2008.
[11] Volf 1996: 57.

become exclusionary. The modern self, suggests Volf, is 'indirectly constituted through the exclusion of the other'.[12] What he has in mind here are the examples Foucault gives of the marginalization of those deemed 'insane' or 'criminal' within modern society. One constitutes oneself in opposition and contrast to the other one defines as 'criminal' or 'insane'. This constitutes oneself as 'sane' or 'law-abiding'. Even the modern self excludes someone, for some reason, and one might add to Foucault's examples one much closer to home: that the modern self, which prides itself on its patterns of inclusion, nevertheless excludes those who do not endorse the ideology of the modern self. Tragically, examples of this abound in contemporary church practice. One thinks of the exclusionary patterns practised towards some evangelical ministers in the Anglican Diocese of New Westminster (including J. I. Packer!), as well as the legal actions of the Episcopal Church against individuals, churches and dioceses within the United States.

Needless to say, much of this has been done, perversely, in the name of inclusion. But Volf aptly comments, 'The very space in which inclusion celebrates its triumph echoes with the mocking laughter of victorious exclusion.'[13]

For Volf exclusion can occur very obviously in cases like ethnic cleansing, but also by assimilation, or by abandonment and indifference.[14] What all three strategies ultimately share is that the other no longer persists as *other*. Their identity as *other* is in some way, or by some strategy, disallowed. In the case of ethnic cleansing the other clearly no longer exists. In the case of assimilation, though, the other no longer exists as other but only as someone like us. In the case of abandonment and indifference one might say the other no longer exists for us, for we refuse to acknowledge him or her as other.

Volf's suggestions about assimilation are very helpful here in considering Jefferts-Schori's proposals for inclusion, that even those who do not agree are included. In important ways they are not permitted to be 'other'. Equally striking, for Jefferts-Schori, faith as well as repentance appear to be irrelevant and misconceived to the appropriation of salvation and inclusion in the people of God. But if one's view is that inclusion works like this, then naturally one will seek to eliminate, assimilate or abandon those who argue for a

---

[12] Ibid. 62.
[13] Ibid. 67.
[14] Ibid. 75.

different version of inclusion. Volf writes, 'The act of exclusion has its own "good reasons".'[15]

It is worth at this point returning to the kind of inclusion that Luke–Acts envisages, and the kind of exclusion that is criticized. There are, of course, kinds of exclusion that are contemplated in Luke–Acts. People are warned about coming judgment and the imperative to repent (Luke 13:1–5). The parable of the great banquet in Luke 14:15–24 envisages that some will be excluded from the banquet, because they will not accept the invitation. The elder son of Luke 15 remains troublingly outside the feast held for his brother's return. But perhaps most striking of all are the descriptions of Jesus to Paul in Acts 26:17–18 as Jesus commissions him for his apostolic ministry. The turning of people from darkness and the realm of Satan to light and the rule of God presupposes precisely that the people to whom Paul is to speak are currently excluded from God's realm of salvation and from the blessing of sins forgiven.

The basis of inclusion in God's realm and in the forgiveness of sins is repentance and faith, and these in turn refer to and depend on God's faithfulness to his promises and his mercy. To that extent the principle of inclusion is grace and mercy. This shapes the nature of the church as a community in the present age, for it is a community of forgiven sinners, who know themselves and others as that. Augustine envisages the church on earth in just this kind of way. He distinguishes schismatics from the life of the church

> inasmuch as it [the church] loves the neighbour, and consequently readily forgives the neighbour's sins, because it prays that forgiveness may be extended to itself by Him who has reconciled us to Himself, doing away with all past things, and calling us to a new life.[16]

It is possible that this basis for inclusion differs very significantly from the kind of inclusion envisaged by the Episcopal Church. Certainly, in the secular account of why people should be 'included', that is, given equal access to goods, services, employment, and so forth, something that bulks very large is a conception of human rights and a politics of equal dignity.

There is a difference of emphasis between inclusion based on a politics of human dignity, a rights-based approach so to speak and

---

[15] Ibid. 96.
[16] *A Treatise on Faith and the Creed* 21 (Schaff 1978, 3: 331).

an approach to inclusion based on grace and mercy. An approach to inclusion based on grace and mercy does not in fact depend on the merit or desert of those who are to be included. Rather, it is a recognition that where God has shown mercy and given repentance, then so should God's people. This was, after all, the basic position adopted by both Peter and the Judaean Christians when faced with the work of God in Samaria and elsewhere in Gentile areas (Acts 11:17–18). They did not resist the inclusion of those whom God had included by his regenerative work.

This, though, is not the same as saying that one must therefore adopt the Jefferts-Schori approach to inclusion. For Peter and Paul, both of whom obediently follow through the principles of God's inclusion, alike call for repentance as the means by which forgiveness of sins and transfer from darkness and the realm of Satan occur. To that extent there is a grace-based principle of inclusion appropriated through repentance, and this is not the same as a principle of inclusion that refuses to distinguish between those who do and do not have faith and repentance, which is the position apparently advocated by Jefferts-Schori.

This gives rise to two related topics, judgmentalism and church discipline. One can indeed see criticism of judgmentalism in passages like Luke 6:37–42, and the fact that this set of warnings can be seen by Jesus as involving hypocrisy suggests that the Pharisees may be associated with such warnings. The Pharisees, moreover, are clearly concerned for matters of discipline and order among the people of God, as their intervention in some of the Sabbath scenes shows.

There is, nevertheless, an inappropriateness to the judgmentalism and 'church discipline' activities of the Pharisees. This is no doubt related to their basic attitude to others, which is one of contempt and superiority. Such superiority is perfectly intelligible if one trusts in oneself for righteousness as the Pharisees are said to do, and regard others as sinners who are not righteous and who should in some sense be excluded. Judgmentalism in its negative sense is then a predictable outcome of unrepentance and the attitudes that unrepentance inculcates towards oneself and others.

However, the attitude of contempt to others is not the only attitude to others associated with the unrepentant by Luke. Luke 14:7–11 recounts Jesus' observation that the guests at the Pharisee's meal sought places of honour. This has been anticipated in his criticism in Luke 11:43 of the urge to seek honour from men. The Pharisees are associated with a need for the good opinion of others. This need is also apparently present in Acts 5:17 with the authorities who are envious of the apostles.

Two observations arise with respect to this need. First, Volf observes that part of the exclusionary approach is to seek to be a hegemonic centre of attention.[17] The need to be hegemonic tends to rule out proper welcome and reception of the other.[18] Yet the need to be hegemonic summarizes very aptly the authorities' reaction of Acts 4 and 5. It also, naturally, provides a challenge to Christian ministers, or seminary professors, who may likewise feel the hegemonic imperative, and who may respond with envy when this is not met. The obvious New Testament counterexample is Paul and his joyful attitude to the proclamation of the gospel by others (Phil. 1:15–18), even when some of that proclamation was from mixed motives.

Second, there is something clearly troubling about where God fits in for those who have this hegemonic need. The stark question is whether someone with this need does not tend to displace God, 'in front of God, against God', as Tertullian put it.[19]

Overall, this pattern of contempt and need displays a strange and wrong treatment of others who are fellow-creatures. For, on the one hand, contempt lords it over others. Yet, curiously on the other hand, needing favour from others risks wronging them as well. Initially, this sounds counterintuitive: How do I wrong someone by needing their approval? We might envisage this as happening in two ways. First, to need their approval in the way we have been discussing risks overvaluing others. This is dubious in several ways. Seeking someone's approval and treating it as a matter of extreme importance can, of course, be apt in some situations, but to seek such approval as a primary thing risks flattering the person or group whose approval is sought. To that extent, the seeking of approval can be a net spread for our neighbours and open the door to vanity for them. Further, it is unfair to require from a fellow-creature the kind of approval that properly comes from God. It places an unfair burden on their wisdom and charity. Finally, and, most obviously, the pattern of seeking approval from others first may be a way of enlisting them as satellites for one's own position. One is in effect seeking to have them treat one

---

[17] Volf 1996: 70.

[18] Naturally, it is here possible to connect the hegemonic attitude with the culture of narcissism that Lasch describes.

[19] Tertullian, *On Idolatry* 4 (Roberts and Donaldson 1980, 3: 63).

as hegemonically central. I earlier related this trait to Lasch's description of the narcissistic cultural personality.[20]

Naturally, one reason why we must reflect so carefully on the approval seeking that Luke recounts in his Gospel with especial reference to the Pharisees is that their example shows us how these behaviours may flourish in what are apparently religious and God-fearing contexts. We know too the pressures on a church leader to seek inappropriate approval from those to whom he ministers, and equally the pressures that a congregation may feel to offer inappropriate approval to a manipulative and Pharisaical church leader. Naturally, 'Pharisaical' in this sense may be more a matter of practice and behaviour than theoretical orthodoxy.

Hypocrisy

We must stay for the present with the dangers of religiosity. This brings us to another great relational vice that Jesus discerns in the character group the Pharisees: hypocrisy. As we approach this, we should bear three things in mind.

First, Luke's Gospel does not envisage hypocrisy as being a uniquely Pharisaical sin, something regarding which we could safely say, 'I am in no danger of this sin.' The warnings in the Gospel are to those whom Jesus is teaching. Moreover, we know in any case that other attitudes Jesus criticizes can be found outside the Pharisees as well as among them. Further, one aspect of the incident featuring Ananias and Sapphira in Acts 5 is their hypocrisy in pretending to be more generous than they were. Hypocrisy has been alive and well, it seems, among the people of God from the earliest times.

My second preliminary point is this. We may well feel that hypocrisy is a vice that flourishes particularly among the religious. The inference may be for some, therefore, that this is a vice that does not flourish among atheists or the irreligious. It would, though, be in order to recall my earlier line of argument about idolatry. There the point was made that even contemporary atheism can be analysed as religious in one sense. Something is treated as of ultimate importance, so that it stands before God against God. Thus we should not necessarily think atheism and similar ideological forms will be hypocrisy-free. In fact, a moment's reflection tells us that hypocrisy can indeed flourish in atheist conditions. Historically, there is naturally the example of

---

[20] Lasch (1979: 38) outlines contempt and need (although not in those terms) with respect to the narcissistic cultural personality.

Stalin's Soviet Union with a theoretical commitment to democracy and proper judicial process, and whose practice fell horribly short at key points, such as the trials of the 1930s under Felix Dzerzhinsky and others.[21] Closer to home comes my own country's theoretical commitment to freedom of speech and belief, but where orthodox bishops are liable to be warned by the police for having suggested sexual orientations can change, even though it was not at the time an offence to make such a suggestion.

Third, we do well to note the importance that is attached to the question of hypocrisy. One frequently heard objection to Christian faith in the UK is the hypocrisy of those inside the church. Very different actions can be construed as examples of this general vice. Thus a pastor's perceived failure to deal consistently with different requests for baptism will be seen as hypocrisy along with the church hierarchy's failure to deal with abuse by clergy. Naturally, some of this outrage at hypocrisy within the church may serve a wider purpose, rationalizing rejection of the claims of Jesus Christ, and one may feel that there is something hypocritical about raising the issue of hypocrisy in this way. Nevertheless, the force with which Jesus criticizes as he does means we should not casually dismiss how hypocrisy may flourish.

We begin with an extended description of hypocrisy from Thomas Watson, from his *Doctrine of Repentance*:

> Hypocrisy is the counterfeiting of sanctity. The hypocrite or stage-player has gone a step beyond the moralist and dressed himself in the garb of religion. He pretends to a form of godliness but denies the power (2 Tim 3:5). The hypocrite is a saint in jest. He makes a magnificent show, like an ape clothed in ermine or purple. The hypocrite is like a house with a beautiful facade, but every room within is dark. He is a rotten post fairly gilded. Under his mask of profession, he hides his plague-sores. The hypocrite is against painting faces, but he paints holiness. He is seemingly good, so that he may be really bad. In Samuel's mantle he plays the devil. Therefore the same word in the original signifies to use hypocrisy and to be profane. The hypocrite seems to have his eyes nailed to heaven, but his heart is full of impure lustings. He lives in secret sin against his conscience. He can be as his company is and act both the dove and the vulture. He hears the word, but is *all ear*.

---

[21] See Conquest 1968.

He is for temple-devotion, where others may look upon him and admire him, but he neglects family and closet prayer. Indeed, if prayer does not make a man leave sin, sin will make him leave prayer. The hypocrite feigns humility, but it is that he may rise in the world. He is a pretender to faith, but he makes use of it rather for a cloak than a shield. He carries his Bible under his arm, but not in his heart. His whole religion is a demure lie.[22]

This is a devastating description. A principal theme is deception, notably the deception of the outside world, our fellow men and women. Such deception and manipulation clearly fit with the attitudes we have just been examining where our fellow human beings are treated wrongly. However, in using the terms of deceit and manipulation the question inevitably arises as to what extent a hypocrite intends to deceive. Is it all a cynical, knowing act? Or is the feigned humility something that deceives the hypocrite too?

This takes us to the question of self-deception. For some this is an unreal category: one cannot deceive oneself, so the argument tends to run, for the following reasons. First, deception is an intentional act. Second, one is immediately aware of one's intentions and beliefs. Third, since one is so aware, one is aware that one's intentions are to deceive, and hence one does not deceive oneself. Language such as 'You're fooling yourself' is a striking turn of phrase but not much more.

However, this invites a number of responses. Biblically, there is language about self-deception, and its attendant evils. James 1 and 1 John 1:8–9 both provide striking examples. But it may be argued these are merely striking turns of phrase. Yet this involves bringing to these texts the assumption that self-deception cannot occur. Is this justifiable?

A key point in the argument outlined above is self-transparency. This refers to the idea that one's intentions and beliefs are in fact known and clear to oneself. In one sense there is much truth in this, for many of one's intentions and beliefs do seem clear and transparent. On reflection, though, it seems difficult to claim one knows all one's intentions and beliefs exhaustively. Without wanting to endorse too uncritically the psychoanalytic movement of men like Sigmund Freud, there is no little plausibility to the idea that not all one's beliefs and intentions are completely transparent to oneself. On occasion there

---

[22] Watson 1668: 68; emphasis original.

are springs of action of which we seem to be unaware: there are times when we surprise ourselves quite genuinely, even when much of our experience of ourselves is regular and predictable.

Of course, there is biblical material that suggests that our intellectual and volitional processes are not intact and transparent after the fall. Thus Romans 1:18–19 depicts a humanity whose thinking has become futile, and at least lacks the awareness that its claims to be wise in fact constitute folly. Ephesians 4:17 likewise indicates a human condition in which thought and will are alike corrupted as they are enmeshed in sin. Moreover, following the more systematic argument I have been laying out, humanity's false faith in God, which is universal post-fall, will also tend to create a false consciousness about ourselves, for the knowledge of God and self are co-relative.

More analytically, G. Bahnsen contends strongly that the idea of self-deception is not a contradiction in terms but one that is quite recognizable.[23] His example is of a mother whose schoolboy son has a reputation as a sneak thief. She vehemently denies it, and has ready explanations of circumstances where things have gone missing. As far as one can tell she is quite sincere as she makes these defences. On the other hand, there are tell-tale signs that she is not entirely at ease with the picture she paints of her son. For at home she is careful not to leave loose change around and always makes sure her handbag is safely stowed away. Bahnsen's point is that though this may be an extreme example, it remains recognizable, and one has to deal both with the mother's sincerity and the way she has induced herself to believe what she does.

The pastoral implications of this are considerable. There is an obvious difference between explaining sin, salvation and repentance to a cynical, genuinely self-knowing, hypocrite and someone who is self-deceived. The self-knowing hypocrite at least will know the truth of what is said, even if this prompts no external public admission. But the case of someone self-deceived is different, for charges of inner sin are likely to be perceived as mere insult and ill-nature, while one remains convinced of one's own righteousness. As Bahnsen's example indicates, undeceiving the self-deceived about their state is not likely to meet with an easy hearing. In fact, Jesus' example indicates that it may very well meet with considerable animosity, for in John 7:7 he relates the hatred of the world for him to his testimony. One might add that teaching the truth of who God is will obliquely yet ultimately

---

[23] Bahnsen 1995: 30.

raise the issue of hypocrisy for a human being, since the knowledge of God and the knowledge of ourselves are so intertwined.

This relates to aspects of presuppositional apologetics. In classic presuppositional apologetics, one works from the basis that any non-Christian ideological outlook or world view will ultimately be inconsistent and a manifestation of human rebellion against God.[24] Aspects of it may be drawn from some secular philosophy but in so far as the world view works it will at some point rely on borrowed Christian intellectual capital, to use the kind of phrase associated with Cornelius Van Til. Thus in classical presuppositional apologetics part of the task is to identify the ideological disjunctions between a worldly philosophy, which finally will not work, and borrowed Christian intellectual capital that is the part of an unbeliever's world view, which does work. It is the disjunction where a world view is vulnerable to criticism and refutation.

However, hypocrisy also features a disjunction, largely between outward presentation and inner reality. Exposing hypocrisy in the way Jesus does is to bring this disjunction into view, with striking images such as the hidden tomb that makes people unclean unbeknown to themselves.

Two objections may arise at this stage. First, Jesus knows the secrets of people's hearts while we do not. Why, then, should we presume to make these points? Second, do we really need to raise these issues of hypocrisy?

In answer to the first, we may say that Jesus warns us emphatically of the dangers of hypocrisy, and in its relation to unrepentance one can see that this is a dangerous spiritual condition indeed. We do well therefore to warn people, ourselves included, of this spiritual reef. Moreover, while we do not know the secrets of the heart in individual cases in the way Jesus did, Jesus has, by expressing certain instances of hypocrisy, nevertheless given us some searching questions on the hypocrisy issue to put to ourselves and others. Thus it may well be profitable to dwell on the question of internal obedience in the heart to commands about adultery, murder, theft, pride and covetousness.

[24] Thus C. Van Til, such a decisively influential advocate of presuppositional apologetics, elegantly comments (1971: 20) that when a non-Christian makes the claim of rationality for his system, 'he cannot make it good'. Since non-Christian systems are the product of human rebellion, immense care must be taken over the terms of contact between Christian and non-Christian. Van Til comments, 'To look for a point of contact with the unbeliever in the unbeliever's notions of himself and his world is to encourage him in his wicked rebellion and to establish him in his self-frustration' (ibid. 17).

This suggests a response to the second question: whether it is worth raising the issue of hypocrisy. No doubt in some cases it will not be in the first instance. Quite conceivably the woman of Luke 7 was quite well aware of her sin, and of its gravity, and thus, in that respect at any rate, was not painting holiness, to borrow Watson's phrasing. On the other hand, there may be cases where it is exactly the issue of hypocrisy and the self-deceiving self-righteousness that goes with it that serve to kill response to the call to repent. It seems in just such cases that Jesus does expose hypocrisy.

We should add to this discussion of hypocrisy some consideration of its systematic place. So far we have been contending that repentance locates us relationally as idolaters, people who have false faith about God our creator, and thus have a false consciousness of ourselves as creatures. We repent among other things of making ourselves other than who we truly are as creatures. Sadly, hypocrisy fits into this picture of false consciousness. Just as the archetypal sin of Genesis 3 involves our accepting lies about God, and so lying about him ourselves, asserting mendaciously that he is not truthful and he is not good, so in hypocrisy we in effect lie about ourselves to ourselves and others, characteristically asserting we are good and denying the inner reality. In this, hypocrisy is part of our construction of false identity, one that we establish for ourselves. It is readily the counterpart and corollary of our rebellion against God. Repentance necessarily stands against hypocrisy, for in repentance we accept not our own publicity about ourselves but God's description and analysis of who we are.

However, while repentance stands as an antithesis of hypocrisy, we must also note how hypocrisy can pervert or distort repentance. Thus within church history there are patterns whereby ongoing repentance in terms of clear public penitential practices can be turned into a meritorious dealing with sin, especially post-conversion sin. As such, they can undermine the principle of salvation by grace alone. Likewise, the understanding of repentance or penitence as a sacrament can undermine genuine repentance. In both cases the risk is that what is public remains at odds with what is internal, and therefore is a species of hypocrisy.

The repentant

At this point we must turn to two major characteristics associated with the repentant and their impact on the treatment of others among the people of God: humility and forgiveness.

Humility

We have already noted how humility is a theme running through Luke's Gospel. Mary's song envisages the humble being lifted up, and Jesus' parable of the guests at the banquet likewise envisages those starting in low positions being elevated by the gracious invitation of the host of the banquet. We have also already seen how Jesus through his teaching does, in the eyes of the reader, bring down the mighty from their seats, revealing how the Pharisee and tax collector in fact stand on level spiritual ground as sinners. We should add that the reader does indeed see the humble being lifted up in the same process. Thus the woman of Luke 7 is implicitly endorsed and approved as one who loves Jesus, Zacchaeus is the object of Jesus' favour as he dines with him, while the repentant criminal is promised paradise alongside Jesus.

Clearly, repentance encourages humility both towards God and towards others. As regards God, pride is clearly precluded because repentance includes an acknowledgment and confession that one has been turned away from God towards that which is not God, that one has wronged him and that one turns to him not in reliance on one's own merit or desert, but in reliance of his promise of mercy. It is an acknowledgment and claiming of his goodness, not ours. In terms of positive characteristics, repentance presupposes and affirms God as merciful and sovereign. It presupposes God's mercy because that is what the repentant plead, as the tax collector does in Jesus' parable of Luke 18. It presupposes God's sovereignty because it accepts that one has broken God's laws. Necessarily, then, any boasting will be in God, not in oneself.

However, just as repentance brings humility in recognizing God's sovereign and merciful action towards oneself, so it can become a springboard for attitude to others in whom God has similarly been working in sovereign mercy. We should recall here the criticism of the Pharisees in Luke 7:30 that in refusing John's baptism of repentance for themselves, they had rejected God's purpose for themselves. But equally in Acts, for example chapter 5, the obstruction of the apostolic message of repentance and forgiveness in Jesus' name is a rejection of God's purpose for others. In both cases God's purpose is being rejected. The corollary of this is that one who is serious about accepting and obeying God's purpose will repent, and endorse and support enthusiastically the authentic Christian repentance of others. This, of course, is precisely what the Jerusalem church does in Acts

11:18 when it has grasped and understood Peter's report about what has happened in Caesarea. Humility before God involves accepting and endorsing what he has sovereignly done in others, no matter how unexpected or, in some sense, how unwelcome.

Such humility before God's action to others is the antithesis of the exclusionary attitudes we see surfacing from time to time in Luke–Acts.

Of course, such exclusionary attitudes spring very readily from a sense of superiority. It is, of course, just such attitudes of superiority that mark the conduct of the Pharisees towards Levi, of Simon towards the woman, of the crowd towards Zacchaeus and quite plausibly of the elder son towards the lost son. It is, moreover, on the basis of such attitudes of superiority that exclusion has been over time so frequently practised towards disfavoured groups, whether that exclusion follows the pattern of obliteration or abandonment and indifference.

However, the self-understanding of the repentant as those who have been turned from away from God in idolatry but who have been graciously turned to him and his Son necessarily tends to eliminate such attitudes of superiority. For a realization that even if one is a Pharisee one stands in need of forgiveness of sins just as much as a tax collector creates an equality. I can no longer call for exclusion on the ground of sin, because that would equally exclude me.

This provides a framework within which we can see a resolution of the patterns of conflict that we have seen in the feast type-scenes in Luke's Gospel. There we saw two relational triangles: the triangles of hospitality and conflict. This created a pattern that looked like this, taking the parable of the lost son of Luke 15 as an example:

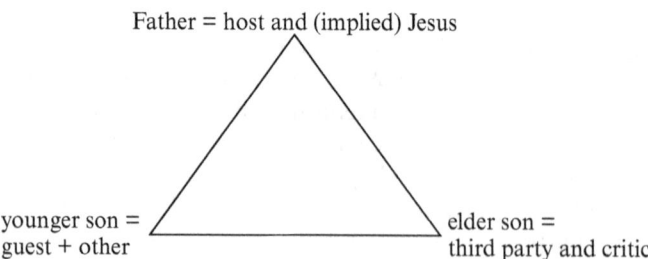

As we have seen, part of the problem that the elder son presents is that he does not share the values of his father in the parable. This, indeed, is one of the themes of Luke 15: that heaven rejoices at the repentant, while those to whom Jesus tells the parables do not rejoice. They do not adopt heaven's outlook and purposes. Rather, they seem deeply estranged from the values and joys of heaven. Similarly, we have seen how the call to repentance in Acts 3:19 arises from a depiction of people who are deeply and tragically opposed to God as life is to death.

However, in repentance we accept God's valuation and estimate of ourselves: that we are sinfully and idolatrously opposed to him. To that extent it is the beginning at least of a participation in the purposes and values of God. The repentant are starting to imitate God by, among other things, accepting his determination of them. But, naturally, for a person who accepts God's determination of himself or herself and accepts again the reality of relation with God as creature with Creator, there is an impetus to accept God's determination of others as well. For if I share God's values about myself as his creature, then by extension I should share his values about my fellows who are also creatures of his.

In repentance, then, there is a movement to a relational triangle like this:

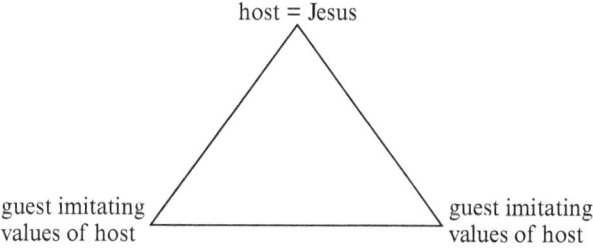

Four observations are pertinent at this point. First, guests at the banquet God holds for the repentant behave in a godly way as they welcome those whom the host welcomes. This is godliness in the sense of Godlikeness.

Second, the guests have a common identity as those on whom the host has had mercy. This is both an individual and a corporate identity and like many corporate identities can benefit from reiteration. Thus the practice of including in morning and evening prayer (in the Anglican Reformation liturgies) prayers of repentance and forgiveness is helpful not least for reaffirming part of the basis on which fellowship takes place, that we are a commonwealth of redeemed sinners.

This coheres closely with the understanding of the life of the church on earth that Augustine outlined.[25] For Augustine, the life of the church on earth is to be marked by bonds of fraternal charity. He writes when expounding 1 John 2:12–17, 'How shall we not be in darkness? If we love the brethren [our fellow-Christians]. How is it proved that we love the brotherhood? By this, that we do not rend unity, that we hold fast charity.'[26]

Yet the distinctive mark of this fraternal charity is its humility. Humility in this Augustinian exegesis has a sharp focus: it is not just the refusal to think highly of oneself but includes the acknowledgment that we do not have our own righteousness but rely on the propitiatory work of Christ. He writes of 1 John 2:1–2:

> Brethren, Jesus Christ the righteous, even Him have we for our advocate with the Father; 'He,' even He, 'is the propitiation for our sins.' This whoso hath held fast, hath made no heresy; this whoso hath held fast, hath made no schism. For whence came schisms? When men say, 'we' are righteous, when men say, 'we' sanctify the unclean, 'we' justify the ungodly; 'we' ask, 'we' obtain.[27]

Pride in Augustine's view wars against this kind of charity.[28] It also has a sharp focus corresponding to the specific humility Augustine has outlined: a denial of this dependence on Christ. Consideration of Pharisaic self-righteousness takes one along similar lines: that self-righteousness wars against the kind of fellowship of forgiven and repentant sinners Luke envisages.

Third, the attitude of welcoming fellow-repentants may often be intertwined with one's own repentance. For, obviously, one of the ways in which we may deny our own creatureliness is by our treatment of others. At its sharpest it may be that the idolatry of which I have to repent is the value I have put on social prominence, acceptance and the good opinions of others.

Fourth, this relational network, in which guests imitate the values of the host and welcome as he does, is indeed an inclusive community. Nevertheless, it is worth at this point returning to the ways in which Volf envisages exclusion as occurring. He mentions exclusion as

---

[25] In large part in response to the Donatist schism.
[26] Augustine, *Homilies on the Epistle of John* 2.3 (Schaff and Wace 1983, 7: 471).
[27] Ibid. 1.8 (464–465).
[28] Ibid. 1.6 (464).

elimination, assimilation, abandonment and indifference.[29] Clearly, the welcome of a fellow-repentant does not constitute either obliteration or abandonment or indifference. But it is natural to ask whether this pattern of welcome is not in fact a strategy of assimilation.

Here another of Volf's considerations about otherness may help us. He suggests that relationship and identity involve not just connectedness, but also separation. In our personal identities we are '*both* separate *and* connected, *both* distinct *and* related'.[30] Without separation and distinction there will indeed be assimilation in a way that denies the other as other.

However, it may well be that the most obvious ways in which this assimilation occurs will be in bipartite, two-party, relationships. Thus, to take a familiar example of assimilation, one ethnic group may assimilate another by suppressing its language and distinctive customs. That which separates or marks off the people group is thus suppressed, and nothing is left for them but that which they share with the majority group.

But in the case we have been examining the relationship is, so to speak, tripartite. One guest accepts and welcomes another for Christ's sake, accepting Christ's determination of that other's identity. There is to this extent 'space' built into the network of relationships, because the relationships between guests are not the only relationships in question. To risk overextending the analogy, a guest does not quarrel with his host's guest list. The existence of relationship between one's fellow-guests and one's host brings space and distance into our relations with our fellow-guests. Because there is the guest–host dimension to the relations others have, which is not controlled by me, this triangular pattern of relations resists the assimilation of one guest by another. In fact, the truly determinative relationships are not between guest and guest, but between guest and host. The guest–host relationship is not itself an assimilative relationship, although it is one of authority and asymmetry, but it is the guest–host relationship that is to govern guest–guest relationships.

This threefold pattern of relation is, naturally, found elsewhere in Christian living. Marriages, parent–child, master–servant relations are all characterized by obligations and privileges that arise because of our relations with Christ, not simply because of the merits, or demerits, of the person with whom we are in relationship.

[29] Volf 1996: 75.
[30] Ibid. 66; emphases original.

Forgiveness and justice

We must now pass from one entailment of repentance to another, the obligation to show mercy. Again this is a case of godlikeness. Thus in Luke 6:36 Jesus enjoins his disciples, 'Be merciful, just as your Father is merciful' (NRSV). Naturally, one might add that a Christian has in particular received God's mercy. In a similar vein Luke 11:4 relates forgiveness of others to divine forgiveness. Most strikingly, Luke 17:3–4 spells out an obligation to forgive a fellow-disciple who is repentant.

Such a position obviously excites strong reactions. Thus Solomon Schimmel, writing from a Jewish perspective, understandably focuses on the nature of the obligation to forgive.[31] His particular concern is the interaction of the principle of forgiveness with other principles of justice and social responsibility. He raises the case of the social responsibility of a woman who in forgiveness will not testify against a rapist, thereby ensuring he will receive an unduly light sentence and be back in the community earlier than, in all justice, he should have been.

We should note, though, several features about the obligation to forgive. First, this is set in the community of the people of God. It deals with relationship in that dimension. There are other dimensions in which we relate to one another, so that, clearly, in the early church, patron and client or master and slave might very well be in the same local church community. It is not clear that these relationships that exist in other dimensions are eradicated merely by being in the same local church. Rather, such relationships may coexist alongside the relationship of one disciple with another, even though that relationship may no doubt mould and influence those other relationships. Philemon, of course, points in just this direction.

Second, the implication of verse 4 is very much that the sin in question lies between the two disciples and perhaps not more generally.[32]

Third, the obligation to forgive arises from repentance. This does meet one of Schimmel's understandably insistent objections to some versions of forgiveness: that it is to be offered to the unrepentant. However, the obligation to forgive at this point bears a close affinity to the forgiveness God offers. Luke–Acts consistently relates

---

[31] Schimmel 2002: 8.
[32] Cf. the preferred reading of Matt. 18:15, that a brother sins 'against you'; although some authorities lack that qualification.

forgiveness to repentance, while continuing liability to judgment is related to lack of repentance. This is the clear implication of Luke 13:1–5 and Acts 17:30–31. In this way the obligation to forgive another does not correspond to what Schimmel describes as 'radical forgiveness', the principle that one must forgive the unrepentant. There may, of course, be other reasons why one might forgive a wrong in some sense: the need to preserve one's own peace of mind, to be able to move on emotionally, psychologically, and so forth. But forgiveness as a means to personal well-being is not the issue in these Lukan passages.

One might add that the idea of obligation to forgive is rightly applied to God as well as to his children. For God is bound to forgive in the sense that he has promised to forgive the repentant and has commissioned his ministers to proclaim this promise. This promise that binds God to forgive does not, naturally, undermine his free grace and sovereignty, for he is not obliged to make the promise. It is a promise freely made. For us, as disciples, the obligation arises differently, in that for the sake of, and under the law of, a third party, we are bound to treat one another in this way. The significance of this third-party presence in our networks of horizontal disciple–disciple relationship is that our obedience in relation to one another obviously bears on our relationship with God.

In all this there are strong elements of a call to imitate God's actions towards one another. Mutual forgiveness based on repentance is part of godlikeness. In that way what may mark out an authentic Christian community is not so much that it stresses that one ought to be like God. After all, this principle is known in Second Temple Judaism and elsewhere. Even in pagan mythology the gods are sometimes seen as exemplars. The issue is not so much whether human beings should model themselves on God, but on differences over what the God is like on whom they model themselves. The true and living God forgives the repentant who turn to his Son.

It is natural to ask what a local church will look like that seriously attempts to practise these principles of mutual repentance and forgiveness. Most obviously there will be a continuity between corporate life and the understanding of the way individuals are saved and forgiven by God. Our understanding of ourselves in salvation is shaped by repentance and the forgiveness of sins, and this understanding extends to one another. It is the basis on which we welcome one another and rejoice at one another's repentance and faith. It should accordingly contour our expectations of one another in corporate life together. If I understand my fellow-disciples as repentant sinners who have turned to God and his Son, then it seems inconsistent to expect them to behave other than as forgiven sinners. My expectations are likely to be tempered and forbearance fostered. Moreover, at its best a group of disciples practising Luke 17 will have a transparency to their relationships. Our understanding of one another as repentant sinners tends to alleviate the pressure to dissimulate and pretend one is holier than one is. This relates, of course, to the themes of false faith and false consciousness. Repentance is an acceptance of the truth about oneself and a rejection of false consciousness and false identity. That rejection of false consciousness should properly extend to our corporate life together.

However, Jesus' commands of Luke 17 obviously prompt the fear that repentance will be abused: that we will be wronged, someone will repent, or say they repent, and then persist in the wrongs they have been doing. Here one has to remember the way that John the Baptist in Luke 3 and the Council of Jerusalem of Acts 15 alike see repentance as bearing fruit in terms of concrete conduct. In the case of actions of which one says one repents, the most obvious fruit is ceasing to do the action in question. There are, of course, clear analogies with the principle that faith is fruit-bearing in terms of personal conduct. Changed conduct is not the root of either faith or repentance, but in practical terms lack of change prompts very serious questions. We may well conclude that struggle with a besetting sin and frequent failure with respect to that sin do not inevitably mean that faith is false and repentance spurious, but the question must still be asked. At this stage, though, we note that the focus has shifted from the fear of wrong being suffered from a persistent and ostensibly repentant offender to the possibility that that offender is not repentant over that sin at all.

One final issue needs to be mentioned with respect to forgiveness and repentance. Such an obligation to forgive is highly countercultural in a rights-based society. Western culture in its American, British and, I think, Australian, forms is heavily focused on rights, and often has a litigious quality to it. There is a strong urge to have oneself and one's rights vindicated, and this is related to the perceived correctness of asserting oneself in a public or group context. Of course, we feel this most intensely precisely when we have been genuinely wronged, and there is a real matter of vindication at stake. What the obligation to forgive, however, involves is a preparedness and a duty to forego entitlement and what one deserves. This again relates to the attitude of humility that should characterize the repentant. For sometimes the urge to vindicate or assert oneself no doubt is related to pride and a contemptuous attitude to others, and not asserting a right that one has can be experienced or construed as a humiliation. Nevertheless, there is a discontinuity between seeing a vertical relationship with God as one shaped by his mercy and grace rather than our own desert and entitlement, on the one hand, and a horizontal attitude to fellow-believers, which insists on relations shaped by strict desert and entitlement: the parable of the unforgiving servant of Matthew 18:23–35 turns on just such a discontinuity. And clearly Jesus is stressing that repentance must shape both our relation with God and our relation with one another.

Concluding reflections

We should move now to some concluding reflections on the question of repentance.

Some sins of omission

The prayer of penitence in the *Book of Common Prayer*'s service of morning prayer speaks not only of sins of commission but also of omission. I am very conscious of such sins of omission in the course of this study, and I think it is important to highlight them so that we are aware of the tentative and incomplete nature of some of the discussion we have been having, even though as regards biblical data I think it both legitimate and important to try to construe repentance in Luke–Acts as a coherent whole.

Clearly, there are texts which I have not dealt with, whole catenae of them. In the New Testament corpus we would of course want to integrate Mark and Matthew with Luke, noting especially that Jesus in Mark and Matthew is described as coming with a message of repentance at the start of his ministry (Matt. 4:17; Mark 1:15). With John, we would want to note the drought of explicit calls to repentance, while noting the significance of John 12:37–43. This passage details the unbelief with which some greet Jesus, and relates this to a fulfilment of Isaiah 6:10 and the hardening of hearts that prevents a turning to God. Tellingly, the lack of open profession by some is related by John to a love of glory from men rather than a glory from God (John 12:43), and this ties neatly with Luke's emphasis on love of prominence and reputation.

Within the Pauline corpus we would, among other things, want to examine 2 Corinthians 7:9–10, because this deals with true and false repentance and what repentance should produce.

However, we should especially note the impact of repentance passages in Hebrews. Two issues are prominent here. First, the possibility that repentance is not always to be found: this argument arises from the example of Esau in Hebrews 12:17. This is certainly explicable within the framework of repentance as a gift, which we have seen in Acts, so that Esau is not granted authentic repentance. Nevertheless, this idea acquires a harder edge here, because Esau seems fruitlessly to seek repentance. If nothing else, this imparts a further dimension to the call to repentance: that response is urgent and should be immediate.

Second, passages such as Hebrews 6:4–12 raise the question of a repentance without perseverance. From this, some might even suggest such a thing as a genuine but temporary faith and a genuine but temporary repentance. This affects very significantly what true faith or true repentance look like, and raises the pastoral question of how one treats someone who has apparent faith or apparent repentance.

It is worth adding here that the position is complicated because real regret over one's actions and character clearly can arise outside the framework of regeneration and salvation. There is a distinction between the promptings of conscience under common grace on the one hand and the promptings of conscience under regeneration on the other. But both may prompt amendment of life and to that extent for some time be indistinguishable at that level. Where over time one would expect a difference would be on the questions of hope and joy, for the promptings of conscience under regeneration are also related to the belief in the promise of forgiveness of sins.

Some personal lessons

I would like to finish with some more personal reflections about the material that we have covered.

To begin with, it seems exceptionally important to me to see repentance as something that helps locate us relationally. Repentance involves questions of identity. It establishes who I truly am: a creature who has been turned away from relationship with his Creator and who is turned back to his Creator through the work of Jesus the Son. Since my relation with my Creator is co-relative, it also establishes who my Creator is, justly angry at his creatures' rebellion but offering forgiveness in his mercy. The implication of this is that a Christianity void of repentance will have weak or simply wrong accounts of anthropology and human identity, and accordingly have a tendency to develop erroneous accounts of who God is.

Second, while all of us, I imagine, rightly see repentance as involving sorrow for sin, regret and mourning at its presence in us, Luke–Acts offers something further in authentic Christian repentance and that is the note of joy, associated with the festal themes of Luke 5 – 19. This joy is, on reflection, utterly to be expected. For repentance is constantly joined to the forgiveness of sins, and this must be an occasion for joy. Further, since repentance is a mark of God's gracious gift to an individual, and an indication of his divine purpose being worked out, we rejoice too at God's purpose being achieved. Joy in repentance we may see in three aspects: the joy of heaven at the repentant; the joy of repentants themselves, like Levi and Zacchaeus; and the joy of believers at seeing others too given the gift of repentance by God and so included in God's forgiven people.

Third, I find it enormously instructive to see the way Acts has linked repentance to repenting of idolatry. A consideration of idolatry and what it involves reminds us of the depths within a person to which repentance goes. It is no mere moralism concerned with externalities. Ministerially, I now find myself thinking of the preaching of repentance as having a significant apologetic dimension: I must try to analyse and understand the forms and kinds of idolatries in which my unbelieving friends and neighbours have been enmeshed.

Bibliography

Ames, W. (1997 [3rd Latin edn 1629]), *The Marrow of Theology*, ed. J. D. Eusden, Grand Rapids: Baker.
Aristotle (1972 [335 BC]), *Poetics* in *Ancient Literary Criticism*, ed. and tr. D. A. Russell and M. Winterbottom, Oxford: Clarendon.
Arnold, C. E. (1992), *Power and Magic: The Concept of Power in Ephesians*, Grand Rapids: Baker.
Bahnsen, G. (1995), 'The Crucial Concept of Self-Deception in Presuppositional Apologetics', *WTJ* 57: 1–31.
Barnett, P. W. (1997), *The Second Epistle to the Corinthians*, Grand Rapids: Eerdmans.
Barrett, C. K. (1973), *The Second Epistle to the Corinthians*, London: A & C Black.
Barth, K. (1958 [1955]), *Church Dogmatics*, IV.2: *The Doctrine of Reconciliation*, ed. G. W. Bromiley and T. F. Torrance, tr. G. W. Bromiley, Edinburgh: T&T Clark.
——— (1960 [1948]), *Church Dogmatics*, III.2: *The Doctrine of Creation*, ed. G. W. Bromiley and T. F. Torrance, tr. K. Knight et al., Edinburgh: T&T Clark.
——— (1975 [1932]), *Church Dogmatics*, I.1: *The Doctrine of the Word of God*, ed. G. W. Bromiley and T. F. Torrance, tr. G. W. Bromiley, Edinburgh: T&T Clark.
Bayer, H. F. (1998), 'The Preaching of Peter in Acts', in I. H. Marshall and D. G. Peterson (eds.), *Witness to the Gospel: The Theology of Acts*, Grand Rapids: Eerdmans, 257–274.
Beale, G. K. (2008), *We Become What We Worship: A Biblical Theology of Idolatry*, Nottingham: Apollos.
Beeke, J. R. (2008), 'Appropriating Salvation: The Spirit, Faith and Assurance, and Repentance (3.1–3, 6–10)', in D. W. Hall and P. A. Lillback (eds.), *A Theological Guide to Calvin's Institutes: Essays and Analysis*, Phillipsburg: P&R, 270–300.
Berger, P. (1979), *The Heretical Imperative: Contemporary Possibilities of Religious Affirmation*, New York: Doubleday.

Berkhof, L. (1939), *Systematic Theology*, repr. 1974, Edinburgh: Banner of Truth.
Berlin, I. (1958), 'Two Concepts of Liberty', repr. 1998, in M. Hardy and R. Hausheer (eds.), *The Proper Study of Mankind*, London: Pimlico, 191–242.
Bock, D. L. (1994), *Luke*, Downers Grove: InterVarsity Press; Leicester: Inter-Varsity Press.
――― (1996), *Luke*, 2 vols., Grand Rapids: Baker.
Bray, G. L. (ed.) (2015 [1547, 1571]), *The Books of Homilies: A Critical Edition*, London: James Clark.
Buber, M. (1953), *The Eclipse of God: Studies in the Relation Between Religion and Philosophy*, London: Gollancz.
――― (1958), *I and Thou*, 2nd edn, tr. R. G. Smith, Edinburgh: T&T Clark.
Burnett, F. W. (1993), 'Characterization and Reader Construction of Character in the Gospels', *Semeia* 63: 3–28.
Calvin, J. (1960 [1559]), *Institutes of the Christian Religion*, ed. J. T. McNeill, tr. F. L. Battles, 2 vols., Philadelphia: Westminster.
――― (1965 [1552]), *The Acts of the Apostles* Vol. 1, tr. J. W. Fraser, and W. J. G. McDonald, Edinburgh: St Andrews Press.
――― (1966 [1554]), *The Acts of the Apostles* Vol. 2, tr. J. W. Fraser and W. J. G. McDonald, Edinburgh: St Andrews Press.
――― (1972a [1555]), *A Harmony of the Gospels Matthew, Mark and Luke* Vol. 1, tr. A. W. Morrison, Edinburgh: St Andrews Press.
――― (1972b [1555]), *A Harmony of the Gospels Matthew, Mark and Luke* Vol. 2, tr. T. H. L. Parker, Edinburgh: St Andrews Press.
―――(1972c [1555]), *A Harmony of the Gospels Matthew, Mark and Luke* Vol. 3, tr. A. W. Morrison, Edinburgh: St Andrews Press.
Campbell, W. K., and R. F. Baumeister (2004), 'Is Loving the Self Necessary for Loving Another? An Examination of Identity and Intimacy', in M. B. Brewer and M. Hewstone (eds.), *Self and Social Identity*, Oxford: Blackwell, 78–98.
Carlston, C. E. (1975), 'Reminiscence and Redaction in Luke 15:11–32', *JBL* 94.3: 368–390.
Carson, D. A. (2004), 'The Vindication of Imputation: On Fields of Discourse and Semantic Fields', in M. Husbands and D. J. Trier (eds.), *Justification: What's at Stake in the Current Debates*, Downers Grove: InterVarsity Press; Leicester: Apollos, 46–78.
Carson, D. A., P. T. O'Brien and M. A. Seifrid (2004), *Justification and Variegated Nomism*, 2 vols., Grand Rapids: Baker Academic.

Catchpole, D. R. (1977), 'The Son of Man's Search for Faith (Luke 18:8b)', *NovT* 19.2: 82–104.
Chalke, S., and A. Mann (2003), *The Lost Message of Jesus*, Grand Rapids: Zondervan.
Chesterton, G. K. (1909), *Orthodoxy*, 2nd edn, London: John Lane.
Colquhoun, J. (1826), *A View of Evangelical Repentance from the Sacred Records*, republished 1965 as *Repentance*, Edinburgh: Banner of Truth.
Conquest, R. (1968), *The Great Terror*, Oxford: Oxford University Press.
Cousar, C. B. (1986), 'Luke 5:29–35', *Int* 40.1: 58–63.
Crocker, J., and D. M. Quin (2004), 'Psychological Consequences of Devalued Identities', in M. B. Brewer and M. Hewstone (eds.), *Self and Social Identity*, Oxford: Blackwell, 124–142.
Darr, J. A. (1998), *Herod the Fox: Audience Criticism and Lukan Characterization*, JSNTSup 163, Sheffield: Sheffield Academic Press.
Domeris, W. R. (1986), 'Biblical Perspectives on Forgiveness', *JTSA* 54.1: 48–50.
Donahue, J. (2001), 'Look in Lost and Found', *America* 185.6: 30.
Downing, G. F. (1992), 'The Ambiguity of "the Pharisee and the Tax Collector" (Luke 18:9–14), in the Greco-Roman World', *CBQ* 54.1: 80–99.
Duke, P. D. (1995), 'A Festive Repentance', *CC* 112.29: 957.
Fee, G. D. (1987), *The First Epistle to the Corinthians*, Grand Rapids: Eerdmans.
Forbes, G. (1999), 'Repentance and Conflict in the Parable of the Lost Son (Luke 15:11–32)', *JETS* 42.2: 211–229.
Forster, E. M. (1927), *Aspects of the Novel*, London: Edward Arnold.
Foucault, M. (1977), 'Truth and Power', repr. 1980 in C. Gordon (ed.), *Power/Knowledge*, New York: Pantheon, 109–133.
France, R. T. (1985), *Matthew*, TNTC, Leicester: Inter-Varsity Press.
Giddens, A. (1991), *Modernity and Self-Identity: Self and Society in the Late Modern Age*, Cambridge: Polity.
Glasscock, E. (1997), *Matthew: Moody Gospel Commentary*, Chicago: Moody.
Gowler, D. B. (1989), 'Characterisation in Luke: A Socio-Narratological Approach', *BTB* 19: 54–62.
—— (1991), *Host, Guest, Enemy and Friend: Portraits of the Pharisees in Luke and Acts*, New York: Peter Lang.
Green, C. M. (2005), *The Word of His Grace: A Guide to Teaching and Preaching from Acts*, Leicester: Inter-Varsity Press.

Green, J. (2002), 'Doing Repentance: The Formation of Disciples in the Acts of the Apostles', *Ex Auditu* 18: 1–23.

Greene, G. (2011 [1938]), *On Brighton Rock*, London: Vintage.

Griffith Thomas, W. H. (1920), *The Catholic Faith: A Manual of Instruction for Members of the Church of England*, rev. W. G. Johnson 1952, London: Church Book Room.

——— (1978 [1930]), *The Principles of Theology: An Introduction to the Thirty-Nine Articles*, 6th edn rev., London: Vine.

Guinness, O. (1992), 'More Victimised Than Thou', in O. Guinness and J. Seel (eds.), *No God but God: Breaking with the Idols of Our Age*, Chicago: Moody, 81–93.

Hamm, D. (1998), 'Prodigal Father, Two Lost Sons', *America* 179.5: 22.

Hansen, G. W. (1998), 'The Preaching and Defence of Paul', in I. H. Marshall and D. G. Peterson (eds.), *Witness to the Gospel: The Theology of Acts*, Grand Rapids: Eerdmans, 295–324.

Haraguchi, T. (2004), 'A Call for Repentance to the Whole Israel – a Rhetorical Study of Acts 3: 12–26', *AJT* 18.2: 267–282.

Harrington, D. (2007), 'Repentance and Forgiveness', *America* 196.9: 39.

Harris, H. A. (1998), 'Should We Say That Personhood Is Relational?', *SJT* 51: 214–234.

Harris, M. J. (1976), '2 Corinthians', in F. Gaebelein (ed.), *EBC*, vol. 10, Grand Rapids: Zondervan, 301–406.

Heil, J. P. (1999), *The Meal Scenes in Luke–Acts: An Audience Oriented Approach*, Atlanta: SBL.

Helm, P. (1986), *The Beginnings: Word and Spirit in Conversion*, Edinburgh: Banner of Truth.

Jodock, D. (1995), 'After Tasting Failure', *CC* 112.8: 265.

Kant, I. (1996 [1784]), 'An Answer to the Question: "What Is Enlightenment?"', in M. J. Gregor (ed. and tr.), *Practical Philosophy*, Cambridge: Cambridge University Press, 17–22.

Kavanaugh, J. F. (1995), 'Lost and Found', *America* 172.9: 39.

Keyes, R. (1992), 'The Idol Factory', in O. Guinness and J. Seel (eds.), *No God but God: Breaking with the Idols of Our Age*, Chicago: Moody, 29–48.

Kierkegaard, S. (1956 [1846]), *Purity of Heart Is to Will One Thing: Spiritual Preparation for the Office of Confession*, tr. D. Steere, New York: Harper & Row.

Lambert, D. (2006), 'The Role and Function of Repentance in Luke–Acts', *NovT* 48.1: 88–90.

BIBLIOGRAPHY

Lane, A. N. S. (1979), 'Calvin's Doctrine of Assurance', *VE* 11: 32–54.

Lasch, C. (1979), *The Culture of Narcissism: American Life in an Age of Diminishing Expectations*, New York: W. W. Norton.

Lewis, C. S. (1942), *The Screwtape Letters: Letters from a Senior to a Junior Devil*, repr. 1964, London: Collins.

——— (1945), *That Hideous Strength*, repr. 1996, New York: Scribner.

Liefeld, W. L. (1984), 'Luke', in F. E. Gaebelein (ed.), *EBC*, vol. 8, Grand Rapids: Zondervan, 797–1059.

Lyman, J. R. (1993), *Christology and Cosmology: Models of Divine Activity in Origen, Eusebius and Athanasius*, OTM, Oxford: Clarendon.

Lyotard, J.-F. (1984), *The Postmodern Condition: A Report on Knowledge*, tr. G. Bennington and B. Massumi, Minneapolis: University of Minnesota Press.

McLaren, B. (2006), *The Secret Message of Jesus*, New York: Thomas Nelson.

McLaren, B., and T. Campolo (2003), *Adventures in Missing the Point*, Grand Rapids: Zondervan.

Malina, B., and J. Neyrey (1991), 'Conflict in Luke–Acts: Labelling and Deviance Theory', in J. Neyrey (ed.), *The Social World of Luke–Acts: Models for Interpretation*, Peabody: Hendrickson, 97–122.

Marshall, I. H. (1980), *Acts*, TNTC, Leicester: Inter-Varsity Press.

——— (1988a), *Luke – Historian and Theologian*, 3rd edn, Carlisle: Paternoster.

——— (1998b), 'How Does One Write on the Theology of Acts?', in I. H. Marshall and D. G. Peterson (eds.), *Witness to the Gospel: The Theology of Acts*, Grand Rapids: Eerdmans, 3–16.

Meadors, E. P. (2006), *Idolatry and the Hardening of the Heart*, New York: T&T Clark.

Millar, J. G. (1998), *Now Choose Life: Theology and Ethics in Deuteronomy*, Leicester: Apollos.

Morris, L. (1974), *The Gospel According to St Luke: An Introduction and Commentary*, TNTC, Leicester: Inter-Varsity Press.

——— (1992), *The Gospel According to Matthew*, Grand Rapids: Eerdmans; Leicester: Apollos.

Murray, J. (1955), *Redemption: Accomplished and Applied*, repr. 1961, Edinburgh: Banner of Truth.

Naugle, D. K. (2002), *Worldview: The History of a Concept*, Grand Rapids: Eerdmans.

Nave, G. D. (2002), *The Role and Function of Repentance in Luke–Acts*, Atlanta: SBL.

Nolland, J. (1989), *Luke 1–9:20*, Word: Dallas.

Oliphint, K. S. (2006), *Reasons {for Faith}: Philosophy in the Service of Theology*, Phillipsburg: P&R.

——— (2008), 'A Primal and Simple Knowledge (1.1–5)', in D. W. Hall and P. A. Lillback (eds.), *A Theological Guide to Calvin's Institutes: Essays and Analysis*, Phillipsburg: P&R, 16–43.

Oyserman, D. (2004), 'Self-Concept and Identity', in M. B. Brewer and M. Hewstone (eds.), *Self and Social Identity*, Oxford: Blackwell, 5–24.

Phillips, T. E. (1998), 'Subtlety as a Literary Technique in Luke's Characterization of Jews and Christians', in R. P. Thompson and T. E. Phillips (eds.), *Literary Studies in Luke–Acts: Essays in Honor of Joseph B. Tyson*, Macon: Mercer University Press, 311–326.

Pictet, B. (1834 [1696]), *Christian Theology*, tr. F. Reyroux, London: Seeley and Burnside.

Porter, S. E. (2007), 'Penitence and Repentance in the Epistles', in M. J. Boda and G. Smith (eds.), *Repentance in Christian Theology*, Wilmington: Michael Glazier, 127–150.

Purves, A. (2007), 'A Confessing Faith: Assent and Penitence in the Reformation Traditions of Luther, Calvin and Bucer', in M. J. Boda and G. Smith (eds.), *Repentance in Christian Theology*, Wilmington: Michael Glazier, 251–266.

Ramachandra, V. (1996), *Gods That Fail: Modern Idolatry and Christian Mission*, Carlisle: Paternoster.

Roberts, A., and J. Donaldson (eds.) (1980), *Ante-Nicene Fathers*, various translators, repr., 10 vols., Grand Rapids: Eerdmans.

Roth, S. J. (1997), *The Blind, the Lame, and the Poor: Character Types in Luke–Acts*, JSNTSup 144, Sheffield: Sheffield Academic Press.

Ryle, J. C. (1878), 'Repentance', in *Old Paths: Being Plain Statements on Some of the Weightier Matters of Christianity*, repr. 1972, London: James Clarke, 403–435.

Schaff, P. (ed.) (1978), *Nicene and Post-Nicene Fathers, First Series*, vol. 3, Grand Rapids: Eerdmans.

Schaff, P., and H. Wace (eds.) (1979), *Nicene and Post-Nicene Fathers, Second Series*, repr., vol. 10, Grand Rapids: Eerdmans.

——— (1983), *Nicene and Post-Nicene Fathers, Second Series*, repr., vol. 7, Grand Rapids: Eerdmans.

——— (1991), *Nicene and Post-Nicene Fathers, Second Series*, repr., vol. 4, Grand Rapids: Eerdmans.

Schimmel, S. (2002), *Wounds not Healed by Time: The Power of Repentance and Forgiveness*, Oxford: Oxford University Press.

Scholes, R., and R. Kellogg (1966), *The Nature of Narrative*, Oxford: Oxford University Press.

Sire, J. (2004), *Naming the Elephant: Worldview as a Concept*, Downers Grove: InterVarsity Press.

Sorabji, R. (2006), *Self: Ancient and Modern Insights About Individuality, Life and Death*, Oxford: Clarendon.

Squires, J. (1998), 'The Plan of God in the Acts of the Apostles', in I. H. Marshall and D. G. Peterson (eds.), *Witness to the Gospel: The Theology of Acts*, Grand Rapids: Eerdmans, 19–39.

Stenschke, C. (1998), 'The Need for Salvation', in I. H. Marshall and D. G. Peterson (eds.), *Witness to the Gospel: The Theology of Acts*, Grand Rapids: Eerdmans, 125–144.

Stirner, M. (1907 [1844]), *The Ego and His Own*, tr. S. T. Byington, New York: Ben Tucker.

Stott, J. (1990), *The Message of Acts*, Leicester: Inter-Varsity Press.

Talbert, C. H. (1998), 'Conversion in the Acts of the Apostles: Ancient Auditors', in R. P. Thompson and T. E. Phillips (eds.), *Literary Studies in Luke–Acts: Essays in Honor of Joseph B. Tyson*, Macon: Mercer University Press, 141–153.

Tannehill, R. C. (1986), *The Narrative Unity of Luke–Acts: A Literary Interpretation*, vol. 1: *The Gospel According to Luke*, Philadelphia: Fortress.

——— (1994), *The Narrative Unity of Luke–Acts: A Literary Interpretation*, vol. 2: *The Acts of the Apostles*, Minneapolis: Fortress.

Thielicke, H. (1966), *A Little Exercise for Young Theologians*, Carlisle: Paternoster.

Thompson, R. P. (1998), 'Believers and Religious Leaders in Jerusalem: Contrasting Portraits of Jews in Acts 1–7', in R. P. Thompson and T. E. Phillips (eds.), *Literary Studies in Luke–Acts: Essays in Honor of Joseph B. Tyson*, Macon: Mercer University Press, 327–344.

Turretin, F. (1992–7 [1674]), *Institutes of Elenctic Theology*, ed. J. T. Dennison, tr. G. M. Giger, 3 vols., Phillipsburg: P&R.

Tyson, J. B. (1978), 'The Opposition to Jesus in the Gospel of Luke', *PRS* 5.3: 144–150.

——— (1984), 'The Jewish Public in Luke–Acts', *NTS* 30: 574–583.

Ussher, J. (1645), *A Body of Divinity: Being the Sum and Sub-*

stance of the Christian Religion, repr. 2007, Watford: Church Society.

VanDrunen, D. (2006), 'To Obey Is Better Than Sacrifice: A Defense of the Active Obedience of Christ in the Light of Recent Criticism', in G. L. W. Johnson and G. P. Waters (eds.), *By Faith Alone: Answering the Challenges to the Doctrine of Justification*, Wheaton: Crossway, 127–146.

Van Til, C. (1971), 'My Credo', in E. R. Geehan (ed.), *Jerusalem and Athens: Critical Discussions on the Philosophy and Apologetics of Cornelius Van Til*, Nutley, N.J.: P&R, 1–21.

Volf, M. (1996), *Exclusion and Embrace: A Theological Exploration of Identity, Otherness and Reconciliation*, Nashville: Abingdon.

Watson, T. (1668), *The Doctrine of Repentance*, repr. 1987, Edinburgh: Banner of Truth.

Wells, D. F. (2005), *Above All Earthly Pow'rs: Christ in a Postmodern World*, Grand Rapids: Eerdmans; Leicester: Inter-Varsity Press.

Westhelle, V. (2006), 'Exposing Zacchaeus', *CC* 123.22: 27–31.

Widdicombe, P. (1994), *The Fatherhood of God from Origen to Athanasius*, Oxford: Clarendon.

Wilkin, R. N. (1985), 'Repentance as a Condition for Salvation in the New Testament', ThD diss., Dallas Theological Seminary.

Witherington, B. (1998), *The Acts of the Apostles: A Socio-Rhetorical Commentary*, Grand Rapids: Eerdmans.

Wright, N. T. (1997), *What St Paul Really Said*, Oxford: Lion.

Young, F. W. (1977), 'Luke 13:1–9', *Int* 31.1: 59–63.

Zizioulas, J. (1985), *Being as Communion: Studies in Personhood and the Church*, Crestwood: St Vladimir's Seminary Press.

——— (2006), *Communion and Otherness: Further Studies in Personhood and the Church*, London: T&T Clark.

Index of authors

Ambrose, 49
Ames, W., 114
Aristotle, 73
Arnold, C. E., 94
Athanasius, 96
Augustine, 138, 150

Bahnsen, G., 144
Barth, K., 79, 80, 91, 108, 121–126
Bayer, H. F., 40, 43
Beale, G., 76, 82, 87
Beeke, J. R., 106, 107, 108, 109, 113
Berger, P., 87
Berlin, I., 96
Bock, D. L., 15, 29, 63, 66
Bray, G. L., 68, 71, 114, 115
Buber, M., 77, 78, 79, 82, 90

Calvin, J., 2, 3, 48, 49, 52, 58–59, 61, 63, 65, 69, 81, 88, 94, 99, 105–113, 119, 123–125, 126, 127
Campbell, W. K., 91
Carson, D. A., 37, 111
Chalke, S., 118–121, 123
Chesterton, G. K., 96

Darr, J. A., 4, 5, 6
Donahue, J., 26

Fee, G. D., 89
Feuerbach, L., 75
Forbes, G., 27
Forster, E. M., 5
Foucault, M., 132, 136–137

Gowler, D. B., 5–6, 14
Green, C. M., 40–41
Green, G., 1
Green, J., 61, 84
Gregory of Nazianzus, 95–96
Griffith Thomas, W. H., 111

Hansen, G. W., 53
Harrington, D., 26
Harris, H. A., 81
Heil, J. P., 12, 18, 19, 21, 23, 24, 25, 26, 27, 30, 32, 38, 51
Helm, P., 127–128, 129

Jefferts-Schori, K., 136, 137, 139

Kant, I., 79, 86, 132
Karpman, S., 12
Keller, T., 99
Keyes, R., 82, 93
Kierkegaard, S., 91
Kuyper, A., 85

Lane, A. N. S., 107, 109, 113
Lasch, C., 132, 141
Lewis, C. S., 100, 131
Liefeld, W. L., 63, 65, 66
Lyotard, J. F., 95

McLaren, B., 116–118, 120, 121
Malina, B., 13, 24
Marshall, I. H., 42, 52, 53, 64, 65
Meadors, E. P., 76, 87
Miller, J. G., 7
Montefiore, C. G., 26

Morris, L., 18, 26, 63, 66
Murray, J., 115–116, 118, 121, 126, 127, 131

Nave, G. D., 15
Nietzsche, F., 78, 81, 89
Nolland, J., 22

Oyserman, D., 73, 91

Porter, S., 3

Ramachandra, V., 88, 89, 95
Roth, S. J., 17
Russell, B., 100

Schimmel, S., 152–153
Shakespeare, W., 69
Shepherd, N., 111
Sire, J., 85
Stenschke, C., 60, 67
Stirner, M., 81, 89
Stott, J., 55, 70, 71, 74, 100

Talbert, C. H., 54, 58
Tannehill, R. C., 4, 5, 11, 12, 16, 21, 30, 31, 32, 40, 41, 50–51, 56, 57, 64–65
Tertullian, Q. S. F., 74, 75, 84, 89, 140
Thielicke, H., 77–78
Tolkien, J. R. R., 43
Turretin, F., 83, 106

Van Till, C., 145
VanDrunen, D., 111
Volf, M., 131, 132, 133, 136–138, 140, 150–151

Watson, T., 142–143, 146
Wells, D. F., 78
Witherington, B., 43, 44, 48, 52–53, 54, 55, 58, 61
Wright, N. T., 2

Zizioulas, J., 81

Index of Scripture references

Note: Primary discussions of a passage are indicated in **bold**.

OLD TESTAMENT

Genesis
1-2 *82*
1:26-30 *77*
2:17 *82, 84*
3 *82, 146*
3:4 *82*
12:3 *44, 84*
15:6 *111*
17:18 *8*

Exodus
3:13-15 *8*
5 *103*
6:2-9 *7*
6:5 *7*
19:5 *8*
34:6-7 *7*

Deuteronomy
30:1 *7*
30:1-3 *8*
30:1-10 *7*
30:2 *7*
30:3 *7*

2 Kings
17:7-23 *84*

Ezra
9:5-15 *7*

Nehemiah
9:6-37 *7*

Psalms
2 *47, 61*
115:8 *88*
130:4 *112*

Isaiah
6:1-13 *87*
6:9-10 *62*
6:10 *155*
40:3-5 *14*
42:6-7 *61*
42:17-20 *87*
43:8-10 *87*
44 *75*
44:18-19 *87*
44:21 *82*

Jeremiah
10 *75, 76*
10:10 *76*
10:11 *76*
10:12 *75, 76*

Ezekiel
22 *88*
23 *88*

Daniel
9 *8, 72, 76*
9:3 *19*
9:3-19 *7, 71*
9:4 *7*
9:7 *7*
9:7-10 *7*
9:10 *7*
9:11-12 *7*
9:12 *7*
9:14 *73*
9:15-19 *7*

Hosea
2:5 *88*

NEW TESTAMENT

Matthew
3:7 *14*
4:17 *155*
11:25 *96*
18:15 *152*
18:23-35 *155*

Mark
1:5 *14*
1:15 *155*

Luke
1:1-4 *4, 14, 33*
1:6 *18, 62, 63, 65*
1:16 *3, 11, 14, 134*
1:17 *18*
1:20 *63*
1:46-55 *134*
1:51-52 *134*
1:52 *39*
1:52-53 *134*
1:67 *63*
1:68-69 *63*
1:68-79 *63*
1:69 *63*

Luke (*cont.*)
1:77 *14, 64*
1:77–79 *61*
1:78–79 *61*
2:25 *18*, *62*
2:25–38 *65*
2:28–32 *64*
2:30–32 *61*
3 *154*
3:1–17 *2*
3:3 *3, 11, 14*
3:7 *14, 18, 24*
3:7–9 *14*
3:8 *14, 15*
3:9 *14*
3:11 *15*
3:12 *15*
3:12–13 *17*
3:13 *15, 29*
3:14 *15*
5 *30, 134*
5 – 19 *157*
5:1–12 *16*
5:1–32 *17*
5:6 *16*
5:8 *16, 17, 29*
5:10 *16*
5:10–11 *16*
5:11 *16, 18*
5:12–14 *17*
5:12–16 *20*
5:17–26 *17, 20*
5:27–32 **16–19**, *31*
5:28 *16, 18*
5:29 *16*
5:29–30 *17*
5:30 *17, 21*
5:31–32 *17, 18*
5:32 *11, 12, 16, 20, 22, 26, 32, 63, 66, 135*
6:1–5 *19*
6:2 *19*
6:7 *19, 134*
6:8 *6*
6:11 *19*
6:36 *152*
6:37–42 *139*
6:39–42 *20*
6:41 *20*
7 *16, 126, 129, 146, 147*
7:29–30 *20*
7:30 *20, 23, 24, 26, 50, 134, 135, 147*
7:34 *20*
7:36 *19, 20*
7:36–50 *13*, **19–22**, *112, 134*
7:37 *21*
7:41 *21*
7:43 *20*
7:44 *21*
7:44–46 *21*
7:45 *21*
7:46 *21*
7:47 *21*
9:46–47 *36*
10:13–15 *22*
10:25–29 *22*
10:27 *29, 84*
10:29–37 *22*
11 *37*
11:14 *152*
11:29–32 *22*
11:30 *22*
11:35 *22*
11:37–52 *13–14*
11:37–54 **22–24**
11:38 *23, 37*
11:39 *23, 24, 30*
11:39–43 *134*
11:39–52 *37*
11:42 *24, 29, 30, 37*
11:42–44 *29*
11:43 *24, 25, 84, 139*
11:44 *24, 37*
11:53–54 *14, 24*
12:1 *20, 134*
12:1–3 *24, 31, 37*
13:1–5 *25, 26, 31, 35, 138, 153*
13:3 *11, 28*
13:5 *11, 28*
13:7–9 *29*
14:1 *12, 25*
14:1–6 *25*
14:1–24 **25**
14:3 *25*
14:5 *25*
14:7 *25*
14:7–11 *25, 139*
14:11 *25*
14:15 *25*
14:15–24 *25, 138*
14:16–24 *12, 28*
15 **25–28**, *30, 31, 67, 134, 138, 148*
15:1 *135*
15:2 *25, 27, 51, 135*
15:4–32 *135*
15:5–7 *26*
15:6 *26, 28*
15:7 *11, 26, 51, 63, 66, 135*
15:9 *26, 28*
15:9–10 *26*
15:10 *11, 26, 51, 135*
15:11–32 *13, 72, 135*
15:17 *72*
15:18–19 *72*
15:20 *27*
15:21 *28*
15:23 *27*
15:24 *72*
15:28 *26, 27, 135*
15:29 *27*
15:32 *14, 26, 27*
16 *37*
16:1–9 *28*
16:9–13 *84*
16:13 *15, 29*
16:14 *29, 37, 84, 134*

INDEX OF SCRIPTURE REFERENCES

16:15 *29*
16:19–31 *15*
16:31 *68*
17 *154*
17:3–4 *152*
17:4 *152*
18 *36, 91, 121, 147*
18:9 *6, 63, 134, 135, 136*
18:9–14 *6, 29, 33, 39, 110, 134*
18:11 *135*
18:11–12 *6, 29*
18:14 *6, 29, 134*
18:18 *30*
18:18–25 *30*
18:21 *30*
18:22 *30, 31*
18:23 *30*
19:1 *30*
19:1–10 *13,* ***28–32****, 30, 39*
19:3 *30, 32*
19:5 *32*
19:6 *31, 32*
19:7 *30, 31, 32, 51*
19:9 *31*
19:9–10 *64*
19:10 *12, 31, 32*
20:27 *39*
22:24–27 *36*
23 *121*
23:11 *16*
23:32 *32*
23:36 *16, 32*
23:39 *32*
23:39–43 ***32–33***
23:42 *33*
23:43 *33*
23:47 *16*
23:50 *62*
24 *38*
24:46 *33*
24:46–48 ***33***

24:47 *2, 3, 11, 35, 39, 65*

John
7:7 *144*
8:34 *61*
12:31 *62*
12:37–43 *155*
12:43 *155*
13:27 *62*
16:11 *62*
19:15 *47*
20:28 *115*

Acts
1 – 7 *38, 39*
1:7–8 *39*
1:8 *48*
1:22 *39*
2 *73*
2 – 7 *70*
2:5 *40*
2:11 *40*
2:14 *40*
2:14–36 *40*
2:14–40 *40, 42*
2:19 *44, 45*
2:19–26 *44*
2:22 *40*
2:22–23 *44*
2:24 *40*
2:25–26 *44*
2:26 *45*
2:29 *40*
2:32 *39, 40*
2:35 *41*
2:35–36 *41*
2:36 *40, 44*
2:36a *42*
2:36b *43*
2:37 *40, 41, 118*
2:37–42 ***39–43***
2:38 *2, 39, 40, 41, 47, 52, 54, 118*
2:38–40 *40*

3:6 *46*
3:10 *46*
3:12 *43*
3:13 *43*
3:13–15 *43*
3:14 *43*
3:14–15 *61, 85*
3:15 *39, 43, 44*
3:16 *46*
3:17 *45, 54*
3:17–26 ***43–45***
3:19 *47, 52, 54, 111, 149*
3:19–26 *113*
3:25–26 *46, 111*
3:26 *48, 51, 84, 113*
4 *45, 140*
4 – 5 *50*
4:1–2 *45*
4:2 *45*
4:7 *46*
4:8–12 *45, 46*
4:10 *39, 46*
4:12 *46, 65*
4:16 *46*
4:18 *46*
4:24–30 *45, 47*
4:25–27 *61*
4:25–28 *32*
4:27–28 *47*
5 *45, 140, 141, 147*
5:1–11 *49*
5:12 *48*
5:12–16 *48*
5:13 *48*
5:14 *48*
5:15–16 *48*
5:16 *48*
5:17 *46, 48, 50, 136, 140*
5:21 *45*
5:24 *47*
5:28 *46, 47*
5:29–32 ***45–48***
5:30 *47*

171

Acts (*cont.*)
5:30–31 *54*
5:31 *47, 52, 113*
5:31–32 *39*
5:31b *118*
6:14 *57*
8 *62*
8:5 *48*
8:10–11 *49*
8:13 *48*
8:18 *49*
8:20–24 **48–49**
8:22 *49*
9:10–16 *50*
9:14 *50*
9:15 *50*
10 *16*
10 – 11 *50*
10:2 *52, 62, 64*
10:22 *62, 64*
10:34 *52*
10:34–48 *50*
10:42–48 *52*
10:43 *52, 54, 64*
10:44 *50*
10:44–46 *51*
10:45–46 *51*
10:47 *51*
11:3 *51, 64*
11:15–18 **50–52**
11:17 *51*
11:17–18 *139*
11:18 *51, 52, 64, 113, 148*
12:2 *52*
13:4–12 *54*
13:6 *57*
13:16 *52*
13:38 *54*
13:38–39 *65*
13:45 *50*
13:47 *38, 61*
13:50 *52*
14:2 *52*
14:4 *52*

14:5–18 **52–53**
14:8–18 *54*
14:10 *52*
14:11–13 *55*
14:11–18 *57*
14:14 *52*
14:15 *2, 3, 53, 120*
14:16 *53*
15 *53, 154*
15:3 *53*
15:29 *53*
16:16–18 *57*
17 *85*
17:16 *53, 55, 70*
17:17 *70*
17:22 *55*
17:22–31 *52*, **53–56**
17:23 *54*
17:24 *55*
17:25 *55*
17:29 *54, 74, 75, 93*
17:29–30 *54*
17:30 *2, 3, 8, 55, 63, 124*
17:30–31 *54, 153*
17:31 *55*
17:32 *56*
19:10 *58*
19:14–16 *57*
19:19–20 *57*
19:23–41 *57, 86*
19:26 *71*
19:27 *57*
19:34 *57, 86*
20:17–24 **58–59**
20:19–20 *58*
20:21 *2, 58, 60, 66, 69, 120*
20:25 *58*
20:26 *57*
26:12–23 **59–62**
26:16–18 *59*
26:17–18 *54, 138*
26:17–20 *3*

26:18 *2, 3, 60, 90, 120*
26:19 *59*
26:20 *2, 3*
26:20–23 *59*
26:21 *60*
28 *38*
28:25–28 *62*
28:26–28 **62**
28:28 *38*

Romans
1:18–19 *144*
1:18–20 *93*
1:18–23 *53*
1:18–32 *53, 71, 83, 87*
1:21 *53, 75*
1:21–22 *75*
1:21–23 *83*
1:24 *53, 83*
1:32 *83*
2:4 *58*
4:1–3 *111*
4:6–8 *111*
4:7 *45*
4:7–9 *45*
4:9 *45*
6:6 *109*
7 *123*

1 Corinthians
8:4 *74*
10:19–20 *61*
10:20–21 *89*
15:16 *4*

2 Corinthians
7:9–10 *156*

Ephesians
2:1 *122*
2:5 *122*
2:12 *84*
4:17 *144*

INDEX OF SCRIPTURE REFERENCES

5:5 *74*
5:14 *121, 122*

Philippians
1:15–18 *140*

Colossians
1:13–14 *62*

1 Thessalonians
1:9 *53*

1:9–10 *53, 55, 58, 71, 106, 118*

2 Timothy
3:5 *142*

Hebrews
6:4–12 *156*
12:17 *156*

James
1 *143*

1 John
1:1–3 *93*
1:8–9 *143*
2:1–2 *150*
2:12–17 *150*

Revelation
4:11 *75, 79*

Titles in this series:

1 *Possessed by God*, David Peterson
2 *God's Unfaithful Wife*, Raymond C. Ortlund Jr
3 *Jesus and the Logic of History*, Paul W. Barnett
4 *Hear, My Son*, Daniel J. Estes
5 *Original Sin*, Henri Blocher
6 *Now Choose Life*, J. Gary Millar
7 *Neither Poverty Nor Riches*, Craig L. Blomberg
8 *Slave of Christ*, Murray J. Harris
9 *Christ, Our Righteousness*, Mark A. Seifrid
10 *Five Festal Garments*, Barry G. Webb
12 *Now My Eyes Have Seen You*, Robert S. Fyall
13 *Thanksgiving*, David W. Pao
14 *From Every People and Nation*, J. Daniel Hays
15 *Dominion and Dynasty*, Stephen G. Dempster
16 *Hearing God's Words*, Peter Adam
17 *The Temple and the Church's Mission*, G. K. Beale
18 *The Cross from a Distance*, Peter G. Bolt
19 *Contagious Holiness*, Craig L. Blomberg
20 *Shepherds After My Own Heart*, Timothy S. Laniak
21 *A Clear and Present Word*, Mark D. Thompson
22 *Adopted into God's Family*, Trevor J. Burke
23 *Sealed with an Oath*, Paul R. Williamson
24 *Father, Son and Spirit*, Andreas J. Köstenberger and Scott R. Swain
25 *God the Peacemaker*, Graham A. Cole
26 *A Gracious and Compassionate God*, Daniel C. Timmer
27 *The Acts of the Risen Lord Jesus*, Alan J. Thompson
28 *The God Who Makes Himself Known*, W. Ross Blackburn
29 *A Mouth Full of Fire*, Andrew G. Shead
30 *The God Who Became Human*, Graham A. Cole
31 *Paul and the Law*, Brian S. Rosner
32 *With the Clouds of Heaven*, James M. Hamilton Jr
33 *Covenant and Commandment*, Bradley G. Green
34 *Bound for the Promised Land*, Oren R. Martin
35 *'Return to Me'*, Mark J. Boda
36 *Identity and Idolatry*, Richard Lints

37 *Who Shall Ascend the Mountain of the Lord?*, L. Michael Morales
38 *Calling on the Name of the Lord*, J. Gary Millar
40 *The Book of Isaiah and God's Kingdom*, Andrew T. Abernethy
41 *Unceasing Kindness*, Peter H. W. Lau and Gregory Goswell
42 *Preaching in the New Testament*, Jonathan I. Griffiths
43 *God's Mediators*, Andrew S. Malone
44 *Death and the Afterlife*, Paul R. Williamson
45 *Righteous by Promise*, Karl Deenick
46 *Finding Favour in the Sight of God*, Richard P. Belcher Jr
47 *Exalted Above the Heavens*, Peter C. Orr
48 *All Things New*, Brian J. Tabb
49 *The Feasts of Repentance*, Michael J. Ovey

An index of Scripture references for all the volumes may be found at http://www.thegospelcoalition.org/article/new-studies-in-biblical-theology

Finding the Textbook You Need

The IVP Academic Textbook Selector is an online tool for instantly finding the IVP books suitable for over 250 courses across 24 disciplines.

ivpacademic.com

www.ingramcontent.com/pod-product-compliance
Lightning Source LLC
Chambersburg PA
CBHW060348190426
43201CB00043B/1761